T0338090

CANNIBAL METAPHYSICS

FOR A POST-STRUCTURAL ANTHROPOLOGY

EDUARDO VIVEIROS DE CASTRO

Translated and Edited by Peter Skafish

A Univocal Book

University of Minnesota Press

Minneapolis

London

Univocal Publishing was founded by Jason Wagner and Drew Burk as an independent publishing house specializing in artisanal editions and translations of texts spanning the areas of cultural theory, media archeology, continental philosophy, aesthetics, anthropology, and more. In May 2017, Univocal ceased operations as an independent publishing house and became a series with its publishing partner the University of Minnesota Press.

Métaphysiques cannibales
by Eduardo Viveiros de Castro
Copyright Presses Universitaires de France, 2009

Originally published by Univocal Publishing, 2014
First University of Minnesota Press edition 2017.

Copyright 2014 by the Regents of the University of Minnesota

Published by the University of Minnesota Press
111 Third Avenue South, Suite 290
Minneapolis, MN 55401-2520
http://www.upress.umn.edu

ISBN 978-1-5179-0531-6

A Cataloging-in-Publication record for this book is available from the Library of Congress.

Printed in the United States of America on acid-free paper

The University of Minnesota is an equal-opportunity educator and employer.

28 27 26 25 24 23   10 9 8 7 6 5 4 3

Acknowledgments

The argument of this book has been nourished by research presented in the following publications that have since been adapted, revised, and considerably re-worked and developed during the course of the book's editorial revisions.

1. "Perspectivismo e multinaturalismo na América idigena," in E. Viveiros de Castro, *A inconstância da alma selvage,* São Paulo, CosacNaify, 2002 (p. 347–399).

2. "And," *Manchester Papers in Social Anthropology,* 7, 2003.

3. "Perspectival anthropology and the method of controlled equivocation," *Tipiti* (Journal of the Society for the Anthropology of lowland South America), 2 (1), 2004, p. 3–22.

4. "Filiação intensiva e aliança demoníaca," *Novos Estudos Cebrap,* 77, 2007, p. 91–126.

5. "Xamanismo transversal: Lévi-Strauss e a cosmopolítica amazônica" in R. Caixeta de Queiroz and R. Freire Nobre, *Lévi-Strauss: leituras brasileiras,* Belo Horizonte, Editora UFMG, 2008 (p. 79–124)

Numerous people have contributed to the realization of these writings. Most of them appear in the bibliography of this present work. Nevertheless, I would like to mention the names of Tânia Stolze Lima, Marcio Goldman, Oiara Bonilla, Martin Holbraad, Peter Gow, Déborah Danowski, Marilyn Strathern, Bruno Latour, Marshall Sahlins, Casper Jensen, Philippe Descola and Anne-Christine Taylor, who should be thanked for having, each in their own way, caused, inspired, supported, translated, critiqued, or in one way or another, improved the ideas put forward in this book.

A first version of this book was presented for the occasion of a series of conferences that took place at L'Institut d'études avancées de Paris (Maison Suger) in January 2009. I want to thank Yves Duroux and Claude Imbert for their generous invitation, the warm welcome, and the stimulating work environment they procured for me during those winter weeks. Last, but certainly not least, I would like to thank Patrice Maniglier who made this book possible by inviting me to take it on as a project and for providing the ideal context in which to publish it as well as for (literally!) making me write it. But more than anything else, I owe him gratitude for his own writings whose themes are quite close to mine and which inspired me to write this book simply by the fact that I had learned something new.

Table of Contents

PART FOUR
The Cannibal Cogito

Introduction

Can anthropology be philosophy? Can it not just contribute to but do, and even aid in reinventing philosophy, in the sense of constructive, speculative metaphysics? And what, in that event, would philosophy be, since most of its best instances begin, end with, and never abandon Western categories? Such questions would be lamely disciplinary were it not for the symmetrically unimaginative, joint response they still receive. For the philosophers, things are often quite simple: anthropology is a source of empirical specifications or exemplifications of matters conceived more universally by themselves, but only rarely does it accede to such a broad level of reflection. The anthropologists, surprisingly, do not exactly balk at the put-down, the large part of them on account of a commitment to examining "reality" in its singularities and particularities (which is to say, out of not just a concern with the concrete but the presumption that intellectual and ethical responsibility is incompatible with posing big questions); and its "theoretical" wing, out of recognition that few people claiming the mantle of philosophy prove sufficiently adept at critique to not end up treating modern ideological values as profound truths, or misconstruing the most simple actualities in their reflections on them.

Although both views might have once characterized actual-ly existing research, too much has happened since to leave them perspicacious, and what has been called the "theoretical bomb" of Eduardo Viveiros de Castro's *Cannibal Metaphysics* will likely leave them a complete shambles.[1] Leaving aside the fact that a

---

1. The characterization is Latour's. See his "Perspectivism: Type or Bomb," *Anthropology Today*, guest editorial, April 2009, vol. 25, no. 2, pp. 21-22. which summarizes the public

9

figure as imposing as Bruno Latour never gave up on doing constructive philosophy (whether as "intraphysics" or the more recent "empirical metaphysics"), the engagements of anthropologists with Islamic political theology, thinking forests, and the modes of truth operant in divination practices, along with the displacement of Western philosophical categories by a nonanthropologist often outdoing on this point the anthropologists—François Jullien—alone upset the received picture of an anthropology speaking concrete truth to a high-flying philosophy congenitally deaf to it. Yet if anthropology and even philosophy indeed no longer match those images, then the rather huge problem opens up of how both can be done together (and what the thing itself then is) without lapsing back into familiar philosophical starting points or the merely critical, nonconstructive position anthropology is most often comfortable with. The question is what the philosophy of this anthropology will be if philosophy is indeed being transformed by the latter, and *Cannibal Metaphysics* is, well past what even an attentive reading might point to, indispensable to answering it; to defining, that is, the problems, terms, methods, political situation, and intellectual disposition of a thinking no longer complacently satisfied with neglecting concepts external to the West and thereby intellectually mimicking the moderns' violent absorption of other peoples, by presuming that such ideas can always be reduced back to their own. To invent the conditions for a thought cognizant, as Viveiros de Castro puts it, of the theoretical imaginations of all peoples, and to thereby contribute to the "permanent decolonization of thought," the *cannibal, multinatural*, and *perspectivist* version of which we will meet below.

But before we get there, some introductions. First published in a French series, entitled "MétaphysiqueS," devoted to novel developments in contemporary philosophy, Viveiros de Castro's book is perhaps the first attempt by a "real" anthropologist at doing speculative philosophy on the basis of ethnographic materials, and to lay out how anthropology has perhaps already been

---

debate held between Viveiros de Castro and Philippe Descola in Paris shortly after the publication of *Métaphysiques Cannibales*.

doing this for a long time.[2] (And actual philosophers apparently agree: the series' editors are a coterie of former *normaliens* that includes Quentin Meillassoux and Patrice Maniglier, and Raymond Ruyer, Étienne Souriau, and Graham Harman count among its authors.) A Jesuit-educated native of Rio and virtuoso of *carioca* irony whose research concerned the Araweté of the eastern Amazon, Viveiros de Castro first became known outside his country in Paris, where his attempt to extend the structuralism of Claude Lévi-Strauss garnered him the attention of this master of anthropology, drew him soon after into debate with one of its chief inheritors (Françoise Héritier), and brought him into contact with another Amazonianist proponent of structuralism from his generation, Philippe Descola, with whom he would maintain a lifelong friendship characterized as much by striking intellectual affinities as by strained theoretical disagreements (their story is central to understanding this book). But Viveiros de Castro was only structuralist or Lévi-Straussian in a very particular, which is to say Deleuzian, sense and the work for which he would become known in anthropology would be most widely received, as has most often been the case with the inheritors of French theory, outside France. The concepts his name has become synonymous with—Amerindian perspectivism and multinaturalism—were given their initial formulation in lectures Viveiros de Castro delivered in Cambridge at the invitation of Marilyn Strathern (his theoretical "impossible twin" in the sense he develops here), where they would influence the generation of European, British-educated anthropologists most identified with the discipline's broader "ontological turn."[3]

2. Paul Rabinow is the other one, if Latour is in a category of his own. Yet *Anthropos Today: Reflections on Modern Equipment* (Princeton: Princeton University Press, 2003) is as anti-philosophical as philosophical (in favor of casuistry over ontology, and pluralistic for moderns alone) and certainly not speculative or metaphysical. Consider *Cannibal Metaphysics* its opposite number.

3. This term, which is owed to Martin Holbraad, has been used to indicate a tendency in anthropology not toward continental philosophy (in fact, most of its practitioners avoid that) but to work that presumes that the collapse of the nature/culture distinction necessitates conceiving comparisons as groundless and thus recursively impactful on our ideas; the turn is most often associated with Holbraad, Morten Pedersen, Casper Bruun Jensen, and their former mentors, Strathern and Viveiros de Castro. It should at the same time be noted that Viveiros de Castro has exercised a decisive influence on a number of inventive anthropologists who are not entirely part of the turn, including Pierre Deléage, Rupert Stasch, and Eduardo Kohn (who has stated that his entire theoretical work began as an

The basic idea was that Amazonian and other Amerindian peoples (from the Achuar and the Runa all the way up to the Kwakiutl) who live in intense proximity and interrelatedness with other animal and plant species, see these nonhumans not as other species belonging to nature but as PERSONS, human persons in fact, who are distinct from "human" humans not from lacking consciousness, language, and culture—these they have abundantly—but because their bodies are different, and endow them with a specific subjective-"cultural" perspective. In effect, nonhumans regard themselves as humans, and view both human humans and other nonhumans as animals, either predator or prey, since predation is the basic mode of relation. Thus the idea that culture is universal to human beings and distinguishes them from the rest of nature falls apart, as we are faced here with what Descola once called "the society of nature," a collective in which humans, animals, plants, and even minerals, tools, and astronomical bodies are all agents, and where all of (human) human life, from kinship to politics to medicine, is arranged and conducted accordingly. Most crucially, the dizzying preponderance of perspectives on the self entails that the other is effectively ontologically prior, and subjectivation requires assuming, through shamanism and other translational means, the perspective of another. Self-consciousness is reached not through confrontation with the other and subsequent self-return but through temporarily occupying, as dramatized by the Tupian cannibalistic sacrificial rituals that this book's title references, the enemy's point of view, and seeing "oneself" from there.[4]

What in this rendering of "perspectivism" resonated with this generation of anthropologists was that Viveiros de Castro treated the suppositions of Amerindian cosmology not only as demanding a critique of ostensibly universal Western concepts but also as a possible and actual basis for our own thinking, and thus too as the products of people(s) who ought to be acknowledged as having a status equal to that of practitioners of modern science.

attempt to specify the practical and semiotic conditions of perspectivism). In philosophy, Patrice Maniglier, who was responsible for the publication of this book's original French version, has extended perspectivism into metaphysics in a way that may prove decisive for philosophy.

4. The other allusions are to Oswalde Andrade's *Manifesto Anthrópofago* and Montaigne's *Of Cannibals*.

The appeal was the idea that anthropology, suddenly deprived of the ground of so many of its comparisons (no nature means no human essence that cultures, histories, and practices differently realize), could and would have to concern itself with the *concepts* organizing different worlds, and with their construals of being: with foreign or marginal and at any rate strange concepts, the ways they exceed those concepts that are our own, and the transformations of the latter that ensue. In other words, anthropology might have (always had) as its object the sort of constructions Gilles Deleuze considered the defining trait of philosophy, and may also for that reason very well be, when it understands enough about them to translate them into our terms, that same art of constructing concepts, but in another version; one in which indigenous, marginal, and countermodern peoples have as much power and right to think as the moderns.

If this anthropological version of that art indeed has a properly metaphysical dimension, it lies in the fact that the concepts it constructs so thoroughly strip modern categories of their universality as to upend our thinking as a whole. How perspectivism does that is by setting off a sort of rapid chain reaction in the main organs of anthropological conceptuality. Once body and soul as well as animality and humanity have been shown to hold a position that is the inverse of the one they do in modernity, a large group of other old master terms become swept into the same reversal: the objects thought by the natural and even the social sciences to populate the world prove to be subjects in Amazonia (all beings have intentionality), and when things look otherwise, it is merely because one has an insufficiently interpreted object; the universal substance of humans and everything else—nature—becomes culture there, even technically speaking (kinship terms apply to animals, most of which are also thought to organize themselves socially, employ technology, inhabit homes and so on); and then the very notions of identity and difference by which these prior terms are distinguished end up reversed. It is at this point that the cascade rips into more traditional metaphysical categories, and becomes most politically deep. Where the identities of objects and substances come first for us, in perspectivism they are second. Because each soul only knows who and what it is on the basis of what its body looks like from the perspective of another soul (which only knows itself on the basis of how its body is seen from the outside, etc.), difference and relations are primary. Finally, not only is the place generality holds in modern thinking accordingly taken by singularity and sheer variety—each "species" is an instance only of itself, and defined only against the others—but "nature" itself is pluralized. Since everything is singularly, psychically human (once again, not just the "human humans"), beings do not distinguish a common, natural substance. A "multinaturalism" of bodies prevails in which here is not *one* "nature."

The fact that rendering Amerindian thought intelligible requires inverting such a large group of modern conceptual dualisms is what places Viveiros de Castro, then, in metaphysics. But so, too, does his need to borrow from philosophy, and Deleuze's in particular, in order to accomplish this. Like nothing else has, *Cannibal Metaphysics* shows that Deleuze, most often when he is writing with Félix Guattari, enables us to understand those other construals of being that Viveiros de Castro likes to call "the metaphysics of the others."[5] Beyond enabling the above analysis of perspectivism and multinaturalism, we discover that he perceived other arrangements of being much like the configurations of it already in place in the kinship systems, political forms, and cosmologies of certain Amerindian and West African peoples. In chapter 7, for instance, we learn that Deleuze and Guattari's engagement in *Anti-Oedipus* with anthropological kinship literature and Dogon myth was a (failed) attempt to correct the Lévi-Straussian theory of marriage alliance by showing that a counternatural, intensive filiation precedes it; in chapter 10, that the references to serial/sacrificial and totemic/structural logic at the outset of the "Becoming-Intense, Becoming-Animal" chapter of *A Thousand Plateaus* indicate that this discussion from *Anti-Oedipus* is being resumed, but now in order to think *alliance* intensively and thus the interspecies "sociality" of peoples whose shamanic and sorcery practices involves animal metamorphosis; and finally, in chapter 12, that the Deleuzian concept of the concept was the linchpin in bringing all of this out.

This is not the whole story, though, to the role Deleuze plays here, with the other part lying in how he ends up, beyond what is explicitly spelled out in this book, transformed by both the

5. Note that he prefers this term to "ontologies." Cf. Marilyn Strathern on "Melanesian metaphysics" at the outset of *Gender of The Gift*.

Amerindian encounter and the other, even less anticipatable "philosophical" intercessor of *Cannibal Metaphysics*: Claude Lévi-Strauss. For although both the philosophical and rhetorical dimensions of the text suggest that it could easily be counted as an instance of the vast corpus of Deleuziana—this is, arguably, one of the most convincing of the remaining deployments of the immanence-intensity-becoming ensemble—readers unfamiliar with Viveiros de Castro (or who are not or no longer Deleuzian) may want to pause before deciding that it is primarily or only that, and reading accordingly. If Deleuze was at all needed, first of all, it was again because he provides the conceptual means for orienting us in a thought-world as strange as Amazonia *so that something can be done with what we learn there*, and Viveiros de Castro is thus right to cast perspectivism and multinaturalism as the becoming-Amazonian of Deleuze (and not the interpretation-through-imposition so much "Deleuze and anthropology" devolves into). Far more important, second, is what this becoming consists of and where exactly it goes. What I will argue is that it upends and transforms one of the conceptual dualisms that most governs Deleuze's thought, and thereby opens a pluralist, comparative approach to thinking that leads philosophy beyond its European confines. This reconverted Deleuze does this, moreover, by reactualizing Lévi-Strauss, himself conceived as a philosopher of Amerindian thought.

The transformation Deleuze's own metaphysics undergoes hinges on what becomes of philosophy, his own definition in particular, after it is put into contact with Amerindian and other anthropological materials. No one aware of what the Deleuze and Guattari of *Anti-Oedipus* and *A Thousand Plateaus* owe to anthropology and thus indigenous and other alien forms of thought can fail to be struck by the effectively conservative, Eurocentric turn they take, fifteen years later, apropos the identity of philosophy in *What is Philosophy?* The relentless diversion of philosophy into foreign and indigenous territories in those prior texts (the long list of these run from the Balinese plateau to Taoist erotic techniques to Sudanese hyena-men) could seem like it never even happened once philosophy and the concept are effectively said, in the famous "Geophilosophy" chapter of the later book, to not have occurred outside ancient Greece, medieval Christendom, and a small group of modern European countries. The manifest reason for this rather broad exclusion—and it absolutely has to be called that—is that the link between the concept and immanence that Deleuze and Guattari argue has existed since the beginning of philosophy either never quite forms or is quickly broken, so they say, in "Chinese," "Hindu," "Jewish," and "Islamic" thought (traditions that are only in some cases sometimes philosophical). The reason *philosophy* is virtually identified with the concept is that this prevents it from being mistaken for an even slightly representational activity, which would cause it to lose its capacity to think immanence. Concepts are distinct, we quickly learn in that text, from propositions expressing truths about the world and instead lead a virtual, self-consistent existence not referring to such actual state of affairs. Whatever it is in "real" situations that provokes thought, concepts constitute a space of their own in which it is their divergences and interconnections, not the degree or quality of their correspondence, that do this work. When their virtual and also plural status is forgotten, as a famous passage in the text goes, "immanence is interpreted as immanent 'to' something," and "confusion […] results, so that the concept has become a transcendent universal."[6] The long list of such interpretations—being immanent to the One, to the *Cogito*, to the Kantian categories—all fail to think immanence because they mistake the transcendent thing they institute for an element of being, and the concept by which they invented it for its representation. Two problems result. Hindered by the presumption that such elements must necessarily be reckoned with, philosophy is unable to turn away from them when faced with new problems and questions, and thus loses its capacity for critique, invention, and change. Possibly worse, it loses touch with the fact it presupposes a preconceptual image of what thinking is that Deleuze and Guattari call, in this context, the plane of immanence, and elaborates one that subordinates thought to normative intellectual dispositions and values (common sense, honesty, and so on). The situation with the other, foreign forms of thought analogous to but distinct from philosophy is said to be merely different, but is effectively

6. Gilles Deleuze and Félix Guattari, *What is Philosophy?* (New York: Columbia University Press, 1994), 44.

cast as inferior. Even if some of them conceive being as immanence—a Tao nowhere gathered together and identifiable, a cosmos initially lacking in order—none decide, as the Greeks did, to take it up with concepts. Rather, they project "figures" onto it that introduce transcendence into it in a more permanent, less controvertible fashion. Comparing what is again identified as a mostly Chinese, Hindu, Jewish, Islamic, and Christian activity with philosophy, this use of figures (respectively, "hexagrams," "mandalas," "sephiroth," "imaginals," and "icons") is essentially said to render being intelligible by "establishing correspondences between divine, cosmic, political, architectural, and organic levels as so many values of one and the same transcendence." The difference from philosophy is not that the large part of being is thereby made subordinate to a transcendent reality or God—philosophy often did the same thing—but that its elements are defined through horizontal and vertical analogies with each other that eventually refer back to that final figure. Where the nonreferential and syntagmatic character of concepts imbricates them with each other and thus forces them to proceed immanently (even attempts to create transcendence with them are done laterally and without any final correspondence to externalities), the referentiality of figures means that they are "essentially paradigmatic" and "hierarchical," which locks thought into transcendence by making them instantiations of an ultimate figure (even an empty one).vv For example, while an "absolutization of immanence," the Tao in this view remains an *image* of being that the hexagrams together embody but can never entirely express or change. Hence the fact that Deleuze and Guattari are content to designate these other traditions as "religions" or "wisdoms" not capable of transforming themselves.

Now a common reaction to this part of *What is Philosophy?* relies on tacit metaphysical presuppositions so conservative that it fails to discern the problem most at stake here. The reflex charge that Deleuze and Guattari present a dehistoricized, idealist account of overly generalized traditions can only with difficulty avoid privileging "history" or "actual practice" as realities to which their thinking should correctly correspond, and thus loses out on precisely the pluralizing, polytraditional potential implicit in the concept of the concept. What such a criticism misses is that immanence is an attempt not only to rid thinking of its theological and humanist residues but also to ensure that no concept is naturalized as a necessary referent so that thought is kept radically, anarchistically plural. Deleuze's famous "empiricism=pluralism" formula means that in the absence of universal theoretical concepts (like the subject, practice, and history), thought operates only in the multiple: in relation to a variety of unequal situations, but also through divergent conceptualizations and construals of them—including, in principle, those from outside modern thought and philosophy. The real failure, then, of Deleuze and Guattari's quick dismissal of "other philosophies" is that it evinces almost no interest in further pluralizing this pluralism by allowing philosophy to engage with and be in essence changed by them.[7]

Although he is, I believe, cognizant of the problem, Viveiros de Castro's means of addressing it is to bypass rather than square off with it directly. To a certain extent, the nonreferentiality and self-consistence of the concept entails, as many other anthropologists have realized, that it has a built-in capacity to overcome the (metaphysical) ethnocentrism of the humanities and social sciences, and Viveiros de Castro simply exploits this to turn philosophy into the self-displacing, decolonizing endeavor that it turned out not to not be in Deleuze. Because the relevance and critical power of the Deleuzian concept does not depend on whether it correctly characterizes things or effectively generalizes them, simply treating Amerindian cosmology as though it were composed of concepts immediately accords an autonomy to it that would be lacking were its significance to depend on its relation to practices or histories supposed to underlie it. Once it is accepted that an alien body of thought is indeed thought, then there is no longer anything to decipher except for what its coordinates, values, suppositions, and truths are, and how these throw our own into disarray by depriving them of universality and transforming them. The permanent mobility philosophy acquires from the concept therefore also entails, in principle, its permanent decoloniality: a constitutive inability to arrogate to itself unlimited intellectual authority, and an equally constitutive dependence on other ontological powers. Such a philosophy

7. Deleuze and Guattari's attempt at pluralism resides in how they say that the exportation of the concept Europeanizes peoples and gives them a basis to critically resist capitalism (the upshot is that they become Uropean/philosophical before this is possible).

cannot be immune to being affected by other "metaphysics," including those of previously or still effectively colonized people, and it will henceforth have no excuse for blowing off their contents and implications. For anthropology, the consequences quickly become clear: not only nature and culture but a series of its other master concepts—the subject, *habitus*, practice, history, ethnographic presence, etc.—can no longer be deployed without being extensively revised, and all the alien concepts they suppressed arise as the source of the change. Inasmuch as anthropology is metaphysics, it is wrested away from the categories of its origins, its belief that it alone is endowed with the right to final interpretations, and the ethnometaphysical underpinnings of its identity. The pluralization is radical, with both the sources and character of thought multiplying.

None of this, however, yet touches on what becomes of Deleuze and Guattari and their notions of philosophy and the concept if they, too, are not spared from the operation. Even if the plural, relational character of the concept makes any veritable philosophy, as Deleuze famously put it, a "system in continuous variation," this variability cannot mean, as *What Is Philosophy?* implies, that it can proceed essentially unperturbed by influences from outside it, particularly where its conception of itself as philosophy is concerned. Where a real disturbance to philosophy arises, as can now be seen, is precisely in the introduction of comparison into it. In metaphysics, to acknowledge Patrice Maniglier, as comparison—in cannibal metaphysics as comparative metaphysics, and thus as what Maniglier has also called a "superior comparativism."[8]

Cannibal Metaphysics' specific comparison of Amerindian and modern ontology is more helped than hindered by *What is Philosophy?* for an additional reason. Deleuze and Guatari's view that having the concept makes Greco-European thought *de facto* function immanently is offset by their acknowledgement that the moderns' Christian origins have caused them to lose the baseline sense of immanence that many other peoples still have. Amerindian thought, as Viveiros de Castro points out early on,

---

8. See his forthcoming "Manifeste pour un comparatisme supérieur en philosophie."

continues to presume such a plane of immanence in its ascription of humanity to everything. "In the beginning," as a particular type of Amerindian myth goes, "there were only human beings, and humans and animals were not yet distinct," and this immanent humanity remains the omnipresent background against which "pockets of transcendence" opened by the transient identification of beings "flicker." The "Amazon" (like "Melanesia" for other anthropologists) reigns supremely immanent, and the moderns thus have a lot to learn, and little to teach. The notion of a *nonconceptual* understanding of immanence is what allows us to perceive this perspectivist version of it, which helps feed the fire the latter started in modern ontology.

As for the fact that Deleuze and Guattari treat the concept as the provenance of the West, perspectivism compensates for this in Viveiros de Castro's view by having its own form of thought—myth—whose basic "unit" is equally, if not more, subversive of transcendence. The classic definition Lévi-Strauss gives of "the gross constituent unit of myth" in "The Structural Study of Myth" already has this "mytheme" being as much of a differential, relational, and plural being as the concept. The sentences or phrases composing a myth involve relations not only with each other but also with those of other variants of the same myth as well as of other myths, both of which will eventually just be called its other versions. Moreover, "the true constituent units of myth," as Lévi-Strauss puts it there, "are not the isolated relations but bundles of such relations" that cut across the myths in such a way that they compose a synchronic plane not apparent when myths are interpreted only in their diachrony.[9] For example, in a Northwest Coast Bella Bella myth (elsewhere made the object of a celebrated analysis), the puzzling matter of why a youth captured by an Ogress is able to frighten her with a clam's siphon (so that his father will be able to distribute her property to the tribe) is answered when the myth is juxtaposed with a similar story from a neighboring, inland mountain tribe called the Chilcotin.[10] In this version, a sorcerer Owl is overcome when the boy he has kidnapped instead brandishes mountain goat horns and obtains

9. Claude Lévi-Strauss, "The Structural Study of Myth," in *Structural Anthropology* (New York: Basic Books, 1963).

10. Claude Lévi-Strauss, "Structuralism and Ecology," *Social Science Information,* February 1973, 12: 7–23.

seashells. The inversion here of both the chief terms of the first myth and their functions—a terrestrial object is the means of obtaining oceanic goods instead of the opposite—arises from the fact that the Chilcotin ascribed no economic value to mountain goat horns but did to shells, like siphons, that the Bella Bella saw as mere waste. Certain such meanings of a myth, then, can be exposed only if it is relinked to a broader group of its variations or versions—a "transformation group," so-called because each one is a transformation of the others—and the logical relations they rearrange reconstituted in this way. Mythemes thus have a relational, extrachronological character much like that ascribed to concepts by Deleuze, and the affinity between them is only heightened when the transphenomenality of mythemes—the fact that they are irreducible to the individual myths constituting them—is emphasized by Lévi-Strauss. A mytheme, he states, is always made up of all its variants, just as a concept is irreducible to the arguments or propositions expressing it. Finally, a last trait—perhaps the most important—is common to both, which is that each one is autonomous of whatever empirical circumstance that set it in motion and that it continues, in part, to reference. The concept's difference from states of affairs has an almost exact analogue in myth's capacity to rework empirical material into increasingly abstract, even hyperlogical, formations.

In regard to its formal properties, then, myth is so theoretical and speculative an operation as to not only have parity with but be superior to the concept—no "mythologist" could have ever formalized myth by making one myth explain or regulate the others—and it is thus understandable that Viveiros de Castro does not explicitly reckon here with the fact that Deleuze granted the concept only to European thought. At the same time, some other problems are raised by his turn to myth and Lévi-Strauss' definition of it, which is that myths' transform each other by inverting each other's semantic distinctions, and both the notion of myth and myth's actual functioning therefore appear to depend on a conception of difference as opposition incompatible with immanent thinking, modern or otherwise. Should the contrasts deployed and changed in myths be between pairs of terms conceived of as the exact opposites of each other, then identity becomes ontologically primary—for meanings to be "opposite" they first have to be entirely stable—and the differential character of Amerindian thought and its consequences are lost. More specifically, if myths simply embody, as Lévi-Strauss until a certain point thought, a more general tendency of the human mind to think through binary distinctions, then we are faced, worse, with a transcendental structure that both Amerindian and modern thought would both simply instantiate but not alter, and the otherness of the former is cancelled.

Viveiros de Castro's way of addressing these issues is to argue that Lévi-Strauss's conception of myth is ultimately based in notions of difference as disequilibrium and dissymmetry (not opposition) and of structure as transformation, and is so because myth's foundations lie in the Amerindian situation of perspectivism, which thinks in exactly those terms. On that basis, he shows that the mythic (perspectivist) method of thinking through contrast and inversion provides the means of relating philosophies to other modes of thought—of making metaphysics from comparisons—that the concept alone could not.

In order to see how it is perspectivism itself that gives rise to these thoughts, we have to absorb the portrait of Lévi-Strauss found in the text's final chapter (its thirteenth, and thus a particularly illumined full moon in the firmament of reason), an image of a differential Lévi-Strauss that flies in the face of the received readings (mostly perpetuated in the absence of actual readings) of him as effectively Kantian, transcendental, and predeconstructive.[11] The Lévi-Strauss that emerges here is the one who, as early as "Introduction to the Work of Marcel Mauss," "de-transcendentalizes" structure, destabilizes the nature/culture distinction, and makes differences—thought under the rubric of a *disymmetry* and *disequilibrium* constitutive of mythic structure—the primary elements and character of being. The strength of the portrait lies, above all else, in the fact that it is based on a perception of the fact that Lévi-Strauss had a second personality, in the sense both of another intellectual

11. The chief ones are Derrida's, in *Of Grammatology*, of a Lévi-Strauss who reproduces Western logocentrism by casting writing and technics as what corrupt the Nabikawara's pure phonocentric relation to nature, and Butler's, who renders sexual difference natural by making the incest prohibition the transcendental condition of kinship exchange; not to mention that of Paul Rabinow (who gave us "Beyond Structuralism and Hermeneutics"), for whom structures are at once obsessed with "meaning" and unamenable to being historically transformed.

identity, corresponding to a late period of his work that begins in the *Mythologiques* proper and culminates in their sequels, and of a distinct persona that sprang from him being dissociated from himself (with regard, precisely, to discontinuity and difference).[12] This other Lévi-Strauss changes and even reverses course in the series on a set of positions—the transcendental status of society, the algebraic character of structure, and kinship, totemism, and myth as effecting a full transition from nature and animality to culture and humanity—once characteristic of his thought and what had been understood to be his structuralism.

This "poststructuralist" Lévi-Strauss first emerges early on in the *Mythologiques*, when it becomes clear that the volume's project of tracing the transposition and recombination of mythic codes from one group of myths to another requires an intersocietal focus that effectively demotes "Society" from a transcendental to an empirical/molecular status, and then crystallizes when the sheer volume and sprawling character of those codes undermines the old presumption (itself once suggested by Lévi-Strauss) that "structure" is the ultimate set of their contents and their final, schematic form. Because their translational character is primary, "structures" are instead nothing but analogues and transformations of each other, and even "break form" enough to innovate new contrastive devices. Structures thus do not express or even total up to a Structure but are only found (the formula is Maniglier's) between two variants, sequences, or levels of a myth inasmuch as they recast each other, and are only "transcendental" in the sense that their relations are not visible in their terms.[13]

Now by itself, this detranscendentalization of society and structure might suggest that there is nothing else to demonstrate about myth apart from (the bad infinity of) its labile variability and reversibility. What is at stake, however, is of course more profound, which is that the structure of myths turns out to be isomorphic with the multinatural perspectivist condition: just

12. See Catherine Malabou, *Following Generation*, vol. 20, n. 2 19-33 for another philosophical treatment of the other Lévi-Strauss.

13. Which is definitely not to say they are not to some extent empirical: it is asserted early on in *The Raw and The Cooked* (Chicago: The University of Chicago Press, 1983), 1, that myths express themselves through the sensible/aesthetic contrasts said to form a "logic of the sensible"—thought that operates through aesthetic materials without discursive mediation—in *The Savage Mind*.

like the perspective-endowing corporeal envelope, each casts or translates the other in terms of itself and is an instance of a vast relational field in which "human" humans and "nonhuman" humans are continuous with each other, and thus not all of them attempt to introduce discontinuity into and thereby render the human distinct. Certain others, instead, stay truer to form by conveying either the basic character of that condition ("the time when humans and animals were not yet distinct") or the reversal entailed when "human" humans are entirely sucked back into it. The detranscendentalization of the structure of myths, in other words, exposes their perspectivist form and the nonnaturalist/nonculturalist character of many of their contents. Myths and the structural study of them reveal not just the passage from nature to culture but the passage "back" to (the other, differential and multi-) "nature," and Lévi-Strauss' "post-structuralism" is the surreptitiously enunciated philosophy of it. (Hence the allusive subtitle of *Cannibal Metaphysics*, which should not be heard in the old sense of "poststructuralism" but as "Post-*Structural Anthropology*": as the resumption, on different grounds, of the project of Lévi-Strauss's 1956 volume.)

Discerning the multinaturalism of myth would be what made it additionally possible, finally, for the other Lévi-Strauss to additionally perceive "perpetual disequilibrium" and an "initial dissymmetry" both as the problem Amerindian thought contemplates when it enters into high speculative mode and as, however remarkable it might seem, "the absolute key to the system" of Amerindian myth. This turn in Lévi-Strauss's thinking, by far the most unanticipated of those Viveiros de Castro exposes, sees him characterizing Amerindian thought as a "bipartite ideology" and "philosophy" in the final instance of the full Mythologiques cycle (which incudes, beyond the four volumes bearing that title, three subsequent books). *The Story of Lynx* begins with Lévi-Strauss explaining that he undertook the project upon realizing that the nature of central Brazilian dual organizations, if they are not institutions but "a method for solving problems," could be understood by pursuing their links to certain Northwest Coast myths. Their "philosophical and ethical sources" are gradually exposed through analyses of myths concerning twins that show them, in contrast to their Indo-European analogues (like the Dioscuri), to reject the idea that they share perfect likenesses and see only inequality between them. Such "impossible twins" reveal that "in Amerindian thought, a sort of philosophical bias seems to make it necessary for things in any sector of the cosmos or of society to not remain in their initial state and for an unstable dualism to always yield another unstable dualism."[14] The dichotomies he obsessively pursued in the Mythologiques turn out, then, not to have been "a universal phenomenon resulting from the binary nature of human thought" but specific to this "explanation of the world." As for the apparently exact oppositions composing these, they are extreme refinements of the far more primary difference figured by twins, the slight divergence or dissymmetry that myth must thoroughly process before symmetrical differences can emerge.

Read superficially, this rewilded Lévi-Strauss looks like he merely reconfirms Deleuze instead of going outside him: virtual differences upon virtual differences are what there is, identities only emerge from them, and some "Amerindians" somewhere are nodding in agreement. Yet the present book's closing affirmation of Deleuze WITH Lévi-Strauss can be read in both directions, and putting the accent on the anthropological end yields a very different perspective—for perspectivism and perspectives themselves really are what is at stake—on what else can be done with the recognizably philosophical part besides endlessly repeating (including through empirical "examples") its main tenets. For conceiving Amerindian thought in terms of concepts changes not only our concepts but our very concept of concepts, pulling the concept, that is, into the orbit of myth and its much greater capacity to effect transformations of not only other myths but also other discursive materials. Think concepts as one would myths—as though they were only ever versions of each other, and in which none of their semantic distinctions are incapable of being transformed—and the radically pluralistic, self-undoing philosophy they had been unable to furnish on their own emerges.[15]

14. Claude Lévi-Strauss, *The Story of Lynx* (Chicago, The University of Chicago Press, 1995), 234.

15. Patrice Maniglier has begun to build an entire metaphysics out of the view that truths are versions of each other. See his forthcoming "The Other's Truths." Reading the vernacular metaphysician Jane Roberts is how I first encountered the idea that things are versions

To see how, we need only contrast one of *Cannibal Metaphysics*' concepts with a properly philosophical one. "Virtual affinity," the last element of the book's metaphysical triad, is the expression by which Viveiros de Castro names the primacy of the ambient relationality he sees as characteristic of Amerindian "sociality" and "kinship," and that resembles Deleuzian virtuality enough to pass for a case of it. In a reversal of what classic kinship theory often took to be the case, the basic Amerindian situation (to again simply explicate Viveiros de Castro) is one in which every being is already in some way a kin relation or "affine," and "consanguinal" (natural or "blood") relations thus have to be established. The perspectivist epistemic formula that "an object is only an insufficiently interpreted subject" concerns not merely the fact that bodies conceal largely inscrutable selves but that life is so saturated with them that identifying oneself in relation to them becomes extremely difficult. Others are everywhere, their points of view are opaque, and inhabiting them is the only way I can know myself; at the same time, these others constitute my "social" universe, are therefore integrally related to me, and collective and personal identity are mixed in with them such that I lack a discrete position from which to go inhabit them.

The consequence, as Viveiros de Castro explains in a text on kinship not reproduced here, is that the collective is always outside "itself" and can only delimit its "natural," consanguinal identity by progressively eliminating the affines to which it is related.[16] For example, an initial delimitation of identity in an otherwise unspecified tribe can be had by treating those living outside one's moieties' residence as distant affines; to define this group further, one treats cross-kin as distant, and parallel kin as close; among these, next, the other sex will be marked as other or merely affinal, and the same sex as consanguinal, and then the self will be naturalized by being distinguished from its ("merely affinal") brothers. Even the individual, finally, will have to isolate its interior by having its body treated, in funerary and other rituals, as consanguinal

(and not only becomings) of each other.

16. See Eduardo Viveiros de Castro, "GUT feelings about Amazonia: potential affinity and the construction of sociality," in Peter Rivière, Laura M. Rival, and Neil L. Whitehead, eds. *Beyond The Visible and The Material: The Amerindianization of Society in The Work of Peter Rivière* (2001): 19-43.

and its soul as "affinal." In sum, consanguinal relations are never given and must instead be perpetually established, through an almost asymptotic pursuit.

Now as soon as it is recalled that that all these "virtual" affines are cultural or conventional in modern terms, this situation stands out as the most bizarre aspect of Amerindian cosmology as it is here presented. The consanguine or "natural" entities sought in the above way are rarities, barely tangible things that not only have to be established but are a matter, to put it in very Viveiros de Castroian terms, of extensive theoretical obsession. In other words, actual beings, beings when they appear to be nothing else but themselves, but their identities, are as apparently unreal and difficult to think within the Amerindian situation as differential/relational beings (multiplicities) are for us. Definitively identifying who all the beings are that give definition to oneself is extremely difficult, and the self thus exists in a kind of atmosphere, as Deleuze put it, that would tear apart a fully formed subject. The virtual—being when relational, unstable, in-between—is the immediate experiential condition, and perceptions of actualities are to be made, even attained. From our vantage, virtual affinity indeed describes an inverted world.

At the same time, something in Deleuze looks upside down if we try to see him and ourselves from this world's point of view. Even if Deleuze and Guattari conceive modern collectivity in *A Thousand Plateaus* by treating virtual, relational dynamics similar to virtual affinity as primary (becomings, micropolitical arrangements, etc.), they nevertheless do not imagine a corresponding experience of it to be possible for the moderns and instead cast it as something to be *achieved*—by "*constructing*" a plane of immanence, "*making* the body without organs," and *dismantling* the actualities, from subjectivity to meaning to the organism, that block the way. The virtual, while primary ontologically and logically, is never conceived as the moderns' basic state of perceptual experience (their "basal metabolism," in Viveiros de Castro's terms) and thus must be continually, again even asymptotically pursued. What comes immediately to the Amerindians must be cautiously elaborated by the moderns, and the concepts by which we make sense of their discrepant ontological arrangements emerge as versions and transformations of each other.

But what exactly gets transformed, and into what? In Deleuze's case, the virtual looks to be the condition of virtual affinity and perspectivism transformed into the concept of a primordial nature prior to speciation and full individuation, and the actual the corollary conversion of the elusive stable identities of Amerindians into a domain of species and objects. A panpsychic, "human" world in which the immediate experience is of nebulous subjects and perspectives demanding (cautious) definition becomes a natural, inhuman world that experience conceals (it is "imperceptible") and that must be engaged through despecification and desubjectivation. Even if being as "nature" in Deleuze is the inorganic life of *natura naturata* and thus neither naturalist nor anthropocentric, it nonetheless basically remains *deanimated* matter that becomes thinkable and (almost) perceivable through the elimination of persons and consciousness.

Viewing Deleuze from this angle amounts, of course, to another transformation. This time it is a sort of back translation of what remain two of our most incisive metaphysical concepts. The virtual/actual couplet stops appearing to be a conceptual distinction that reveals everything—"nature"—to be initially preindividual and always outside genre and form, and begins instead to look more like an apprehension of this initial, prespeciated condition as involving only bodies, not souls, and thus as its de-animization. The Amerindian soul and body, that is, displaces the virtual/actual pair by showing it to be a merely local construal of being, and thereby forces metaphysics into a truly multinatural space in which no concept has, even though purely situational and variable use, anything resembling universal extension.

It is indeed in perspectivism, then, that we find the radical pluralism that was missing from *What is Philosophy?* When juxtaposed with an Amerindian "concept," one of the very concepts by which philosophy was defined proves to be comparable in the way a myth would be, and to even function like one—the virtual/actual can be read as a distinction that replaces soul/body, assigns new functions to the latter terms (the soul as explication of an the mutually implicated bodies), and switches the problem—and the result for us is that it is rendered relative and even transformed, in the other direction: again, the materialist, modern character of the virtual is exposed, and seeing this flips the position of "the subject" (psyche, person, and even consciousness are better words) from derivative to primary. This transformation, though, does not just affect these concepts but extends to the very form or concept by which we think them, and in two ways. First, by making the basic state differences between perspectives rather than between deanimated bodies, Amerindian thought also makes "concepts" indissociable from (individual and collective) persons and their relations. Once perspectivism is being practiced as philosophy, as it just was, thinking cannot *not* concern the problem of identity as it arises when the other person comes first, and this "enemy's point of view" must for that reason be inhabited in order to bring definition to the self. Concepts become inherently (and politically) comparative, and comparison the means of arriving at a definition of self.

Second, the mythic thinking by which such comparisons are undertaken reconceives the concept in precisely such contrastive terms and thereby provides the very multiversal "philosophical" form that we have been seeking. Myths are, as we saw, intelligible only in comparison with each other not only on account of the fact that they translate and rearrange each other's semantic distinctions but because they only do so from being perspectivist from the outset. Like Amazonian persons, myths are versions of each other whose specific point of view is given by the "bodies" formed by their particular codes, and their significance can be uncovered only by tracking how they convert and often reverse the perceptual forms of their (sometimes literal) neighbors, who thus in a sense always come first. Myth is thus thinking that occurs against the backdrop of the other as a possible world, even as it translates the latter into and thus adheres to its point of view. In this crucial respect, they are quite different from concepts as Deleuze defined them. Where concepts maintain immanence by always in fact coming (even if unwittingly) in the plural, myths go a step further by having to actively contend with other myths (or concepts, or narratives, or discursive materials, and so on) and their divergent perspectives. Immanence becomes much more a matter of worlds and psyches that can at best be translated, and whose otherness need not be preserved because it is always stubbornly there.

◎ ◎ ◎

But is this indeed philosophy? Could myth *cum* concept, thought and critique as comparison, and being as differences of perspective really provide the main aspects of a metaphysics? In other words, does it do justice to actual philosophies to approach them from such a panpsychist perspective and as though we were comparing myths? And would we even then still be in the vicinity of anything resembling anthropology?

Turning to a few instances of contemporary philosophy in its relation to ecology will not yield negative answers. Set next to the exemplary myth of perspectivism, the paradigmatic case of speculative realism itself looks like myth. In "l'Arrêt de Monde," a recent essay on ecology, Amerindian thought, catastrophism, and the Anthropocene coauthored with the Leibnizian philosopher Deborah Dankowski, Viveiros de Castro and her argue that Quentin Meillassoux's work remains curiously anthropocentric due to its inattention to these very things.[17] The archefossil, Meillassoux's figure for being in its primary qualities prior to the emergence of biological life and human beings, describes a "time"—at once an original past and an effectively precosmological situation—not when humans and animals were indistinct but when neither they nor any other perspective existed, and that demonstrates being's autonomy respective to human thought. Read in light of an ecological crisis that demands the reinvention of the relations between humans and nonhumans, this aspect of the case against correlationism amounts to an anthropocentrism different from the one it criticizes. Making the emptiest universe the most real one effectively restores the exceptionality of (a certain) human being, ignoring the "planetary objectification of correlationism" that occurs with the Anthropocene. By contemplating so abstractly "our" irrelevance, this metaphysics skips over the perspectival universe right now looking back at us and engages only a deanimated reality that suspiciously resembles a catastrophic future in which we imagine ourselves inevitably extinct.

Proceeding in this way might seem to imply that philosophy itself will never hold up or is merely a genre of discourse with

17. See Deborah Dankowski and Eduardo Viveiros de Castro, "l'Arrête de Monde," in *Émilie Hache, ed, De l'univers clos au monde infini* (Paris: Éditions Dehors, 2014), and the forthcoming translation from Polity Press.

no specificity of its own. Apart from reiterating that Lévi-Strauss emerges here as a strange kind of metaphysician (which forces anew the issue of how other comparative thinkers, from Foucault to Agamben, also are), a brief gloss of Bruno Latour's recent *An Inquiry Into Modes of Existence* (subtitled, crucially, *An Anthropology of The Moderns*) shows the exact opposite. In that text, which is billed as a metaphysics both empirical and anthropological, Latour offers a proposal for how "the moderns" (and not modernity: it is again a question of identities and perspectives) might account for themselves to the other collectives of the Earth at the moment when ecological crisis demands a radically cooperative politics. In lieu of defining the moderns on the basis of their institutions and history, Latour enumerates the different modes or ways of being constituting their collective existence (dispensing with the text's nomenclature, these include politics, religion, life, technology, art, the psyche, and so on) in order that the moderns associated with each can become more understandable to both each other and the rest of the world. Despite its centrist political tone, there is a perspectivist dimension to the project, and it first of all lies in its extension of what Latour long ago dubbed a "symmetrical anthropology" that takes the moderns for a collective as alien as the Araweté out of an awareness of the divergent ontological arrangements of other collectives. Where it intensifies is in the argument that the very modes deemed by the moderns to form the bedrock of being—nature and science, object and subject—are in fact merely two of an ensemble of twelve, and the claim has as much to do with Latour's own project of undermining the nature/culture distinction as with the influence Amerindian thought has exercised on his work (Descola and Viveiros de Castro have both influenced it at various points). The deepest resonance, though, lies in the fact that the notion of ontological difference(s) at the core of the project requires a novel form of philosophical interlocution in which it is not intellectuals and scientists alone who have the right to speak about the essences of things but a throng of others (from lawyers and activists to animals and spirits) with expertise concerning certain modes. The difficulty many have in perceiving how the *AIME* book is a metaphysics has everything to do with how it must contrastively distinguish beings and modes in order to legitimate their discrepant perspectives and diplomatically coordinate their relations.

Defining the moderns by drawing internal contrasts among them is not entirely flush with perspectivism's demand to push them outside themselves, and Latour's symmetrization of anthropology is thus probably asymmetrically achieved (the moderns look very different from the outside than they do from within). Yet at the same time, Latour's metaphysics is perhaps the very first to constrain itself to the ontology of a people, and it is in this respect entirely amenable to being joined to an account of the ontologies of others. This is where the Amerindian soul/body distinction emerges full force. Despite the difference between it and the present book, Descola's *Beyond Nature and Culture* characterizes the moderns in terms of the contrast between their deployment of the soul/body and that of what it calls "animism" but also that of two other ontologies—"totemism" and "analogism"—such that the moderns' ontology becomes the most exotic, provincial, and temporally local of the four. Refracted through Viveiros de Castro, Descola's quartet yields what is likely the first instance of a sort of geographic ontology capable of remapping the Earth, in something like a theoretical Gall-Peter projection, from a perspectivist angle.

And finally, the question. Is all this philosophy in fact still anthropology? Neither the metaphysics of *Cannibal Metaphysics* nor my account of it will seem to confirm this if the concept, the myth, of perspectivism does not enable us to enter the perspectives not just of peopleS, but of *people,* of other "subjects," or, more exactly, of the interlocutors of anthropologists that, in the course of fieldwork and beyond, are teachers as well as philosophers to them, in the archaic sense (wise enough to love wisdom but not to claim it). But perspectivism *does* do this, and quite well, by allowing us to heed people engaged in nothing else but "ontological self-determination." Just after the original French publication of the present work came *La chute du ciel: Paroles d'un chamun yanomani,* the account of the life and cosmopractical thought of one Davi Kopenawa as dictated by him to the anthropologist Bruce Albert. Can we really, if we have heard Viveiros de Castro and given up on turning other people's concepts into "social realities" to be explained, not hear how its myths impact us? "Since the beginning of time," as Kopenawa says of the

Yanomani demiurge and while giving an account of his life of political struggle against the expropriation of their forestland

> *Omama* has been the center of what the white people call ecology. It's true! Long before these words existed among them and they started to speak about them so much, they were already in us, though we did not name them the same way. [...] In the forest, we human beings are the "ecology." But it is equally the *xapiri* [spirits], the game, the trees, the rivers, the fish, the sky, the rain, the wind, and the sun.... The white people who once ignored all these things are starting to hear them a little [and] now they call themselves the "people of the ecology."[18]

This is why, perhaps, some of us have begun to see, through eyes like Kopenawa's, that "the tapirs, the peccaries, the macaws that we hunt in the forest were once also humans" and "this is why today we are still the same kind." It is also why, realizing that such a myth necessarily transforms our concepts, we who recently became "people of the ecology" had better strain to elaborate another understanding— panpsychic, transpecific, metamorphic—of "human" perspective.[19]

Peter Skafish
Montreal, November 2014

---

18. Davi Kopenawa and Bruce Albert, *The Falling Sky: Words of a Yanomami Shaman*, (Cambridge: The Belknap Press of Harvard University Press, 2013), 393.

19. Initial work on this translation was done while I was a Fondation Fyssen Postdoctoral Fellow and *chercheur invité* at the Laboratoire d'Anthropologie Sociale, and the bulk of it undertaken during an Andrew W. Mellon Foundation Postdoctoral Fellowship in the Department of Anthropology at McGill University. I would like to thank each of those institutions for their generosity, and also to express my gratitude to Sheehan Moore, Philippe Descola, William Hanks, Eduardo Kohn, Patrice Maniglier, Diane Leclair and Gregory Paquet, Dimitra Papandreou, and Toby Cayouette for the various forms of support and assistance they offered. Drew Burk and Jason Wagner deserve endless thanks for the patience, encouragement, resources, and work they put into this project, and for having the courage and intelligence to run a publishing house like *Univocal*. Finally, a special thanks to Eduardo Viveiros de Castro for his readiness to answer my questions, and the radically collaborative spirit and wicked sense of humor with which he did so from start to finish.

Everything must be interpreted as intensity
—Anti-Oedipus

PART ONE

Anti-Narcissus

Chapter One

A Remarkable Reversal

I once had the intention of writing a book that would have been something of a homage to Deleuze and Guattari from the point of view of my discipline; it would have been called *Anti-Narcissus: Anthropology as Minor Science*. The idea was to characterize the conceptual tensions animating contemporary anthropology. From the moment I had the title, however, the problems began. I quickly realized that the project verged on complete contradiction, and the least misstep on my part could have resulted in a mess of not so anti-narcissistic provocations about the excellence of the positions to be professed.

It was then that I decided to raise the book to the rank of those fictional works (or, rather, invisible works) that Borges was the best at commenting on and that are often far more interesting than the visible works themselves (as one can be convinced of in reading the accounts of them furnished by that great blind reader). Rather than write the book itself, I found it more opportune to write about it as if others had written it. *Cannibal Metaphysics* is therefore a beginner's guide to another book, entitled *Anti-Narcissus*, that because it was endlessly imagined, ended up not existing—unless in the pages that follow.

The principal objective of *Anti-Narcissus*, in order to place my mark on the "ethnographic" present, is to address the following question: what do anthropologists owe, conceptually, to the people they study? The implications of this question would doubtlessly seem clearer were the problem approached from the other end. Are the differences and mutations internal to anthropological theory principally due to the structures and conjunctures (criticohistorically understood) of the social formations, ideological debates, intellectual fields and academic contexts from which anthropologists themselves emerge? Is that really the only relevant hypothesis? Couldn't one shift to a perspective showing that the source of the most interesting concepts, problems, entities and agents introduced into thought by anthropological theory is in the imaginative powers of the societies—or, better, the peoples and collectives—that they propose to explain? Doesn't the originality of anthropology instead reside there, in this always-equivocal but often fecund alliance between the conceptions and practices that arise from the worlds of the so-called "subject" and "object" of anthropology?

The question of *Anti-Narcissus* is thus epistemological, meaning political. If we are all more or less agreed that anthropology, even if colonialism was one of its historical *a prioris*, is today nearing the end of its karmic cycle, then we should also accept that the time has come to radicalize the reconstitution of the discipline by forcing the process to its completion. Anthropology is ready to fully assume its new mission of being the theory/practice of the permanent decolonization of thought.

But perhaps not *everyone* is in agreement. There are those who still believe that anthropology is the mirror of society. Not, certainly, of the societies it claims to study—of course no one is as ingenuous as that anymore (whatever …)—but of those whose guts its intellectual project was engendered in. We all know the popularity enjoyed in some circles by the thesis that anthropology, because it was supposedly exoticist and primitivist from birth, could only be a perverse theater where the Other is always "represented" or "invented" according to the sordid interests of the West. No history or sociology can camouflage the complacent paternalism of this thesis, which simply transfigures the so-called others into fictions of the Western imagination in which they lack a speaking part. Doubling this subjective phantasmagoria with the familiar appeal to the dialectic of the objective production of the Other by the colonial system simply piles insult upon injury, by proceeding as if every "European" discourse on peoples of non-European tradition(s) serves only to illumine our "representations of the other," and even thereby making a certain theoretical postcolonialism the ultimate stage of ethnocentrism. By always seeing the Same in the Other, by thinking that under the mask of the other it is always just "us" contemplating ourselves, we end up complacently accepting a shortcut and an interest only in what is "of interest to us"—ourselves.

On the contrary, a veritable anthropology, as Patrice Maniglier has put it, "returns to us an image in which we are unrecognizable to ourselves," since every experience of another culture offers us an occasion to engage in experimentation with our own—and far more than an imaginary variation, such a thing is the putting into variation of our imagination (Maniglier 2005b: 773-4). We have to grasp the consequences of the idea that those societies and cultures that are the object of anthropological research influence, or, to put it more accurately, coproduce the theories of society and culture that it formulates. To deny this would be to accept a particular kind of constructivism that, at the risk of imploding in on itself, inevitably ends up telling the same simple story: anthropology always poorly constructed its objects, but when the authors of the critical denunciations put pen to paper, the lights came on, and it begin to construct them correctly. In effect, an examination of the readings of Fabian's *Time and the Other* (1983) and its numerous successors makes it impossible to know if we are once again faced with a spasm of cognitive despair before the inaccessibility of the thing in itself or the old illuminist thaumaturgy where an author purports to incarnate a universal reason come to scatter the darkness of superstition—no longer that of indigenous peoples, rest assured, but of the authors who proceeded him. The de-exoticization of the indigenous, which is not so far from all this, has the counter-effect of a rather strong exoticization of the anthropologist, which is also lurking nearby. Proust, who knew a thing or two about time and the other, would have said that nothing appears older than the recent past.

Disabling this type of epistemo-political reflex is one of the principal objectives of *Anti-Narcissus*. In order to accomplish this, however, the last thing we should do is commit anthropology to a servile relationship with economics or sociology whereby it would be made, in a spirit of obsequious emulation, to adopt the meta-narratives promulgated by these two sciences, the principal function of which would seem to be the repressive recontextualization of the existential practice(s) of all the collectives of the world in terms of "the thought collective" of the analyst (Englund and Leach 2000: 225-48).[1] The position argued here, on the contrary, affirms that anthropology should remain in open air continuing to be an art of distances keeping away from the ironic recesses of the Occidental soul (while the Occident may be an abstraction, its soul definitely is not), and remain faithful to the project of the externalization of reason that has always so insistently pushed it, much too often against its will, outside the stifling bedroom of the Same. The viability of an authentic endoanthropology, an aspiration that has for numerous reasons come to have first priority on the disciplinary agenda, thus depends in a crucial way on the theoretical ventilation that has always been favored by exoanthropology—a "field science" in a truly important sense.

The aim of *Anti-Narcissus*, then, is to illustrate the thesis that every nontrivial anthropological theory is a *version* of an indigenous practice of knowledge, all such theories being situatable in strict structural continuity with the intellectual pragmatics of the collectives that have historically occupied the position of object in the discipline's gaze.[2] This entails outlining a performative description of the discursive transformations of anthropology at the origin of the internalization of the transformational condition of the discipline as such, which is to say the (of course theoretical) fact that it is the discursive anamorphosis of the ethnoanthropologies of the collectives studied. By using the example, to speak of something close at hand, of the Amazonian notions of perspectivism and multinaturalism—the author is an Americanist ethnologist—the intention of *Anti-Narcissus* is to show that the styles of thought proper to the collectives that we study are the motor force of anthropology. A more profound examination of these styles and their implications, particularly from the perspective of the elaboration of an anthropological concept of the concept, should be capable of showing their importance to the genesis,

---

1. See also Lévi-Strauss' distinction between anthropology, a "centrifugal science" adopting "the perspective of immanence," and economics and sociology, the "centripetal sciences" that attribute a "transcendental value" to the societies of the observer (1978[1964]: 307-8).

2. This does not at all mean that the former and the latter are epistemologically homogeneous from the point of view of the techniques in play and the problems implied. See Strathern (1987).

now underway, of a completely different conception of anthropological practice. In sum, a new anthropology of the concept capable of counter-effectuating a new concept of anthropology, after which the descriptions of the conditions of the ontological self-determination of the collectives studied will absolutely prevail over the reduction of human (as well as nonhuman) thought to a *dispositif* of recognition: classification, predication, judgment, and representation.... Anthropology as comparative ontography (Holbraad 2003: 39–77)—*that* is the true point of view of immanence.[3] Accepting the importance of and opportunity presented by this task of thinking thought otherwise is to incriminate oneself in the effort to forge an anthropological theory of the conceptual imagination, one attuned to the creativity and reflexivity of every collective, human or otherwise.

Thus the intention behind the title of the book I am describing is to suggest that our discipline is already in the course of writing the first chapters of a great book that would be like its *Anti-Oedipus*. Because if Oedipus is the protagonist of the founding myth of psychoanalysis, our book proposes Narcissus as the candidate for patron saint or tutelary spirit of anthropology, which (above all in its so-called "philosophical" version) has always been a little too obsessed with determining the attributes or criteria that fundamentally distinguish the subject of anthropological discourse from everything it is not: *them* (which really in the end means us), the non-Occidentals, the nonmoderns, the nonhumans. In other words, what is it that the others "have not" that constitutes them as non-Occidental and nonmodern? Capitalism? Rationality? Individualism and Christianity? (Or, perhaps more modestly, *pace* Goody: alphabetic writing and the marriage dowry?) And what about the even more gaping absences that would make certain others nonhumans (or, rather, make the nonhumans the true others)? An immortal soul? Language? Labor? The *Lichtung*? Prohibition? Neoteny? Metaintentionality?

---

3. This perspective on immanence is not exactly the same as that of Lévi-Straus in the passage cited above.

All these absences resemble each other. For in truth, taking them for the problem is exactly the problem, which thus contains the form of the response: the form of a Great Divide, the same gesture of exclusion that made the human species the biological analogue of the anthropological West, confusing all the other species and peoples in a common, privative alterity. Indeed, asking what distinguishes us from the others—and it makes little difference who "they" are, since what really matters in that case is only "us"—is already a response.

The point of contesting the question, "what is (proper to) Man?" then, is absolutely not to say that "Man" has no essence, that his existence precedes his essence, that the being of Man is freedom and indetermination, but to say that the question has become, for all-too obvious historical reasons, one that it is impossible to respond to without dissimulation, without, in other words, continuing to repeat that the chief property of Man is to have no final properties, which apparently earns Man unlimited rights to the properties of the other. This response from our intellectual tradition, which justifies anthropocentrism on the basis of this human "impropriety," is that absence, finitude and lack of being [*manque-à-être*] are the distinctions that the species is doomed to bear, to the benefit (as some would have us believe) of the rest of the living. The burden of man is to be the universal animal, he for whom there exists a universe, while nonhumans, as we know (but how in the devil do we know it?), are just "poor in world" (not even a lark …). As for non-Occidental humans, something quietly leads us to suspect that where the world is concerned, they end up reduced to its smallest part. We and we alone, the Europeans,[4] would be the realized humans, or, if you prefer, the grandiosely unrealized: the millionaires, accumulators, and configurers of worlds. Western metaphysics is truly the *fons et origio* of every colonialism.

In the event that the problem changes, so too will the response. Against the great dividers, a minor anthropology would make small multiplicities proliferate—not the narcissism of small differences but the anti-narcissism of continuous variations; against all the finished-and-done humanisms, an "interminable humanism" that constantly challenges the constitution of

---

4. I include myself among them out of courtesy.

humanity into a separate order (see Maniglier 2000: 216-41). I will re-emphasize it: such an anthropology would make multiplicities proliferate. Because it is not at all a question, as Derrida opportunely recalled (2008), of preaching the abolition of the borders that unite/separate sign and world, persons and things, "us" and "them," "humans" and "nonhumans"—easy reductionisms and mobile monisms are as out of the question as fusional fantasies—but rather of "unreducing" [*irréduire*] (Latour) and undefining them, by bending every line of division into an infinitely complex curve. It is not a question of erasing the contours but of folding and thickening them, diffracting and rendering them iridescent. "This is what we are getting at: a generalized chromaticism" (D. G. 1987). Chromaticism as the structuralist vocabulary with which the agenda for its posterity will be written.

The draft of *Anti-Narcissus* has begun to be completed by certain anthropologists who are responsible for a profound renewal of the discipline. Although they are all known figures, their work has not at all received the recognition and diffusion it deserves—even, and especially in the instance of their own countries of origin. I am referring in the last case to the American Roy Wagner, who should be credited with the extremely rich notion of "reverse anthropology," a dizzying semiotics of "invention" and "convention," and his visionary outline of an anthropological concept of the concept; but I am also thinking of the English anthropologist Marilyn Strathern, to whom we owe the deconstruction/potentiation of feminism and anthropology, just as we do the central tenets of an indigenous aesthetic and analysis forming the two flanks of a Melanesian anti-critique of Occidental reason, and even the invention of a properly post-Malinowskian mode of ethnographic description; and to that Bourguignon Bruno Latour and his transontological concepts of the collective and the actor-network, the paradoxical movement of our never-having-been modern, and the anthropological re-enchantment of scientific practice. And to these can be added many others, recently arrived, but who will go unnamed since it would be largely impossible to do otherwise without some injustice, whether by omission or commission.[5]

But well before all of them (cited or not) there was Claude Lévi-Strauss, whose work has a face turned toward anthropology's past, which it crowns, and another looking into and anticipating its future. If Rousseau, by the former's account, ought to be regarded as the founder of the human sciences, then Lévi-Strauss deserves to be credited not only with having refounded them with structuralism but also with virtually "un-founding" them by pointing the way toward an anthropology of immanence, a path he only took "like Moses conducting his people all the way to a promised land whose splendor he would never behold" and perhaps never truly entered.[6] In conceiving anthropological knowledge as a transformation of indigenous practice—"anthropology," as he said, "seeks to elaborate the social science of the observed"— and the *Mythologiques* as "the myth of mythology," Lévi-Strauss laid down the milestones of a philosophy to come (Hamberger 2004: 345) one positively marked by a seal of interminability and virtuality.[7]

Claude Lévi-Strauss as the founder, yes, of *post*-structuralism…. Just a little more than ten years ago, in the afterward to a volume of *L'Homme* devoted to an appraisal of the structuralist heritage in kinship studies, the dean of our craft made this equally penetrating and decisive statement:

> One should note that, on the basis of a critical analysis of the notion of affinity, conceived by South American Indians as the point of articulation between opposed terms—human and divine, friend and foe, relative and stranger—our Brazilian colleagues have come to extract what could be called a metaphysics of predation. […] Without a doubt, this approach is not free from the dangers that threaten any hermeneutics: that we insidiously begin to think on behalf of

---

5. An exception must be made for Tim Ingold, who (along with Philippe Descola, about whom we will have occasion to speak later) is doubtlessly the anthropologist who has done the most to undermine the ontological partitions of our intellectual tradition, particularly those that separate "humanity" from the "environment" (see Ingold 2000). However insightful, Ingold's work as a whole nonetheless owes a great deal to phenomenology, which means that its relations with the concepts and authors at the heart of the present book are largely indirect.

6. This allusion to Moses can be found in *Introduction to the Work of Marcel Mauss* (L.-S. 1987a).

7. On the philosophy to come of Lévi-Strauss, see Klaus Hamberger (2004).

those we believe to understand, and that we make them say more than what they think, or something else entirely. Nobody can deny, nonetheless, that it has changed the terms in which certain big problems were posed, such as cannibalism and headhunting. From this current of ideas, a general impression results: whether we rejoice in or recoil from it, philosophy is once again center stage. No longer our philosophy, the one that my generation wished to cast aside with the help of exotic peoples; but, in a remarkable reversal [*un frappant retour des choses*], theirs. (L.-S. 2000: 719-20)

The observation marvelously sums up, as we will see, the content of this present book, which is, in fact, being written by one of these Brazilian colleagues.[8] Indeed, not only do we take as one of our ethnographic axes this properly metaphysical use South American Indians make of the notion of affinity, but we sketch, moreover, a reprise of the problem of the relation between, on the one hand, the two philosophies evoked by Lévi-Strauss in a mode of non-relation—"ours" and "theirs"—and, on the other hand, the philosophy to come that structuralism projected.

For whether we rejoice in it or recoil from it, what is really at stake is philosophy…. Or, rather, the re-establishment of a certain connection between anthropology and philosophy via a new consideration of the transdisciplinary problematic that was constituted at the imprecise frontier between structuralism and poststructuralism during that brief moment of effervescence and generosity of thought that immediately preceded the conservative revolution that has, in recent decades, showed itself particularly efficacious at transforming the world, both ecologically and politically, into something perfectly suffocating.

A double trajectory, then: an at once anthropological and philosophical reading informed, on the one hand, by Amazonian thought—it is absolutely essential to recall what Taylor (2004: 97) has stressed are "the Amerindian foundations of structuralism"—and, on the other, by the "dissident structuralism" of Gilles Deleuze (Lapoujade 2006). The destination, moreover, is also double, comprising the ideal of anthropology as a

---

8. See my (2001a) "A propriedade do conceito: sobre o plano de imanência amerindio" for another commentary on this passage, which has also been brilliantly discussed by Maniglier (2005a).

permanent exercise in the decolonization of thought, and a proposal for another means besides philosophy for the creation of concepts.

But in the end, anthropology is what is at stake. The intention behind this tour through our recent past is in effect far more prospective than nostalgic, the aspiration being to awaken certain possibilities and glimpse a break in the clouds through which our discipline could imagine, at least for itself qua intellectual project, a denouement (to dramatize things a bit) other than mere death by asphyxia.

Chapter Two

Perspectivism

Such a requalification of the anthropological agenda was what Tânia Stolze Lima and I wanted to contribute to when we proposed the concept of Amerindian *perspectivism* as the reconfiguration of a complex of ideas and practices whose power of intellectual disturbance has never been sufficiently appreciated (even if they found the word relevant) by Americanists, despite its vast diffusion in the New World.[9] To this we added the synoptic concept of *multinaturalism*, which presented Amerindian thought as an unsuspected partner, a dark precursor if you will, of certain contemporary philosophical programs, like those developing around theories of possible worlds, others that refuse to operate within the vicious dichotomies of modernity, or still others that, having registered the end of the hegemony of the kind of critique that demands an epistemological response to every ontological question, are slowly defining new lines of flight for thought under the rallying cries of transcendental empiricism and speculative realism.

The two concepts emerged following an analysis of the cosmological presuppositions of "the metaphysics of predation" evoked

9. For the chief formulations of the idea, see Tânia Stolze Lima, "The Two and Its Many: Reflections on Perspectivism in a Tuna Cosmology" (1999[1996]), and *Um Peixe Olhou para Mim: O Povo Yudjá e a Perspectiva* (2005). See also Viveiros de Castro "Cosmological Deixis and Amerindian Perspectivism" (1998), 'Perspectivisimo e multinaturalismo na América indígena' (2002a), "Perspectival Anthropology and the Method of Controlled Equivocation" (2004a), and "Exchanging Perspectives: The Transformation of Objects into Subjects in Amerindian Cosmologies" (2004b). In what follows, I repeat themes and passages from these articles already known to the anthropological public, but which other readers will benefit from having reprised.

in the last chapter. We found that this metaphysics, as can be deduced from Lévi-Strauss' summary of it, reaches its highest expression in the strong speculative yield of those indigenous categories denoting matrimonial alliance, phenomena that I translated with yet another concept: *virtual affinity*.[10] Virtual affinity is the schematism characteristic of what Deleuze would have called the "Other-structure"[11] of Amerindian worlds and is indelibly marked by cannibalism, which is an omnipresent motif in their inhabitants' relational imagination. Interspecific perspectivism, ontological multinaturalism and cannibal alterity thus form the three aspects of an indigenous alter-anthropology that is the symmetrical and reverse transformation of Occidental anthropology—as symmetrical in Latour's sense as it is reverse in the sense of Wagner's "reverse anthropology." By drawing this triangle, we can enter into the orbit of one of the philosophies of "the exotic peoples" that Lévi-Strauss opposed to ours and attempt, in other words, to realize something of the imposing program outlined in the fourth chapter, "Geophilosophy," of *What Is Philosophy?* … even if it will be at the price—but one we should always be ready to pay—of a certain methodological imprecision and intentional ambiguity.

Our work's perfectly contingent point of departure was the sudden perception of a resonance between the results of our research on Amazonian cosmopolitics—on its notion of a perspectivist multiplicity intrinsic to the real—and a well-known parable on the subject of the conquest of the Americans recounted by Lévi-Strauss in *Race and History*:

> In the Greater Antilles, some years after the discovery of America, while the Spaniards sent out investigating commissions to ascertain whether or not the natives had a soul, the latter were engaged in the drowning of white prisoners in order to verify, through prolonged watching, whether or not their corpses were subject to putrification. (L.-S. 1978b[1952]: 329)

10. Viveiros de Castro 2001b; 2002b. See below, chapter 11.

11. Deleuze 1990a.

In this conflict between the two anthropologies, the author perceived a baroque allegory of the fact that one of the typical manifestations of human nature is the negation of its own generality. A kind of congenital avarice preventing the extension of the predicates of humanity to the species as a whole appears to be one of its predicates. In sum, ethnocentrism could be said to be like good sense, of which perhaps it is just the apperceptive moment: the best distributed thing in the world. The format of the lesson is familiar, but that does not lessen its sting. Overestimating one's own humanity to the detriment of the contemptible other's reveals one's deep resemblance with it. Since the other of the Same (of the European) shows itself to be the same as the Other's other (of the indigenous), the Same ends up unwittingly showing itself to be the same as the Other.

The anecdote fascinated Lévi-Strauss enough for him to repeat it in *Tristes Tropiques*. But there he added a supplementary, ironic twist, this time noting a difference (rather than this resemblance) between the parties. While the Europeans relied on the social sciences in their investigations of the humanity of the other, the Indians placed their faith in the natural sciences; and where the former proclaimed the Indians to be animals, the latter were content to suspect the others might be gods. "Both attitudes show equal ignorance," Lévi-Strauss concluded, "but the Indian's behavior certainly had greater dignity" (1992: 76). If this is really how things transpired,[12] it forces us to conclude that, despite being just as ignorant on the subject of the other, the other of the Other was not exactly the same as the other of the Same. We could even say that it was its exact opposite, if not for the fact that the relation between these two others of humanity—animality and divinity—is conceived in indigenous worlds in completely different terms than those we have inherited from Christianity. The rhetorical contrast Lévi-Strauss draws succeeds because it

---

12. As Marshall Sahlins observed in *How "Natives" Think: About Captain Cook, for Example* (1995), the association of colonial invaders with local divinities, a phenomenon observed in diverse encounters between the Moderns and indigenous peoples, says much more about what the Indians thought about divinity than about what they thought of Europeanness or modernity.

appeals to *our* cosmological hierarchies rather than those of the Taino.[13]

In any case, consideration of this disequilibrium was what led us to the hypothesis that Amerindian ontological regimes diverge from those widespread in the West precisely with regard to the inverse semiotic functions they respectively attribute to soul and body. The marked dimension for the Spanish was the soul, whereas the Indian emphasized the body. The Europeans never doubted that the Indians had bodies—animals have them too—and the Indians in turn never doubted that the Europeans had souls, since animals and the ghosts of the dead do as well. Thus the Europeans' ethnocentrism consisted in doubting that the body of the other contained a soul formally similar to the one inhabiting their own bodies, while the ethnocentrism of the Indians, on the contrary, entailed doubting that the others' souls or spirits could possess a body materially similar to theirs.[14]

◊ In the semiotic terms of Roy Wagner, a Melanesianist who will quickly reveal himself to be a crucial intercessor in the theory of Amerindian perspectivism, the body belongs to the innate or spontaneous dimension of European ontology ("nature"), which is the counter-invented result of an operation of conventionalist symbolization, while the soul would be the constructed dimension, the fruit of a "differentiating" symbolization that "specifies and renders concrete the conventional world by tracing radical distinctions and concretizing the singular individuals of this world" (Wagner 1981: 42). In indigenous worlds, on the contrary,

13. The anecdote was taken from Oviedo's *History of the Indians*; it would have taken place in Hispanolia, in the inquiry undertaken in 1517 by priests of the order of St. Jerome in the colonies, and Puerto Rico, with the submergence of a young Spaniard, who was caught and then drowned by Indians. It is an argument that, moreover, demonstrates the necessity of pushing the archaeology of the human sciences back until at least the controversy of Valladolid (1550–51), the celebrated debate between Las Casas and Sepúlveda on the subject of the nature of American Indians. See Anthony Pagden, *The Fall of Natural Man: The American Indian and the Origins of Comparative Ethnology* (1982).

14. The old notion of the soul has been going incognito ever since it was rechristened as culture, the symbolic, mind, etc.... The theological problem of the soul of others became the philosophical puzzle of "the problem of other minds," which currently extends so far as to include neurotechnological inquiries on human consciousness, the minds of animals, the intelligence of machines (the gods have apparently transferred themselves into Intel microprocessors). In the last two cases, the question concerns whether certain animals would not, after all, have something like a soul or a consciousness—perhaps even a culture—and, reciprocally, if certain material non-autopoietic systems lacking, in other words, a true body could show themselves capable of intentionality.

the soul "is experienced as … a manifestation of the conventional order implicit in everything" and "sums up the ways in which its possessor is similar to others, over and above the ways in which he differs from them" (Wagner 1981: 94); the body, on the contrary, belongs to the sphere of what comes from the responsibility of agents and is one of the fundamental figures of something that has to be constructed against a universal and innate ground of an "immanent humanity" (Wagner 1981: 86-9).[15] In short, European praxis consists in "making souls" (and differentiating cultures) on the basis of a given corporeal-material ground—nature—while indigenous praxis consists in "making bodies" (and differentiating species) on the basis of a socio-spiritual continuum, itself also given … but in myth, as we will see.

Wagner's conceptually dense and quite original theoretical system resists didactic summary; thus we request that the reader directly engage its most elegant and realized presentation in *The Invention of Culture*. *Grosso modo*, the Wagnerian semiotic can be said to be a theory of human and nonhuman practice conceived as exhaustively consisting in the reciprocal, recursive operation of two modes of symbolization: (1) a collectivizing, conventional (or literal) symbolism where signs are organized in standardized contexts (semantic domains, formal languages, etc.) to the extent that they are opposed to a heterogeneous plane of "referents"— that is, they are seen as symbolizing something other than themselves; and (2) a differentiating, inventive (or figurative) mode in which the world of phenomena represented by conventional symbolization is understood to be constituted by "symbols representing themselves," that is, events that simultaneously manifest as symbols and referents, thereby dissolving the conventional contrast. It should be observed, first of all, that the world of referents or the "real" is defined here as a semiotic effect: what is other to a sign is another sign having the singular capacity of "representing itself." The mode of existence of actual entities qua events or occasions is a tautegory. It should be stressed that the contrast between the two modes is itself the result of a conventionalist operation (and perception): the distinction between invention and convention is itself conventional, but at the same time every convention is produced through a counter-invention. The contrast is thus intrinsically recursive, especially if we understand that human cultures are fundamentally in conflict over the mode of symbolization they (conventionally) privilege as an element appropriated for action or invention, in reserving to the other the function of the "given." Cultures, human macrosystems of conventions, are distinguished by what they define as belonging to the sphere of the responsibilities of agents—the mode of the constructed—

---

15. Here I am myself "innovating" on Wagner, who does not raise in *The Invention of Culture* the question of the status of the body in the "differentiating" cultures.

and by what belongs (because it is counter-constructed as belonging) to the world of the given or non-constructed.

> The core of any and every set of cultural conventions is a simple distinction as to what kind of contexts—the nonconventionalized ones or those of convention itself—are to be deliberately articulated in the course of human action, and what kind of contexts are to be counter-invented as "motivation" under the conventional mask of "the given" or "the innate." Of course […] there are only two possibilities: a people who deliberately differentiate as the form of their action will invariably counter-invent a motivating collectivity as "innate," and a people who deliberately collectivize will counter-invent a motivating differentiation in this way. (Wagner 1981: 51)

The anthropological chiasm Lévi-Strauss opened up via the Antilles incident is in accord with two characteristics of Amazonian cosmology recently distinguished by its ethnography. First, it unexpectedly confirmed the importance of an economy of *corporeality* at the very heart of those ontologies recently redefined (in what will be seen to be a somewhat unilateral fashion) as animist.[16] I say "confirmed" because this was something that had already been abundantly demonstrated in the *Mythologiques*, as long as they are taken literally and thus understood as a mythic transformation of the mythic transformations that were their object. In other words, they describe, in prose wedding Cartesian rigor to Rabelaisian verve, an indigenous anthropology formulated in terms of organic fluxes, material codings, sensible multiplicities, and becomings-animal instead of in the spectral terms of our own anthropology, whose juridical-theological grisaille (the rights, duties, rules, principles, categories and moral persons conceptually formative of the discipline) simply overwhelms it.[17]

16. The theme of animism was recently reanimated by Philippe Descola (1992, 1996) who of course pays unstinting attention to Amazonian materials.

17. See A. Seeger, R. DaMatta and E. Viveiros de Castro, 1979 for a first formulation of the problematic of corporeality in indigenous America. Because it explicitly relied on the *Mythologiques*, this work was developed without the least connection to the theme of embodiment that would take anthropology by storm in the decades to follow. The structuralist current of Amerindian ethnology, deaf to what Deleuze and Guattari called the "at once pious and sensual" appeal to phenomenological "fleshism"—the appeal to "rotten wood," as a reader of *The Raw and The Cooked* would say—always thought incarnation from the perspective of the culinary triangle rather than the holy Trinity.

Second, Amazonianists have also perceived certain theoretical implications of this non-marked or generic status of the virtual dimension or "soul" of existents, a chief premise of a powerful indigenous intellectual structure that is *inter alia* capable of providing a counter-description of the image drawn of it by Western anthropology and thereby capable, again, of "returning to us an image in which we are unrecognizable to ourselves." This double, materialist-speculative twist, applied to the usual psychological and positivist representation of animism, is what we called "perspectivism," by virtue of the analogies, as much constructed as observed, with the philosophical thesis associated with this term found in Leibniz, Nietzsche, Whitehead and Deleuze.

As various ethnographers have noted (unfortunately too often only in passing), virtually all peoples of the New World share a conception of the world as composed of a multiplicity of points of view. Every existent is a center of intentionality apprehending other existents according to their respective characteristics and powers. The presuppositions and consequences of this idea are nevertheless irreducible to the current concept of relativism that they would, at first glance, seem to evoke. They are, in fact, instead arranged on a plane orthogonal to the opposition between relativism and universalism. Such resistance on the part of Amerindian perspectivism to the terms of our epistemological debates casts suspicion on the transposability of the ontological partitions nourishing them. This is the conclusion a number of anthropologists arrived at (although for very different reasons) when asserting that the nature/culture distinction—that first article of the Constitution of anthropology, whereby it pledges allegiance to the ancient matrix of Western metaphysics—cannot be used to describe certain dimensions or domains internal to non-Occidental cosmologies without first making them the object of rigorous ethnographic critique.

In the present case, such a critique demanded the redistribution of the predicates arranged in the paradigmatic series of "nature" and "culture": universal and particular, objective and subjective, physical and moral, the given and the instituted, necessity and spontaneity, immanence and transcendence, body and spirit, animality and humanity, and so on. The new order of this other conceptual map led us to suggest that the term "multinaturalism" could be used to designate one of the most distinctive traits of Amerindian thought, which emerges upon its juxtaposition with modern, multiculturalist cosmologies: where the latter rest on the mutual implication between the unicity of nature and the multiplicity of cultures—the first being guaranteed by the objective universality of bodies and substance, and the second engendered by the subjective particularity of minds and signifiers (cf. Ingold 1991)—the Amerindian conception presupposes, on the contrary, a unity of mind and a diversity of bodies. "Culture" or subject as the form of the universal, and "nature" or object as the particular.

The ethnography of indigenous America is replete with references to a cosmopolitical theory describing a universe inhabited by diverse types of actants or subjective agents, human or otherwise—gods, animals, the dead, plants, meteorological phenomena, and often objects or artifacts as well—equipped with the same general ensemble of perceptive, appetitive, and cognitive dispositions: with the same kind of soul. This interspecific resemblance includes, to put it a bit performatively, the same mode of apperception: animals and other nonhumans having a soul "see themselves as persons" and therefore "are persons": intentional, double-sided (visible and invisible) objects constituted by social relations and existing under a double, at once reflexive and reciprocal—which is to say collective—pronominal mode. What these persons see and thus are as persons, however, constitutes the very philosophical problem posed by and for indigenous thought.

The resemblance between souls, however, does not entail that what they express or perceive is likewise shared. The way humans see animals, spirits and other actants in the cosmos is profoundly different from how these beings both see them and see themselves. Typically, and this tautology is something like the degree zero of perspectivism, humans will, under normal conditions, see humans as humans and animals as animals (in the case of spirits, seeing these normally invisible beings is a sure indication that the conditions are not normal: sickness, trance and other "altered states"). Predatory animals and spirits, for their part, see humans as prey, while prey see humans as spirits or predators. "The human being sees himself as what he is. The loon, the snake, the jaguar, and The Mother of Smallpox, however, see him as a tapir or a pecari to be killed," remarks Baer apropos the Matsiguenga of Amazonian Peru (Baer 1994). In seeing *us* as nonhumans, animals and spirits regard themselves (their own species) as human: they perceive themselves as (or become) anthropomorphic beings when they are in their houses or villages, and apprehend their behavior and characteristics through a cultural form: they perceive their food as human food—jaguars see blood as manioc beer, vultures see the worms in rotten meat as grilled fish—their corporeal attributes (coats, feathers, claws, beaks) as finery or cultural instruments, and they even organize their social systems in the same way as human institutions, with chiefs, shamans, exogamous moieties and rituals.

Some precisions prove necessary. Perspectivism is only rarely applied to all animals (even as it encompasses nearly all other beings, and at the very least the dead), as the species it seems most frequently to involve are the big predators and scavengers, like jaguars, anacondas, vultures and harpies, and the typical prey of humans—wild boar, monkeys, fish, deer and tapirs. In fact, one of the fundamental aspects of perspectivist inversions concerns the relative, relational status of predator and prey. The Amazonian metaphysics of predation is a pragmatic and theoretical context highly favorable to perspectivism. That said, there is scarcely an existent that could not be defined in terms of its relative position on a scale of predatory power.

For if all existents are not necessarily *de facto* persons, the fundamental point is that there is *de jure* nothing to prevent any species or mode of being from having that status. The problem, in sum, is not one of taxonomy, classification or so-called ethnoscience.[18] All animals and cosmic constituents are intensively and virtually persons, because all of them, no matter which, can reveal themselves to be (transform into) a person. This is not a simple logical possibility but an ontological potentiality. Personhood

---

18. Compare with what Lienhardt says on the heteroclite collection of species, entities and phenomena that served the clan-divinities of the Dinka of Sudan. "The Dinka have no theory about the principle upon which some species are included among clan-divinities, and some omitted. There is no reason, in their thought, why anything might not be the divinity of some clan" (1961: 110).

and perspectiveness—the capacity to occupy a point of view—is a question of degree, context and position rather than a property distinct to specific species. Certain nonhumans actualize this potential more fully than others, and some, moreover, manifest it with a superior intensity than our species and are, in this sense, "more human than humans" (see Irving 1960). Furthermore, the question possesses an essentially *a posteriori* quality. The possibility of a previously insignificant being revealing itself (to a dreamer, sick person or shaman) as a prosopomorphic agent capable of affecting human affairs always remains open; where the personhood of being is concerned, "personal" experience is more decisive than whatever cosmological dogma.

If nothing prevents an existent from being conceived of as a person—as an aspect, that is, of a biosocial multiplicity—nothing else prevents another human collective from *not* being considered one. This is, moreover, the rule. The strange generosity that makes peoples like Amazonians see humans concealed under the most improbable forms or, rather, affirm that even the most unlikely beings are capable of seeing themselves as humans is the double of the well-known ethnocentrism that leads these same groups to deny humanity to their fellow men [*congénères*] and even (or above all) to their closest geographical or historical cousins. In contrast with the courageously disenchanted maturity of the old Europeans and their longstanding resignation to the cosmic solipsism of the human condition (a bitter pill for them, however sweetened it is by the consolation of intraspecific intersubjectivity), it is as if our exotic people perpetually oscillate between two infantile narcissisms: one of small differences between fellow people(s) [*congénères*] that often resemble each other too much, and another of big resemblances between entirely different species. We see how the other(s) can never win: at once ethnocentric and animist, they are inevitably immoderate, whether by omission or commission.

The fact that the condition of the person (whose universal apperceptive form is human) could be "extended" to other species while "denied" to other collectives of our own immediately suggests that the concept of the person—a center of intentionality constituted by a difference of internal potential—is anterior and logically superior to the concept of the human. Humanity is in the position of the common denominator, the reflexive mode of the collective, and is as such derived in relation to the primary positions of predator and prey, which necessarily implicates other collectives and personal multiplicities in a situation of perspectival multiplicity.[19] This interspecific resemblance or kinship arises from the deliberate, socially produced suspension of a given predatory difference and does not precede it. This is precisely what Amerindian kinship consists of: "reproduction" as *the intensive stabilization and/or deliberate non-achievement of predation*, in the fashion of the celebrated Batesonian (or Balinese) intensive plateau that so inspired Deleuze and Guattari. It is not by chance that in another text of Lévi-Strauss' that deals with cannibalism, this idea of identity-by-subtraction receives a formulation perfectly befitting Amerindian perspectivism:

> [T]he problem of cannibalism … would not be a search for the "why?" of the custom, but, on the contrary, for the "how?" of the emergence of this lower limit of predation by which, perhaps, we are brought back to social life. (L.-S. 1987b: 113; see also L.-S. 1981: 690)

This is nothing more than an application of the classic structuralist precept that "resemblance has no reality in itself; it is only a particular instance of difference, that in which difference tends toward zero" (L.-S. 1981: 38).[20] Everything hinges on the verb "to tend," since, as Lévi-Strauss observes, difference "is never completely annulled." We could even say that it only blooms to its full conceptual power when it becomes as slight as can be: like the difference between twins, as an Amerindian philosopher might say.

---

19. "Human" is a term designating a relation, not a substance. Primitive peoples' celebrated designations of themselves as "the human beings" and "the true men" seem to function pragmatically, if not syntactically, less as *substantives* than as *pronouns* marking the subjective position of the speaker. It is for this reason that the indigenous categories of collective identity possess this great contextual variability so characteristic of pronouns, marking the self/other contrast through the immediate kinship of the "I" with all other humans, or, as we have seen, with all other beings endowed with consciousness. Their sedimentation as "ethnonyms" seems to be mostly an artifact produced through interactions with the ethnographer.

20. The precept is classic, but few of the so-called "structuralists" truly understood how to push the idea to its logical conclusion and thus beyond itself. Might that be because they would be pulled with it into the orbit of *Difference and Repetition*?

◎ ◎ ◎

The notion that actual nonhumans possess an invisible prosopo-morphic side is a fundamental supposition of several dimensions of indigenous practice, but it is only foregrounded in the particular context of shamanism. Amerindian shamanism could be defined as the authorization of certain individuals to cross the corporeal barriers between species, adopt an exospecific subjective perspective, and administer the relations between those species and humans. By seeing nonhuman beings as they see themselves (again as humans), shamans become capable of playing the role of active interlocutors in the trans-specific dialogue and, even more importantly, of returning from their travels to recount them; something the "laity" can only do with difficulty. This encounter or exchange of perspectives is not only a dangerous process but a political art: diplomacy. If Western relativism has multicultural-ism as its public politics, Amerindian shamanic perspectivism has multinaturalism as its cosmic politics.

Shamanism is a mode of action entailing a mode of knowledge, or, rather, a certain ideal of knowledge. In certain respects, this ideal is diametrically opposed to the objectivist epistemology encouraged by Western modernity. The latter's telos is provided by the category of the object: to know is to objectify by distinguishing between what is intrinsic to the object and what instead belongs to the knowing subject, which has been inevitably and illegitimately projected onto the object. To know is thus to desubjectify, to render explicit the part of the subject present in the object in order to reduce it to an ideal minimum (and/or to amplify it with a view to obtaining spectacular critical effects). Subjects, just like objects, are regarded as the results of a process of objectification: the subject constitutes or recognizes itself in the object it produces, and knows itself objectively when it succeeds in seeing itself "from the outside" as a thing. Our epistemological game, then, is objectification; what has not been objectified simply remains abstract or unreal. The form of the Other is the thing.

Amerindian shamanism is guided by the inverse ideal: to know is to "personify," to take the point of view of what should be known or, rather, *the one* whom should be known. The key is to know, in Guimarães Rosa's phrase, "the who of things," with-out which there would be no way to respond intelligently to the question of "why." The form of the Other is the person. We could also say, to utilize a vocabulary currently in vogue, that shamanic personification or subjectivation reflects a propensity to universalize the "intentional attitude" accorded so much value by certain modern philosophers of mind (or, more accurately, philosophers of *modern* mind). To be more precise, since the Indians are perfectly capable of adopting "physical" and "functional" attitudes *sensu* Dennett (1978) in everyday life, we will say that here we are faced with an epistemological ideal that, far from seeking to reduce "ambient intentionality" to its zero degree in order to attain an absolutely objective representation of the world, instead makes the opposite wager: true knowledge aims to reveal a maximum of intentionality through a systematic and deliberate abduction of agency. To what we said above about shamanism being a *political* art we can now add that it is a political *art*.[21] For the good shamanic interpretation succeeds in seeing each event as being, in truth, an *action,* an expression of intentional states or predicates of an agent. Interpretive success, then, is directly proportional to the successful attribution of intentional order to an object or *noeme*.[22] An entity or state of things not prone to subjectivation, which is to say the actualization of its social relation with the one who knows it, is shamanically insignificant—in that case, it is just an epistemic residue or impersonal factor resistant to precise knowledge. Our objectivist epistemology, there is no need to recall, proceeds in the opposite direction, conceiving the intentional attitude as a convenient fiction adopted when the aimed-for object is too complex to be decomposed into elementary physical

21. The relation between artistic experience and the process of the "abduction of agency" was analyzed by Alfred Gell in *Art and Agency* (1998).

22. I am referring here to Dennett's notion of the n-ordinality of intentional systems. A second-order intentional system is one in which the observer ascribes not only (as in the first order) beliefs, desires and other intentions to the object but, additionally, beliefs, etc. about other beliefs (etc.). The standard cognitive thesis holds that only humans exhibit second- or higher-order intentionality. The shamanistic "principle of the abduction of a maximum agency" runs afoul of the creed of physicalist psychology: "Psychologists have often appealed to a principle known as 'Lloyd Morgan's Canon of Parsimony,' which can be viewed as a special case of Occam's Razor: it is the principle that one should attribute to an organism as little intelligence or consciousness or rationality or mind as will suffice to account for its behavior" (Dennett 1978: 274).

processes. An exhaustive scientific explanation of the world, it is thought, should be capable of reducing every object to a chain of causal events, and these, in turn, to materially dense interactions (through, primarily, action at a distance).

Thus if a subject is an insufficiently analyzed object in the modern naturalist world, the Amerindian epistemological convention follows the inverse principle, which is that an object is an insufficiently interpreted subject. One must know how to personify, because one must personify in order to know. The object of the interpretation is the counter-interpretation of the object.[23] The latter idea should perhaps be developed into its full intentional form—the form of a mind, an animal under a human face—having at least a demonstrable relation with a subject, conceived as something that exists "in the neighborhood" of an agent (see Gell 1998).

Where this second option is concerned, the idea that non-human agents perceive themselves and their behavior under a human form plays a crucial role. The translation of "culture" in the worlds of extrahuman subjectivities has for its corollary the redefinition of several natural objects and events as indexes from which social agency can be inferred. The most common case is the transformation of something that humans regard as a brute fact into another species' artifact or civilized behavior: what we call blood is beer for a jaguar, what we take for a pool of mud, tapirs experience as a grand ceremonial house, and so on. Such artifacts are ontologically ambiguous: they are objects, but they necessarily indicate a subject since they are like frozen actions or material incarnations of a nonmaterial intentionality. What one side calls nature, then, very often turns out to be culture for the other.

Here we have an indigenous lesson anthropology could benefit from heeding. The differential distribution of the given and the constructed must not be taken for an anodyne exchange, a simple change of signs that leaves the terms of the problem intact. There is "all the difference of/in the world" (Wagner 1981: 51) between a world that experiences the primordial as bare transcendence

---

23. As Marilyn Strathern observes of an epistemological regime similar to that of Amerindians: "The same convention requires that the objects of interpretation—human or not—become understood as other persons; indeed, the very act of interpretation presupposes the personhood of what is being interpreted. [...] What one thus encounters in making interpretations are always counter-interpretations" (1991: 23).

and pure anti-anthropic alterity—as the nonconstructed and non-instituted opposed to all custom and discourse[24]—and a world of immanent humanity, where the primordial assumes a human form. This anthropomorphic presupposition of the indigenous world is radically opposed to the persistent anthropocentric effort in Western philosophies (some of the most radical included) to "construct" the human as the nongiven, as the very being of the nongiven (Sloterdijk 2000). We should nevertheless stress, against fantasies of the narcissistic paradises of exotic peoples (a.k.a. Disney anthropology), that this presupposition renders the indigenous world neither more familiar nor more comforting. When everything is human, the human becomes a wholly other thing.

So there really are more things in heaven and earth than in our anthropological dream. To describe this multiverse, where every difference is political (because every relation is "social"), as though it were an illusory version of our universe—to *unify* them by reducing the inventions of the first to the conventions of the second—would be to decide for a simplistic and politically puerile conception of their relationship. Such facile explanations end up engendering every sort of complication, since the cost of this ersatz ontological monism is its inflationary proliferation of epistemological dualisms—emic and etic, metaphoric and literal, conscious and unconscious, representation and reality, illusion and truth (I could go on…). Those dualisms are dubious not because all such conceptual dichotomies are in principle pernicious but because these in particular require, if they are to unify (any) two worlds, discriminating between their respective inhabitants. Every Great Divider is a mononaturalist.

24. "Yet nature is different from man: it is not instituted by him and is opposed to custom, to discourse. Nature is the primordial–that is, the nonconstructed, the noninstituted" (Merleau-Ponty 2003: 3-4).

Chapter Three

Multinaturalism

"We moderns possess the concept but have lost sight of the plane of immanence...." (D. G. 1994: 104). All the foregoing is merely the development of the founding intuition, deductively effectuated by indigenous theoretical practice, of the mythology of the continent, which concerns a milieu that can rightly be called prehistorical (in the sense of the celebrated absolute past: the past that has never been present and which therefore is never past, while the present never ceases to pass), and that is defined by the ontological impenetrability of all the "insistents" populating and constituting this milieu—the templates and standards of actual existents.

As the *Mythologiques* teach us, the narrativization of the indigenous plane of immanence articulates in a privileged way the causes and consequences of speciation—the assumption of a specific corporeality—by the personae or actants therein, all of whom are conceived as sharing a general unstable condition in which the aspects of humans and nonhumans are inextricably enmeshed:

> I would like to ask a simple question. What is a myth?
> It's the very opposite of a simple question [...]. If you were to ask an American Indian, he would most likely tell you that it is a story of the time before men and animals became distinct beings. This definition seems very profound to me. (L.-S. and Éribon: 1991: 139)

In fact, the definition is profound, even if showing this requires taking a slightly different direction than the one Lévi-Strauss had in mind in his response. Mythic discourse registers the movement by which the present state of things is actualized from a virtual, precosmological condition that is perfectly transparent—a cha-osmos where the corporeal and spiritual dimensions of beings do not yet conceal each other. Far from evincing the primordial iden-tification between humans and nonhumans commonly ascribed to it, this precosmos is traversed by an infinite difference (even if, or because, it is internal to each person or agent) contrary to the finite and external differences constituting the actual world's species and qualities. Whence the regime of qualitative multiplic-ity proper to myth: the question, for example, of whether the mythic jaguar is a block of human affects having the form of a jaguar or a block of human affects having a human form is strictly undecidable, as mythic "metamorphosis" is an event, a change on the spot: an intensive superposition of heterogeneous states rather than an extensive transposition of homogenous states. Myth is not history because metamorphosis is not a process, was not yet a process and will never be a process. Metamorphosis is both anterior and external to the process of process—it is a figure (a figuration) of becoming.

The general line traced by mythic discourse thus describes the instantaneous sorting of the precosmological flux of indiscern-ibility that occurs when it enters the cosmological process. Fol-lowing that, the feline and human dimensions of jaguars (and of humans) will alternately function as figure and potential ground for each other. The original transparence or infinitely bifurcated *complicatio* gets explicated in the invisibility (of human souls and animal spirits) and opacity (of human bodies and animal somatic "garb"[25]) that mark the constitution of all mundane beings. This invisibility and opacity are, however, relative and reversible, even as the ground of virtuality is indestructible or inexhaustible; the great indigenous rituals of the recreation of the world are pre-cisely *dispositifs* for the counter-effectuation of this indestructible ground.

The differences coming into effect within myths are, again, infinite and internal, contrary to the external, finite differences between species. What defines the agents and patients of mythic

---

25. The motif of perspectivism is nearly always accompanied by the idea that the visible form of each species is a simple envelope (a "clothing") hiding an internal human form that is only accessible, as we have seen, to the gaze of members of the same species, or certain perspectival "commutators," like shamans.

events is their intrinsic capacity to be something else. In this sense, each persona infinitely differs from itself, given that it is initially supposed by mythic discourse only in order to be replaced, which is to say transformed. Such "self-"difference is the characteristic property of the notion of "spirit," which is why all mythic beings are conceived of as spirits (and as shamans), and every finite mode or actual existent, reciprocally, can manifest as (for it was) a spirit when its reason to be is recounted in myth. The supposed lack of differentiation between mythic subjects is a function of their being constitutively irreducible to essences or fixed identities, whether generic, specific, or even individual.[26]

In sum, myth proposes an ontological regime ordered by a fluent intensive difference bearing on each of the points of a heterogeneous continuum, where transformation is anterior to form, relations superior to terms, and intervals interior to being. Each mythic subject, being a pure virtuality, "was already previously" what it "would be next" and this is why it is not something actually determined. The extensive differences, moreover, introduced by post-mythic speciation (*sensu lato*)—the passage from the continuous to the discrete constituting the grand (my)theme of structural anthropology—is crystallized in molar blocks of infinitely internal identity (each species is internally homogeneous, and its members are equally and indifferently representatives of the species as such).[27] These blocks are separated by external intervals that are quantifiable and measurable, since differences between species are finite systems for the correlation, proportioning, and permutation of characteristics of the same order and same nature.

26. I have in mind the detotalized, "disorganized" bodies that roam about Amerindian myths: the detachable penises and personified anuses, the rolling heads and characters cut into pieces, the eyes transposed from anteaters to jaguars and *vice versa*, etc.

27. As we know, myths contain various moments where this convention is "relativized" (in the sense of Wagner's 1981 book) since, given that infinite identity does not exist, difference is never entirely annulled. See the humorous example from *The Origin of Table Manners* on the subject of poorly matched spouses: "What do the myths proclaim? That it is wicked and dangerous to confuse physical differences between women with the specific differences separating animals from humans, or animals from each other.... [A] s human beings, women, whether beautiful or ugly, all deserve to obtain husbands. [...] When contrasted in the mass with animal wives, human wives are all equally valid; but if the armature of the myth is reversed, it cannot but reveal a mysterious fact that society tries to ignore: all human females are not equal, for nothing can prevent them from being different from each other in their animal essence, which means that they are not all equally desirable to prospective husbands" (L.-S. 1979: 76).

The heterogeneous continuum of the precosmological world thus gives way to a discrete, homogeneous space in whose terms each being is only what it is, and is so only because it is not what it is not. But spirits are the proof that all virtualities have not necessarily been actualized, and that the turbulent mythic flux continues to rumble beneath the apparent discontinuities between types and species.

Amerindian perspectivism, then, finds in myth a geometrical locus where the difference between points of view is at once annulled and exacerbated. In this absolute discourse, each kind of being appears to other beings as it appears to itself—as human—even as it already acts by manifesting its distinct and definitive animal, plant, or spirit nature.[28] Myth, the universal point of flight of perspectivism, speaks of a state of being where bodies and names, souls and actions, egos and others are interpenetrated, immersed in one and the same presubjective and preobjective milieu.

The aim of mythology is precisely to recount the "end" of this "milieu"; in other words, to describe "the passage from Nature to Culture," the theme to which Lévi-Strauss attributed a central role in Amerindian mythology. And contrary to what others have said, this was not without reason; it would only be necessary to specify that the centrality of this passage by no means excludes its profound ambivalence—the *double sense* (in more than one sense) it has in indigenous thought, as becomes evident the farther one advances through the *Mythologiques*. It is likewise important to emphasize that what results from this passage is not exactly what has been imagined. The passage is not a process by which the human is differentiated from the animal, as the evolutionist Occidental vulgate would have it. *The common condition of humans and animals is not animality but humanity.* The great mythic division shows less culture distinguished from nature than nature estranged from itself by culture: the myths recount how animals lost certain attributes humans inherited or conserved. Nonhumans are ex-humans—and not humans are ex-nonhumans. So where our popular anthropology regards humanity as standing upon animal foundations ordinarily occluded by culture—having

28. "No doubt, in mythic times, humans were indistinguishable from animals, but between the non-differentiated beings who were to give birth to mankind on the one hand and the animal kingdom on the other, certain qualitative relationships pre-existed, anticipating specific characteristics that were still in a latent state" (L.-S. 1981: 588).

once been entirely animal, we remain, at bottom, animals—indigenous thought instead concludes that having formerly been human, animals and other cosmic existents continue to be so, even if in a way scarcely obvious to us.[29]

The more general question raised for us, then, is why the humanity of each species of existent is subjectively evident (and at the same time highly problematic) and objectively non-evident (while at the same time obstinately affirmed). Why is it that animals see themselves as humans? Precisely because we humans see them as animals, while seeing ourselves as humans. Peccaries cannot see themselves as peccaries (or, who knows, speculate on the fact that humans and other beings are peccaries underneath the garb specific to them) because this is the way they are viewed by humans. If humans regard themselves as humans and are seen as nonhumans, as animals or spirits, by nonhumans, then animals should necessarily see themselves as humans. What perspectivism affirms, when all is said and done, is not so much that animals are at bottom like humans but the idea that as humans, they are at bottom something else—they are, in the end, the "bottom" itself of something, its other side; they are different from themselves. Neither animism, which would affirm a substantial or analogic resemblance between animals and humans, nor totemism—which would affirm a formal or homological resemblance between intrahuman and interanimal differences—perspectivism affirms an intensive difference that places human/nonhuman difference *within each existent.* Each being finds itself separated from itself, and becomes similar to others only through both the double subtractive condition common to them all and a strict complementarity that obtains between any two of them; for if every mode of existent is human for itself, none of them are human to each other such that humanity is reciprocally reflexive (jaguars are humans

---

29. The revelation of this ordinarily hidden side of beings (which is why it is conceived in different ways as "more true" than its apparent side) is intimately associated with violence in both intellectual traditions: the animality of humanity, for us, and the humanity of the animal, for the Amerindians, are only rarely actualized without destructive consequences. The Cubeo of the Northwest Amazon say that "the ferociousness of the jaguar has a human origin" (Irving Goldman).

to other jaguars, peccaries see each other as humans, etc.), even while it can never be mutual (as soon as the jaguar is human, the peccary ceases to be one and vice versa).[30] Such is, in the last analysis, what "soul" means here. If everything and everyone has a soul, nothing and no one coincides with itself. If everything and everyone can be human, then nothing and no one is human in a clear and distinct fashion. This "background cosmic humanity" renders the humanity of form or figure problematic. The "ground" constantly threatens to swallow the figure.

But if nonhumans are persons who see themselves as persons, why then do they not view all other kinds of cosmic persons as the latter view themselves? If the cosmos is saturated with humanity, why is this metaphysical ether opaque, or why is it, at best, like a two-way mirror, returning an image of the human from only one of its sides? These questions, as we anticipated apropos the Antilles incident, grant us access to the Amerindian concept of the body. They also make it possible to pass from the quasi-epistemological notion of perspectivism to a veritable ontological one—multinaturalism.

The idea of a world that comprises a multiplicity of subjective positions immediately evokes the notion of relativism. Frequent mention, both direct and indirect, is made of it in descriptions of Amerindian cosmologies. We will take, almost at random, the conclusion of Kaj Arhem, an ethnographer of the Makuna. After describing the perspectival universe of this Northwest Amazonian people in minute detail, he concludes that the idea of a multiplicity of perspectives on reality entails, in the case of the Makuna, that "every perspective is equally valid and true" and "a true and correct representation of the world does not exist" (1993: 124).

This is no doubt correct, but only in a certain sense. There is a high probability that the Makuna would say, on the contrary, that where humans are concerned, there *is* a true and accurate representation of the world. If a human begins to see, as a vulture would, the worms infesting a cadaver as grilled fish, he will draw the following conclusion: vultures have stolen his soul, he himself is in the course of being transformed into one, and he and his kin will cease being human to each other. In short, he is gravely ill, or

---

30. We can thus see that if for us "man is a wolf to man," for the Indians, the wolf can be man for wolves—with the proviso that man and wolf cannot be man (or wolf) simultaneously.

even dead. In other words (but this amounts to the same thing), he is en route to becoming a shaman. Every precaution, then, has to be taken to keep perspectives separate from each other on account of their incompatibility. Only shamans, who enjoy a kind of double citizenship in regard to their species (as well as to their status as living or dead), can make them communicate—and this only under special, highly controlled conditions.[31]

But an important question remains. Does Amerindian perspectivist theory in fact postulate a plurality of *representations* of the world? It will suffice to consider the testimony of ethnographers in order to perceive that the situation is exactly the inverse: all beings see ("represent") the world *in the same way*; what changes is *the world they see*. Animals rely on the same "categories" and "values" as humans: their worlds revolve around hunting, fishing, food, fermented beverages, cross-cousins, war, initiation rites, shamans, chiefs, spirits.... If the moon, serpents, and jaguars see humans as tapirs or peccaries, this is because, just like us, they eat tapirs and peccaries (human food par excellence). Things could not be otherwise, since nonhumans, being humans in their own domain, see things as humans do—like we humans see them in our domain. But the things *they see* when they see them *like we do* are *different*: what we take for blood, jaguars see as beer; the souls of the dead find a rotten cadaver where we do fermented manioc; what humans perceive as a mud puddle becomes a grand ceremonial house when viewed by tapirs.

At first glance, this idea would appear to be somewhat counterintuitive, seeming to unceasingly transform into its opposite, like the multistable objects of psychophysics.[32] Gerald Weiss, for example, describes the world of the Peruvian Amazonian Ashakinka people as "a world of relative semblances, where different kinds of beings see the same things differently" (Weiss 1972: 170). Once again, this is true, but in a different way than intended. What Weiss "does not see" is precisely the fact that different types of beings see the same things differently is merely a consequence of

31. To paraphrase F. Scott Fitzgerald, we could say that the sign of a first-rank shamanic intelligence is the capacity to simultaneously hold two incompatible perspectives.

32. The Necker cube is the perfect example, since its ambiguity hinges on an oscillating perspective. Amazonian mythology contains numerous cases of characters that, when encountered by a human, change rapidly from one form to another—from human (seductive) to animal (terrifying).

the fact that different types of beings see different things in the same way. What, after all, counts as "the same thing?" And in relation to who, which species, and in what *way*?

Cultural relativism, which is a multiculturalism, presumes a diversity of partial, subjective representations bearing on an external nature, unitary and whole, that itself is indifferent to representation. Amerindians propose the inverse: on the one hand, a purely pronominal representative unit—the human is what and whomever occupies the position of the cosmological subject; every existent can be thought of as thinking (it exists, therefore it thinks), as "activated" or "agencied" by a point of view[33]—and, on the other, a real or objective radical diversity. Perspectivism is a multinaturalism, since a perspective is not a representation.

A perspective is not a representation because representations are properties of mind, whereas a *point of view is in the body*. The capacity to occupy a point of view is doubtlessly a power of the soul, and nonhumans are subjects to the extent to which they have (or are) a mind; but the difference between points of view—and a point of view is nothing but a difference—is not in the soul. The latter, being formally identical across all species, perceive the same thing everywhere. The difference, then, must lie in the specificity of the body.

Animals perceive in the same way as us but perceive different things than we do, because their bodies are different than ours. I do not mean by this physiological differences—Amerindians recognize a basic uniformity of bodies—but the affects, or strengths and weakness, that render each species of the body singular: what it eats, its way of moving or communicating, where it lives, whether it is gregarious or solitary, timid or fierce, and so on. Corporeal morphology is a powerful sign of these differences, although it can be quite deceiving; the human figure, for instance, can conceal a jaguar-affection. What we are calling "body," then, is not the specific physiology or characteristic anatomy of something but an ensemble of ways or modes of being that constitutes a *habitus*, ethos, or ethogram. Lying between the formal subjectivity of souls and the substantial materiality of organisms

---

33. The point of view creates not its object, as Saussure would say, but rather the subject itself. "Such is the basis of perspectivism, which does not mean a dependence in respect to a pregiven or defined subject; to the contrary, a subject will be what comes to the point of view, or rather what remains in the point of view" (D. 1993: 19).

is a middle, axial plane that is the body qua bundle of affects and capacities, and that is at the origin of perspectivism. Far from being the spiritual essentialism of relativism, perspectivism is a corporeal mannerism.

Multinaturalism does not suppose a Thing-in-Itself partially apprehended through categories of understanding proper to each species. We should not think that Indians imagine that there exists a something=X, something that humans, for example, would see as blood and jaguars as beer. What exists in multinature are not such self-identical entities differently perceived but immediately relational multiplicities of the type blood/beer. There exists, if you will, only the limit between blood and beer, the border by which these two "affinal" substances communicate and diverge.[34] Finally, there is no X that would be blood to one species and beer to another; just a "blood/beer" that from the very start is one of the characteristic singularities or affections of the human/jaguar. The resemblance Amazonians frequently draw between humans and jaguars, which is that both of them drink "beer," is only made so that what creates the difference between humans and jaguars can be better perceived. "One is either in one language *or* another—there is no more a background-language than a background-world" (Jullien 2008, 135). In effect, one is *either* in the blood *or* in the beer, with no one drinking a drink-in-itself. But every beer has a background-taste of blood and vice-versa.

We are beginning to be able to understand how *Amerindian perspectivism* raises the problem of translation, and thus how to address the problem of translating perspectivism into the onto-semiotic terms of Occidental anthropology. In this way, the possession of similar souls implies the possession of analogous concepts on the part of all existents. What changes from one species of existent to another is therefore body and soul as well as the referents of these concepts: the body is the site and instrument of the referential disjunction between the "discourses" (the semiograms) of each species. Amerindian perspectivism's problem is thus not

---

34. Etymologically, the affine is he who is situated *ad-finis*, whose domain borders on mine. Affines are those who communicate by borders, who hold "in common" only what separates them.

to find the referent common to two different representations (the Venus behind the morning star and the evening star) but instead to circumvent the equivocation that consists in imagining that a jaguar saying "manioc beer" is referring to the same thing as us simply because he means the same thing as us. In other words, perspectivism presumes an epistemology that remains constant, and variable ontologies. The same "representations," but different objects. One meaning, multiple referents. The goal of perspectivist translation—which is one of the principle tasks of shamans—is therefore not to find in human conceptual language a *synonym* (a co-referential representation) for the representations that other species employ to indicate the same thing "out there"; rather, the objective is to not lose sight of the difference concealed by the deceiving *homonyms* that connect/separate our language from those of other species. If Western anthropology is founded on the principle of interpretive charity (goodwill and tolerance as what distinguishes the thinker from the rest of humanity in its exasperation with the other), which affirms a natural synonymy between human cultures, Amerindian alter-anthropology contrarily affirms a counter-natural homonymy between living species that is at the source of all kinds of fatal equivocations. (The Amerindian principle of precaution: a world entirely composed of living foci of intentionality necessarily comes with a large dose of bad intentions.)

In the end, the concept of multinaturalism is not a simple repetition of anthropological multiculturalism. Two very different conjugations of the multiple are at stake. Multiplicity can be taken as a kind of plurality, as happens in invocations of the "the multiplicity of cultures" of beautiful cultural diversity. Or, on the contrary, multiplicity can be the multiplicity *in* culture, or culture *as* multiplicity. This second sense is what interests us. The notion of multiculturalism becomes useful here on account of its paradoxical character. Our macroconcept of nature fails to acknowledge veritable plurality, which spontaneously forces us to register the ontological solecism contained in the idea of "several natures" and thus the corrective displacement it imposes. Paraphrasing a formula of Deleuze's on relativism (1993: 21), we could say that Amazonian multinaturalism affirms not so much a variety of natures as the naturalness of variation—variation *as* nature. The inversion of the Occidental formula of multiculturalism bears not simply on its constitutive terms—nature and culture—as they are mutually determined by their respective functions of unity and diversity, but also on the values accorded to term and function themselves. Anthropological readers will recognize here, of course, Lévi-Strauss' canonical formula (1963e[1955]: 228): perspectivist multinaturalism is a transformation, through its double twist, of Occidental multiculturalism, and signals the crossing of a historico-semiotic threshold of translatability and equivocation—a threshold, precisely, of perspectival transformation.[35]

---

35. For "the crossing of a threshold" in Lévi-Strauss, see 2001: 29; see also the essential commentary on this by Mauro Almeida (2008).

Chapter Four

Images of Savage Thought

In calling perspectivism and multinaturalism an indigenous cosmopolitical theory, I am using the word "theory" by design.[36] A widespread tendency in the anthropology of the past several decades has consisted in refusing savage thought [*la pensée sauvage*] the status of a veritable theoretical imagination. What this denial primarily enlightens us about is a certain lack of theoretical imagination on the part of anthropologists. Amerindian perspectivism, before being a possible object of a theory extrinsic to it—a theory, for example, conceived as the derived epistemological reflex of a more primary animist ontology (Descola 2013) or an emergent phenomenological pragmatics peculiar to the "mimetic" cultures of hunting peoples (Willerslev 2004)—invites us to construct other theoretical images of theory. Anthropology cannot content itself with describing in minute detail "the indigenous point of view" (in the Malinowskian sense) if it is only subsequently going to be gratified to identify, in the best critical tradition, the blind spots in that perspective, and thereby absorb it in the point of view of the observer. Perspectivism demands precisely the opposite, symmetric task, which is to discover what a point of view is *for* the indigenous: the *concept* of the point of view at work in Amerindian cultures, which is also the indigenous point of view on the anthropological concept of the point of view.

---

36. There is no need to recall that cosmopolitics is a term that lays claim to a link with the work of Isabelle Stengers (2010[1996]) and Bruno Latour. The latter, for his part, adopted the Amazonian concept of mulitnaturalism in order to designate the nonviability, from a cosmopolitical perspective, of the modernist couplet of multiculturalism/mononaturalism.

Obviously, the indigenous concept of the point of view does not coincide with the concept of the point of view of the indigenous, just as the point of view of the anthropologist cannot be the same as that of the indigenous (this is not a fusion of horizons) but only its (perspectival) relation with the latter. This relation, moreover, is one of reflexive dislocation. Amerindian perspectivism is an intellectual structure containing a theory of its own description by anthropology—for it is precisely another anthropology, superimposed over ours.[37] That is exactly why perspectivism is not, *pace* Descola, a subtype of animism, i.e., a schema of practice whose reasons can be known only by the reason of the anthropologist. It is not a type but a concept, and the most interesting use for it consists not so much in classifying cosmologies that appear exotic to us but in counter-analyzing those anthropologies that have become far too familiar.

Apart from a lack of theoretical imagination (a factor that should never be underestimated) there are other, quite often contradictory reasons for the common acceptance of the double standard that denies the nonmoderns the power, or perhaps the impotence, of theory: the tendency, on the one hand, to define the essence of indigenous practice in terms of Heideggerian *Zuhandenheit*, and, on the other, the refusal to grant what Sperber calls "semi-propositional representations" the status of authentic knowledge, a move which takes the savage mind [*la pensée sauvage*] hostage each time it threatens to slip free of the modest, reassuring limits of encyclopedic categorization.

---

37. As Patrice Maniglier said, "Because structure is most rigorously defined as a system of transformation, it cannot be represented without making its representation a part of itself (2000, 238). Concerning this point, Anne-Christine Taylor offers the following felicitous definition of anthropology: "A discipline that aims at placing side by side the point of view of the ethnologist and that of the subjects of the inquiry in order to make from this an instrument of knowledge." What still needs to be emphasized is that said juxtaposition requires a deliberate conceptual effort, given that the points of view in question mostly work at cross purposes with each other, and that the point where they join is not the geometrical space of human nature but rather the crossroads of equivocation (see below). The Korowai of Western New Guinea conceive the relation of mutual invisibility and inverse perspectives between the world of the living and that of the dead via the image of tree trunk that has fallen onto another (Stasch 2009: 27).

The problem resides in the fact that the faculty of thought is identified with "the system of judgment," and knowledge with the model of the proposition. Whether from its phenemenologico-constructivist or cognitivo-instructionist wings, contemporary anthropology has long discoursed on the severe limitations of this model in accounting for intellectual economies of the non-Occidental variety (or, if you prefer, of the nonmodern, nonliterate, nondoctrinal, and other "constitutive" absence varieties). In other words, anthropological discourse has devoted itself to the paradoxical enterprise of heaping proposition upon proposition on the subject of the nonpropositional essence of the discourse of the others, going on endlessly about what supposedly goes without saying. We find ourselves (theoretically) content when indigenous peoples confirm their putatively sublime disdain for self-interpretation and even scarcer interest for cosmologies and systems: the absence of indigenous interpretation has the big advantage of allowing for the proliferation of anthropological interpretations of that absence, and their disregard for cosmological architecture permits for the construction of beautiful anthropological cathedrals wherein societies are arranged according to their greater or lesser disposition toward systematicity. In short, the more practical the indigenous, the more theoretical the anthropologist. Let me add that this nonpropositional mode is conceived as being so strongly dependent on its "contexts" of transmission and circulation as to stand diametrically opposite to what scientific discourse, in its miraculous capacity for universalization, is imagined to be. So while we are all necessarily circumscribed by our "circumstances" and "relational configurations," *theirs* are (and how!) even more systematically circumscribed—more circumstantial, more configured—than others.

The point, though, is first of all not to dispute the thesis that nondomesticated thought is inherently nonpropositional; this is not a fight to re-establish the others' right to a rationality that they never claimed themselves. Lévi-Strauss' profound idea of *savage thought* should be understood to project another *image of thought*, not yet another *image of the savage*. What is being contested, then, is the implicit idea that the proposition should continue to serve as the prototype of rational enunciation and the atom of theoretical discourse. The nonpropositional is regarded as being essentially primitive, as non- or even anti-conceptual. The thesis, naturally, could be defended in a way "for" (and not just "against") these Others that lack concepts. This absence of the rational concept, that is, could be taken as a positive sign of the existential dis-alienation of the peoples in question—the manifestation of a state in which knowledge and action, thought and sensation, and so on are inseparable. Yet even if done "for" them, this would still be to concede way too much to the proposition and to reaffirm a totally archaic concept of the concept that persists in conceiving it as an operation subsuming the particular in the universal (as an essentially classificatory and abstracting process). But instead of deciding on that basis to reject the concept, the task is to know how to detect the infraphilosophical in the concept, and, reciprocally, the virtual conceptuality in the infraphilosophical. To put it another way, we have to arrive at an anthropological concept of the concept that takes for granted the extrapropositionality of every creative ("savage") thought in its integral positivity, and that develops in a completely different direction those traditional notions of category (whether innate or acquired), representation (propositional or semi-propositional), and belief (like flowers, simple or divided).

Multinaturalist Amerindian perspectivism is one of the anthropological contenders for this concept of the concept. It has not, however, been received that way in certain academic milieus.[38] Most often, it has been construed as a descriptive generalization of certain properties of the content of a discursive object radically external to anthropological discourse and thus incapable of producing structural effects within the latter. Little surprise, then, that we have witnessed discussions more or less animated by the question of whether the Bororo or Kuna are indeed perspectivist (as if it could be demonstrated that "perspectivists" are traipsing around the forest); some have even asked, in the spirit of *The Persian Letters*, "How can one be perspectivist?" Reciprocally, the skeptics have not refrained from mocking declarations that perspectivists are nowhere to be found, that the whole affair merely concerns longstanding knowledge about minor details of Amerindian mythologies, and that perspectivism is not an indigenous theory but just some special effect of certain

38. The Amerindianists to whom I presented these ideas about their ideas quickly perceived their implications for the relations of force between indigenous "cultures" and the Occidental "sciences" that would circumscribe and administer them.

pragmatic constraints whose principles escape the parties concerned, who are supposed to talk to jaguars without realizing that it is because they talk to jaguars that jaguars seem to talk back (a disorder of language, that's all…). From *the second it started*, all of this thwarted the possibility of a serious consideration of the consequence of perspectivism for anthropological theory, which is the transformation it imposes on the entire practice of the concept in the discipline: in a word, the idea that the ideas indicated by this label constitute not yet another object for anthropology but another idea of anthropology, an alternative to Western "anthropological anthropology," whose foundations it subverts.

◊ In part, the naturalist (or rather, analogist) interpretation of perspectivism, which treats the latter as merely one property among others of a certain, animist schema of objectivation of the world, has opened a path in our local anthropological space on the basis of the large place Philippe Descola grants it in his magnum opus, *Beyond Nature and Culture*. It would be impossible here to do this monumental work justice, which often turns its focus to my own work; the divergences between us that I have found necessary to mark below are expressed in the context of a longstanding, mutually enriching dialogue that presupposes profound agreement on our part concerning many other anthropological questions.

In *Beyond Nature and Culture*, Descola reprises, corrects, and completes the panorama laid out in *The Savage Mind* by refining the concept of totemism by juxtaposing it with three other "ontologies" or "modes of identification" (the synonymy, it should be noted, is not without interest): "animism," "analogism," and "naturalism." The author constructs a four-part matrix in which the four basic ontologies are distributed according to how they configure the relations of continuity or discontinuity between the corporeal and spiritual dimensions of different species of beings[39]—dimensions conceived in terms of the neologisms "physicality" and "interiority." This matrix translates, as Descola generously notes, a particular schema that I proposed in my article on Amerindian perspectivism (Viveiros de Castro 1998/1996). In that text (the one partially reprised in the second chapter of the present book), I drew perhaps an all too-brief distinction between two internally contrastive

---

39. The different species are reduced, in the final analysis, to the human/nonhuman polarity. Modern naturalism, for example, is said to be "one of the possible expressions of the more general schemas that govern the objectivization of the world and of others" (Descola 2013: xviii). Although the duality between nature (the world) and culture or society (other) is subjected to critique, it continues, perhaps inevitably, to function as a background presupposition.

ontological schemas, which are, first, the combination of metaphysical continuity (the generic soul) and physical discontinuity (the specific body) between kinds of existents that are proper to indigenous psychomorphic multinaturalism and, second, the combination of physical continuity and metaphysical discontinuity typical of modern anthropocentric multiculturalism, where humans, even as they communicate with the rest of creation via corporeal matter, are absolutely separated from it on account of their spiritual substance (and its contemporary avatars).[40] This contrast is of course largely reminiscent of Descola's animist and naturalist schemas; but for him, it is necessary to add two other cases, where "parallel" relations of either continuity or discontinuity between the physical and the metaphysical predominate, in order to engender the two other schemas of, respectively, totemism and analogism (2013: 121).[41]

The original impetus behind *Beyond Nature and Culture* was probably the same one that guided so many anthropologists and philosophers of our generation: dissatisfaction with structuralism's sometimes unilateral interest in the discontinuist/classificatory, metaphoric/symbolic, totemic/mythological side of the savage mind, which worked toward the detriment of its continuist/transcategorical, metonymic/indexical, pragmatic/ritual side. In short, years of proceeding alongside Lévi-Strauss had us suspecting that the time had come to re-explore Lévy-Bruhl's path—without forgetting, (as was also the case with Méséglise and Guermantes), that there was not just one way to join their itineraries (which, in any case, were not as far from the narrator's perspective as was believed). Animism, the first of the ontologies Descola identified, was a step in this very direction. It will suffice to recall that animism has as a basic presupposition the idea that nonhuman beings are persons, i.e., the terms of social relations: in contrast with totemism, a system of classification that signifies intrahuman relations through natural diversity, animism deploys social

40. When contrasted with Descola's previous works on the spiritual/mental continuity between beings in "animistic" worlds, one of the great breakthroughs of *Beyond Nature and Culture* is its diacritical inclusion of the corporeal dimension. My dear friend and colleague could thus rightfully declare to me, as the Canaque Boesoou so memorably had to Maurice Leenhardt, that "What I brought to theory was the body!"

41. I have not hidden my reservations about whether these two parallel schemas are in fact well founded (or at least about the question of whether they belong to the same onto-typological category as the two internally contrastive schemas). The problem is that they presuppose mutually independent definitions of interiority and physicality that function to substantialize them, while the internally contrastive schemas simply require "positional" values determinable through an internal contrast where one pole functions as the figure or ground for the other. This marks an important difference between Descola's animism and what I call perspectivism: the latter should not be taken for a type or particular specification of the former but rather as a *mode of functioning* of the distinction between soul and body.

categories to signify the relations between humans and nonhumans alike. There would thus be a single series—that of persons—instead of two, while the relations between "nature" and "culture" would involve metonymic contiguity rather than metaphoric resemblance.[42]

Where my own work is concerned, I attempted to escape what seemed to me the excessively combinatory dimension of *The Savage Mind* by valorizing the "minor" pole of the rather problematic opposition Lévi-Strauss draws there between totemism and sacrifice (see below, chapters 8 and 9). What I put in the column of sacrifice in my analysis of Amerindian shamanism and cannibalism, Descola attributed to animism, and it was largely due to this conceptual "synonymy" that we fed each other's work so well: we thought we were talking about the same things.... But where I was aiming, well beyond sacrificial metonymies, for an "other" of classificatory reason, or, more precisely, a noncombinatory or alogical interpretation of the central notion of structuralism—transformation—the author of *Beyond Nature and Culture* followed a quite different trajectory. While attenuating the generic sense Lévi-Strauss granted to the notion of totemism (by which it ends up being synonymous with all acts of signification), the procedure by which the four basic ontologies are deduced is clearly of an inspiration that is totemic in Lévi-Strauss' sense instead of "sacrificial."[43] Descola conceives his object as a closed combinatory play whose objective is to establish a typology of schemas of practice—forms of objectivation of the world and the other—by means of finite rules of composition. In this sense, the book could also be said to be as much analogistic as totemist, which is no surprise, given that its contribution to classic structuralism consists of splitting Lévi-Straussian totemism into the two subtypes of totemism *sensu* Descola and analogism. Without casting any doubt on the fact that the definition of analogism magnificently accommodates a series of phenomena and civilizational styles (particularly those of several peoples once considered "barbaric"), it should nonetheless be said that the place analogism most exists is in *Beyond Nature and Culture* itself, a book of admirable erudition and analytic fineness but whose theory and method are completely analogist. Hence its penchant and taste for total classifications, identifications, systems of correspondence, properties, schemas of micro/macrocosmic projections.... In effect, its design makes it impossible for Descola's system to not predominately express one of the four ontologies he identifies: the very idea of identification is an analogist idea. An animist or naturalist would probably have some

42. As I already mentioned, the introduction of differential corporeality rendered this model more complex.

43. In Descola's book, sacrifice also received a more restrained or literal interpretation, as it is considered a characteristic of analogist rather than animist ontology.

different ideas—like perspectivist ideas, which the present work's ideas are versions of.

The problem, for me, is not how to extend and thus amplify structuralism but how to interpret it intensively, and thus in a "post-" structural direction. We could say, then, that if the challenge Descola confronted and overcame was that of rewriting *The Savage Mind* after having profoundly assimilated *The Order of Things*, mine was to know how to rewrite the *Mythologiques* on the basis of everything that *A Thousand Plateaus* disabused me of in anthropology.[44]

That being said, perspectivism is not allergic to every problematic of classification, and does not necessarily condemn it for logocentrism or comparable sins. In fact, if one examines things up close, the rest of us anthropologists are also a little analogist, and in this sense, perspectivism is the reduplication or intensification of the classificatory libido, particularly inasmuch as its characteristic problem can be put as follows: *What happens when the classified becomes the classifier?* What happens when it is no longer a matter of ordering the species which nature has been divided into but of knowing how these species themselves undertake this task? And when the question is raised: which nature do they thereby make (how do jaguars objectivate "the world and the other?"). What happens when the question becomes to know how the totemic operator functions from the point of view of the totem? Or, more generally (but exactly in the same sense), what happens when we ask indigenous people what anthropology is?

Anthropology is "social" or "cultural," (or rather, should be), not in contradistinction with "physical" or "biological" anthropology but because the first question it should be dealing with is that of working out what holds the place of the "social" or "cultural" for the people that it studies; what, in other words, the anthropologies of those peoples are if the latter are taken as the agents, instead of the patients, of theory. This is equivalent to

---

44. The proximity of *Beyond Nature and Culture* to *The Order of Things* should not prevent us from remarking that Foucault's great book shows itself to be radically implicated in (and complicated by) its own periodization, while the question of knowing if *Beyond Nature and Culture* ever situates itself in its own typology or, on the contrary, excludes itself as a mode of thought from the modes of thought it identifies, seems to me to find a clear response in the book. It should also be noted that the difference between our respective references to the Lévi-Straussian corpus is just as (if not more) significant than the difference between the Kantianism of *The Order of Things* and the post-correlationist nomadology of *A Thousand Plateaus*.

saying that doing anthropology is not much more than comparing anthropologies—but also nothing less. Comparison, then, would not only be our principal analytic tool but also our raw material and ultimate horizon, what we compare always and already being more comparisons in the same sense that, in structuralist method (the one of the *Mythologiques*) the object of every transformation is just another transformation, and not some original substance. (Things could not be otherwise, once every comparison is seen to be a transformation.) If culture, according to Strathern's elegant processual definition "consists in the way people draw analogies between different domains of their worlds" (1992a: 47), then every culture is a gigantic, multidimensional process of comparison. As for anthropology, if it, following Roy Wagner, "studies culture through culture," then "whatever operations characterize our investigations must also be general properties of culture" (1981: 35). In brief, anthropologist and native alike are engaged in "directly comparable intellectual operations" (Herzfeld 2001: 7), and such operations are, more than anything else, comparative. Intracultural relations, or internal comparisons (the Strathernian "analogies between domains"), and intercultureal relations, or external comparisons (Wagner's "invention of culture") are in strict ontological continuity.

But direct comparability does not necessarily entail immediate translatability, just as ontological continuity does not mean epistemological transparency. So then how do we render the analogies drawn by Amazonian peoples in terms of our own analogies? What happens to our comparisons when they are compared to indigenous comparisons?

I will propose *equivocation* as a means of reconceptualizing, with the help of Amerindian perspectivist anthropology, this emblematic procedure of our academic anthropology. The operation I have in mind is not the explicit comparison of two or more sociocultural entities external to the observer, done with the intention of detecting constants or concomitant variations having a nomothetic value. While that has certainly been one of anthropology's most popular modes of investigation, it remains just one among others at our disposal, and is merely a "regulative rule" of the discipline's method. Comparison as I conceive it, on the contrary, is a "constitutive rule" of method, the procedure involved when the practical and discursive concepts of the observed are translated into the terms of the observer's conceptual apparatus. So when I speak of comparison, which is more often than not implicit and automatic—making it an explicit topic is an essential moment of anthropological method—the anthropologists' discourse is included as one of its terms, and it should be seen as being at work from the first moment of fieldwork or even of the reading of an ethnographic monograph.

These two comparative modalities are neither independent of each other nor equivalent. The first of them is often extolled for providing an objectifying triangulation of the dual imaginary of ego and other (which ostensibly marks the second operation) and thus granting access to properties entirely attributable to the observed, yet is less innocent than it appears. We have a triangle which is not truly triangular—2+1 does not necessarily make 3—because it is always the anthropologist (the "1") who defines the terms by which two or more cultures foreign to his own (and also often to each other) will be related. When the Kachin and the Nuer are compared, it is not at the request of the Kachin or the Nuer, and what the anthropologist does by means of this usually disappears from the comparative scene, by concealing the problem that he himself (im)posed on the Kachin and the Neur so that it would seem that both parties are comparing each other.... They then exist only internally to anthropological discourse and are seen as having a common objectivity as sociocultural entities that would be comparable by virtue of a problem posed by another sociocultural entity that, in deciding the rules of the comparative game, reveals itself to stand outside its bounds. And if this recalls Agamben's idea of the state of exception, it's because *that's the idea* (the very same one)....

Contrary to learned *doxa*, then, the symmetrization internal to the object, which is achieved through its comparative pluralization, does not confer on it some magic power of symmetrizing the subject-object relation or of transforming the subject into a pure comparative mind. Nor does this by itself render explicit the other, subjacent comparison that, as we saw, *implicates* the observer in his relation with the observed.

This kind of implication is also known as *translation*. It has, of course, become a cliché to say that translation is the distinctive task of cultural anthropology.[45] The real problem is to know precisely what translation can or should be, and how to undertake it. Yet this is where things become complicated, as Talal Asad has shown (1986) in terms that I will adopt (or translate) here. In anthropology, comparison is in the service of translation, and not the reverse. Anthropology compares for the sake of translation, and not in order to explain, generalize, interpret, contextualize, say what goes without saying, and so forth. And if, as the Italian saying goes, translation is always betrayal, then any translation worthy of the name, to paraphrase Benjamin (or rather, Rudolf Pannwitz) betrays the destination language, and not that of the source. Good translation succeeds at allowing foreign concepts to deform and subvert the conceptual apparatus of the translator such that the *intentio* of the original language can be expressed through and thus transform that of the destination. *Translation, betrayal ... transformation.* In anthropology, this process was called myth, and one of its synonyms was structural anthropology.

So to translate Amerindian perspectivism is first of all to translate its image of translation, which is of a "controlled equivocation" ("controlled" in the sense that walking is a controlled way of falling). Amerindian perspectivism is a doctrine of equivocation, of referential alterity between homonymous concepts. Equivocation is the mode of communication between its different perspectival positions and is thus at once the condition of possibility of the anthropological enterprise and its limit.

The indigenous theory of perspectivism emerges from an implicit comparison between the ways the different modes of corporeality "naturally" experience the world as affective multiplicity. Such a theory would thus appear to be a *reverse anthropology*, the inverse of our own ethno-anthropology as an explicit comparison of the ways that different mentalities "culturally" represent a world that would in turn be the origin of these different conceptual versions of itself. A culturalist description of perspectivism therefore amounts to the negation and delegitimation of its object, the retrospective construal of it as a primitive or fetishistic form of anthropological reasoning—an anti- or pre-anthropology.

---

45. Well, it is a cliché in only *certain* milieus; in others, defenses are frequently made of the idea that the true task of anthropology is not to carry out cultural translation, whatever this would be, but rather to reduce it naturally.

The concept of perspectivism, on the contrary, proposes an inversion of this inversion. Now for the native's turn! Not "the return of the native," as Adam Kuper (2003) ironically called the great ethnopolitical movement inspiring this reflexive displacement (what Sahlins [2000] called "the indigenization of modernity"), but a turn—an unexpected turning, *kairos*, thing, or detour. Not Thomas Hardy, but Henry James, the consummate genius of perspectivism: a turn of the indigenous that would be like the "the turn of the screw"... rather than the "screw the native" seemingly preferred by certain of our colleagues. In Kuper's view, the narrative told here would be a horror story: an *altermondialiste* cognitive anthropology or, as Patrice Maniglier once let drop, an *"altercognitivisme."*

In the end, this is what was at stake in Lévi-Strauss' anecdote about the Antilles incident. It does not comment from a distance on perspectivism but is itself perspectivist. It should be read as a historical transformation, in more than one sense, of several Amerindian myths that thematize interspecific perspectivism. I am thinking, for example, of the tales in which a protagonist lost in the forest happens upon a strange village whose inhabitants invite him to drink a refreshing gourd of "manioc beer," which he accepts enthusiastically ... until he realizes, with horrified surprise, that it is full of human blood. Which leads him to conclude, naturally, that he is not really among humans. The anecdote, as much as the myth, turns on a type of communicative disjunction where the interlocutors are neither talking about nor cognizant of the same thing (in the case of the Puerto Rican anecdote, the "dialogue" takes place on the plane of Lévi-Strauss' own comparative reasoning about reciprocal ethnocentrism). Just as jaguars and humans use the same name for different things, the Europeans and the Indians were talking about "humanity" while wondering if this self-description was really applicable to the Other. But what Europeans and Indians understood to be the defining criterion or intension of that concept was radically different. In sum, Lévi-Strauss' anecdote and the myth equally hinge on equivocation.

The Antilles anecdote resembles innumerable others recounted in the ethnographic literature and also present in my own fieldwork. In fact, it encapsulates the anthropological event or situation par excellence. The celebrated episode of Captain Cook in Hawaii, for example, can be viewed, following Sahlins' famous but now-neglected analysis of it, as a structural transformation of the doubled experiment of Puerto Rico: each would be one version of the archetypical anthropological motif of intercultural equivocation. Viewed from indigenous Amazonia, the intercultural is nothing more than a particular case of the interspecific, and history only a version of myth.

It should be stressed that equivocation is not merely one among the numerous pathologies that threaten communication between anthropologists and indigenous peoples, whether linguistic incompetence, ignorance of context, lack of empathy, literalist ingenuity, indiscretion, bad faith, and sundry other deformations or shortcomings that can afflict anthropological discourse at an empirical level.[46] But in contrast with all these contingent pathologies, equivocation is a properly transcendental category, a constitutive dimension of the project of cultural translation proper to the discipline.[47] Not at all a simple negative facticity, it is a condition of possibility of anthropological discourse that justifies the latter's existence (*quid juris?*). To translate is to take up residence in the space of equivocation. Not for the purpose of cancelling it (that would suppose that it never really existed) but in order to valorize and activate it, to open and expand the space imagined not to exist between the (conceptual) languages in contact—a space in fact hidden by equivocation. Equivocation is not what prevents the relation, but what founds and impels it. To translate is to presume that an equivocation always exists; it is to communicate through differences, in lieu of keeping the Other under gag by presuming an original univocality and an ultimate redundancy—an essential similarity—between what the Other and we are saying.

Michael Herzfeld recently observed that "anthropology is about misunderstandings, including anthropologists' own

---

46. "Communicative pathologies," from those of the Graal to the Asdiwal, are of course a major topic Lévi-Strauss examines in the *Mythologiques*.

47. These considerations are obviously a paraphrase—a Strathernian analogy between domains—of a well-known passage from Deleuze and Guattari (1994: 51-2).

misunderstandings, because they are usually the outcome of the mutual incommensurability of different notions of common sense—our object of study" (2003: 2). No disagreement here. Well, not exactly: I would insist on the point that, if anthropology in principle exists, it is precisely because "common sense" in not so common. I would also add that the incommensurability of the clashing "notions," far from being an impediment to their comparability, is exactly what permits and justifies it (as Lambek [1998] argues). For only the incommensurate is worth comparing—comparing the commensurate, I think, is a task best left to accountants. Lastly, I will have to say that "misunderstanding" should be conceived in the specific sense equivocation is in perspectivist multinaturalism: an equivocation is not failed interpretation but "excess" interpretation, and is such to the extent that one realizes that there is always more than one interpretation in play. And above all, these interpretations are necessarily divergent, not in relation to imaginary modes of perceiving the world but through their relations with real, perceived worlds. In Amerindian cosmologies, the real world of different species *depends* on their points of view, for the "world in general" *consists* only of different species, being the abstract space of divergence between them *as* points of view. For as Deleuze would say, there are not points of view on things, since things and beings are themselves points of view (1988: 203).

Anthropology, then, is interested in equivocations in the "literal" sense: *inter esse*, betweenness, existing among. But, as Roy Wagner said of his initial time with the Daribi of New Guinea (1981: 20), "their misunderstanding of me was not the same as my misunderstanding them," (which may very well be the best definition of culture ever proposed). The critical point, of course, is not the mere fact that there were empirical misunderstandings, but the "transcendental fact" that they were not the same. The question, accordingly, is not who was wrong and still less who misled whom. Equivocation is not error, deception, or falsehood but the very foundation of the relation implicating it, which is always a relation with exteriority. Deception or error, rather, can be defined as something peculiar to a particular language game, while equivocation is what happens in the interval between different language games. Deception and error assume preconstituted, homogeneous premises, while equivocation not only presumes heterogeneous premises but also conceives them as heterogeneous and supposes them as premises. More than being determined by its premises, equivocation defines them.

Equivocation, in sum, is not a subjective weakness but a machine for objectification; nor is it an error or illusion (not objectification conceived according to the language of reification, fetishization, and essentialization) but the limit condition of every social relation, a condition that itself becomes superobjectified in the limit case of that relation we call "intercultural," where language games maximally diverge. It should go without saying that such divergence includes the relation between the anthropologist's discourse and that of the indigenous. Thus the anthropological concept of culture, as Wagner argues, is the equivocation that arises as an attempt at resolving intercultural equivocation; and it is equivocal to the extent that it rests on the "paradox created by imagining a culture for people who do not imagine it for themselves" (1981: 27). This is why, even when misunderstandings are transformed into understandings (even when, that is, the anthropologist transforms his initial incomprehension about the indigenous in "their culture," or when the indigenous understand, for example, that what the Whites call a "gift" is in fact "merchandise"), the equivocations do not remain the same. The Other of the Others is always other. And if equivocation is neither error nor illusion nor lie but the very form of the relational positivity of difference, its opposite is not truth but "univocation," the aspiration to exist of a unique, transcendent meaning. Error or illusion par excellence would consist in imagining a univocation lying beneath each equivocation, with the anthropologist as its ventriloquist.

So we really are dealing with something other than a *return of the native*. If there is a return at all, it is Lévi-Strauss' "striking return to things": the return of philosophy to center stage. Not, however, according to his suggestion that this would entail a mutually exclusive choice between our philosophy and theirs (yet another case of homonymy? So much the better!) but in terms of a disjunctive synthesis between anthropology understood as experimental metaphysics or field geophilosophy, and philosophy conceived as the *sui generis* ethno-anthropological practice of the creation of concepts (D. G. 1994). This traversalization of anthropology and philosophy, which is a "demonic alliance" à la *A Thousand Plateaus*, is established in view of a common objective, which is the entry into a state (a plateau of intensity) of the permanent decolonization of thought.

It would be useful to recall that sociocultural anthropology has always been thoroughly saturated with philosophical problems and concepts, from that philosophical concept of ours—myth—to the quite philosophical problem, evoked by Lévi-Strauss, of how to exit philosophy, which is to say the cultural matrix of anthropology. The question, then, is not of knowing if anthropology should renew its constantly interrupted dialogue with philosophy but of determining which philosophy it should take the time to link into. Clearly it depends both on what one wants and on what one can do. Defining an image of savage thought with the help of Kant, Heidegger, or Wittgenstein is entirely possible. And it is no less the case that direct parallelisms can be established between the contents on both sides: Amazonian cosmologies, for example, have rich, equivocating resemblances to the distinction between the worlds of essence and appearance and could thus seem to lend themselves to a Platonic reading (the sole interest of which, however, would be to show how this Indian Platonism is merely apparent). But everything, I will repeat, depends on the problem that savage thought poses to us, which is the question of what the *interesting* philosophical problems are among all those to be discerned in the innumerable, complex semiopratical arrangements invented by the collectives anthropology has studied.

The philosophy of Deleuze, and more particularly the two volumes of *Capitalism and Schizophrenia* that were written with Guattari, is where I found the most appropriate machine for retransmitting the sonar frequency that I had picked up from Amerindian thought. Perspectivism and multinaturalism, which are, again, objects that have been resynthesized by anthropological discourse (indigenous theories, I dare say, do not present themselves in such conveniently pre-packaged fashion!), are the result of the encounter between a certain becoming-Deleuzian of Amerindian ethnology and a certain becoming-Indian of Deleuze and

Guattari's thought—a becoming-Indian that decisively passes, as we will see, through the chapter concerning becomings in *A Thousand Plateaus*.

Does that come down to saying that the Indians are Deleuzians, as I once cheekily declared?[48] Yes and no. *Yes*, first because Deleuze and Guattari do not ring hollow when struck with indigenous ideas; second, because the line of thinkers privileged by Deleuze, inasmuch as they constitute a minor lineage within the Western tradition, allows for a series of connections with the outside of the tradition. But in the last analysis, *no*, the Indians are not Deleuzians, for they can just as much be Kantians as Nietzscheans, Bergsonians as Wittgensteinians, and Merleau-Pontyeans, Marxists, Freudians, and, above all, Lévi-Straussians…. I believe that I have even heard them referred to as Habermasians, and in that case, anything is possible.

Yes and no. Obviously, "the problem is poorly posed." Because from the point of view of a multinaturalist counter-anthropology, which is what is at stake, the philosophers are to be read in light of savage thought, and not the reverse: it is a matter of actualizing the innumerable becomings-other that exist as virtualities of our own thinking. To think an outside (*not necessarily* China[49]) in order to run against the grain of the thought of the Outside, by starting from the other end. Every experience of another thinking is an experience of our own.

48. Viveiros de Castro, 2006.

49. *Penser d'un dehors (la Chine)* is the title of one of François Jullinen's books (Jullien and Marchaisse 2000) and is, like the rest of his work, an absolutely paradigmatic reference for *Anti-Narcissus*, even in the rare moments where I do not succeed at being in complete agreement with it.

PART TWO

Capitalism and Schizophrenia
from an Anthropological Point of View

Chapter Five

A Curious Chiasm

For my generation, the name of Gilles Deleuze immediately evokes the change in thought that marked the period circa 1968, when some key elements of our contemporary cultural apperception were invented. The meaning, consequences and very reality of this change have given rise to a still-raging controversy.

For the spiritual servants of order, "the yes-men that labor for the majority,"[50] this change foremost represents something from which future generations ought to have been and still must be protected—the guardians of today having been the protégés of yesterday and *vice versa* (and so on)—so as to reinforce the conviction that the event of '68 was consumed without being consummated. By which they mean that nothing actually happened. The real revolution supposedly happened contra that event, and "Reason," to employ the usual euphemism, was what delivered it; the reason-power that consolidated the planetary machine of Empire, in which the mystical nuptials of Capital and the Earth—globalization—climaxed, and that saw itself coroneted by the glorious emanation of that Noosphere more commonly known as the information economy. Even if capital does not always act with reason, one nonetheless gets the impression that reason always delights in letting itself be roughly taken by capital.

Yet for countless others who romantically insist (as the usual insult goes) that another world remains possible, both the propagation of the neoliberal plague and the technopolitical consolidation of the societies of control—where the Market equals the

---

50. Pignarre and Stengers 2011: 31-35.

State, the State equals the Market, and there is no choice outside them—can be confronted only if we retain our capacity to connect with the flux of desire that briefly broke the surface some forty years prior. For them, the pure event that was '68 had never ceased occurring or else has not yet even begun, inscribed as it seems to be in a kind of historical future subjunctive.

I would like, "rightly" or wrongly, to count myself among the latter, and I would for that reason say the same thing about the influence of Gilles Deleuze and his longtime collaborator Félix Guattari, the authors of the most important oeuvre, where the politics of the concept is concerned, in the philosophy of the second half of the 20th century. What I mean by "the same thing" is that this influence is far from having actualized its full potential. The presence of Deleuze and Guattari in certain disciplines and contemporary fields of investigation is indeed far less evident than would be expected, and one discipline in which this presence has proved even weaker is social anthropology.

The influence of Deleuze and Guattari on anthropology has been far less extensive than that of Foucault or Derrida, both of whose work has been extensively absorbed by what could be called the dominant counter-currents of the contemporary human sciences, including those found in anthropology. These counter-currents have not had the easiest time in France in the last decade-and-a-half. The relations between anthropology and philosophy have intensified remarkably in the last thirty years, but this development primarily occurred in Anglophone universities, where anthropology proved itself, like many other disciplines, to be more open to so-called continental philosophy than French anthropology has been. Heidegger's existential analytic, Merleau-Ponty's phenomenology of corporeality, Foucault's microphysics of power, and Derridean deconstruction whipped up in the 1980s and 1990s the continental winds that had already been blowing in the 1970s, and that carried the lingering odors of the old European Marxisms into American and British anthropology—a succession of influences that can, at any rate, be seen as immunological reactions to structuralism, which was the chief

European menace in the 1960s. In Old Europe, particularly France, the relations between philosophy and anthropology were instead slowly whitewashed until structuralism lost its paradigmatic élan and was reconstituted on pre- rather than post-structuralist bases (Lévi-Strauss and Eribon, 1988: 131), at least where the anthropological side of the story is concerned. Philosophical post-structuralism, French theory par excellence, had little effect on anthropology in France, while it was, on the contrary, the party most responsible for the rapprochement between the two disciplines in Anglophone countries (not without provoking, of course, quite violent reactions from all the local academic powers).

To be sure, there is no lack of examples of the unintended humor caused by French theory's appropriation by anthropologists and their peers in the transhexagonal world. But the blasé indifference, if not open hostility, that the French human sciences have as a rule demonstrated toward the constellation of problems designated by this label (which was already doubly pejorative for the Americans) is more than regrettable, having created a sort of developmental lag in the discipline by producing extreme, reciprocal, and in the end reflexive incomprehension between its principle national traditions. Lévi-Strauss' disenchanted proposal (1992: 414) to rechristen the discipline *"entropology"* seems to have become self-referential. Such discontent in the theory of civilization.

A curious chiasm all the same. Whereas contemporary Anglophone anthropology unhesitatingly appropriates French and continental philosophy from the 1960s and 1970s, inventively grafting it onto its autochthonous empiricopragmatic *habitus*, French anthropology (save for the usual exceptions, the most notable of whom, Bruno Latour and François Jullien, remain taxonomically as well as politically marginal to the academic mainline, despite their renown) is showing symptoms of being absorbed back into its Durkheimian substratum, which nevertheless has not prevented it from also being seduced by the local drivers of the franchising of English scholastic logic (which over the past decades has undergone an expansion in France as rapid and inexplicable as the expansion of McDonald's there). Another tendency that ought to be registered (but with ennui: so much more would have to happen to counteract the previous development) is the vast sociocognitive naturalization, in anthropology's unconscious, of a certain psychocognitive naturalism (projected onto the unconscious of its object) that justifies an economy of knowledge where the anthropological concept, in perfect coherence with the axiomatics of cognitive capitalism, effectively becomes a figure of the symbolic surplus value the "observer" extracts from the existential labor of the "observed."[51]

Let's be clear: things have not really gone that far.[52] Where anthropology is concerned, examples of its creativity and dynamism have been more numerous than the mere mention of Latour and Jullien could lead one to believe, and a generational changing of the guard is underway that may not (not necessarily …) exacerbate the above-mentioned tendencies. Furthermore, there has always been discerning researchers who defend in no uncertain terms a reciprocity of perspectives as a constitutive requirement of the anthropological project, and who thus refuse to join in with what Bob Scholte has dubbed the "epistemocide" of its objects. Hence the reactionary tidal wave, which counts among those riding it a small but no less illustrious contingent of anthropologists—certain of whom, as we know, have invoked the name of Lévi-Strauss as justification for their role as Republican censors—has not entirely crashed down on the bastions of resistance, those of anthropologists, like Favret-Saada (2000), as much as philosophers … with Isabelle Stengers being the philosopher who should be given the biggest mention, for having done more than

---

51. If the two directions French thought took after the structuralist moment—cognitivism and poststructuralism—are considered, it is clear that the country's anthropology has drifted in a quasi-unanimous fashion toward the former attractor, to the point where the word "cognitive" has become the dominant operator of the phatic function in the recent discourse of the discipline. Anthropological cognitivism has shown itself, at the end of the day (the institutional and psychological proximity of the gigantic figure of Lévi-Strauss might explain it), to be far more anti-structuralist than the different philosophical cases of post-structuralism constituted by Foucault, Deleuze, and Derrida. Moreover, this second direction has developed, as we know, into a tense but fecund imbrication with the "hyperstructuralism" whose roots lie in the works of Althusser and Lacan and that bloomed in Badiou, Balibar, Jacques-Alain Miller, J-C Milner, and others (Maniglier 2009).

52. In the interval between typing this paragraph and its publication, I felt certain that I would no longer agree with it and would have to add some lengthy amendments. But this is still how things sit from my vantage, here and now. And *naturally*, I immediately excluded my fellow Americanists (we have always been superstructuralists!) from this atypical assessment.

anyone else to fully (that is, from the left) realize the Latourian principle of generalized symmetry.

Some reasons for optimism thus remain. We are witnessing, for instance, a historical-theoretical re-evaluation of the structuralist project. While it is difficult to anticipate the intellectual effects that the "structural event" of the recent inclusion of Lévi-Strauss in the *Bibliothéque de la Pléiade* might have, his work has begun to be reexamined in a context where it is not only "behind us" and "around us" but also "before us," to evoke the final words of "Race and History" (1952: 49). The appearance of the *Pléiade* volume, moreover, is one of those "remarkable reversals" that its author was so fond of observing: anthropological structuralism's heritage is now, outside of some notable exceptions and homages, better cared for by philosophy than anthropology. I am referring here to the rehabilitation of Lévi-Strauss being undertaken by a new generation of philosophers, with the aim of redeeming the originality and radicality of French thought during the 1960s.[53]

Of everyone in this generation, special mention should be made of the philosopher Patrice Maniglier. He has offered one of the most original interpretations of structuralism by unearthing from Saussurian semiology a quite singular ontology of the sign that is also consubstantial with Lévi-Strauss' anthropology. As for Manigler's reading of Lévi-Strauss himself, it discretely bears what is nonetheless the explicit influence of Deleuze. It goes without saying that it would have been quite difficult to get either thinker to assent to such a reading, and the situation is worse (yet already for that reason more interesting) where their self-proclaimed disciples are concerned. But the line has been drawn: Structural anthropology, Maniglier unflinchingly affirms, is "at once empiricist and pluralist," and the philosophy it contains is, "in all respects, a practical philosophy." An empiricist, pluralist, and pragmatic Lévi-Strauss? Finally, someone has said it! The reader no doubt gets that we are 180 degrees from that "Lévi-Straussology"

---

53. I am thinking here of the group making up the *Centre international d'étude de la philosophie française contemporaine*, which includes Patrice Maniglier and Frédéric Keck. Gildas Salmon's excellent work on Lévi-Strauss and myth (2013) is also of great importance; had it been available during the writing of the present book, I might not have dared to say much that I do in later chapters about the *Mythologiques* and their author. It is obviously also necessary to go a little further back, to the pioneering efforts of Jean Petitot, who reconceived the theoretical genealogy of structuralism. See Petitot, 1999.

[*"la-pensée-Lévi-Strauss"*] that Jeanne Favret-Saada lambasted with such admirable sarcasm.

The novelty of Deleuze's philosophy was rapidly seized upon in the counter-cultural political spaces born out of '68, from experimental art to minority politics to feminism. Shortly thereafter, it was incorporated into the conceptual repertoire of the new strategic projects of symetrico-reflexive anthropology, like science studies, and then further deployed in certain well-known analyses of the dynamics of late capital. In seeming compensation, the attempts at articulating classic anthropology—the study of minoritarian subjects and objects, in all the senses of these three words—to Deleuzian concepts surprisingly remain both rare and, where they have occurred, overly timid. For in the end, the diptych of *Capitalism and Schizophrenia* supports a number of its claims with a vast bibliography on non-Occidental peoples, from the Guayaki to the Kachin to the Mongolians, thereby developing theses rich in implications for anthropology—too rich, perhaps, for certain delicate intellectual constitutions. Beyond that, the work of certain anthropologists who have recently left a major mark on the discipline—such as Roy Wagner, Marilyn Strathern, Bruno Latour, and the rest—contain suggestive connections to Deleuze's ideas. And the connections between these connections have not really been made. In Wagner's case, they seem purely virtual, the results either of what Deleuze called an "aparallel evolution" or of independent invention, in the Wagnerian sense; which renders them no less real or astonishing. Where Strathern is concerned, the connections are "partial," as would befit the author of *Partial Connections*, or else highly indirect (but isn't "indirection" her preferred procedure?). That said, the onetime Cambridge dame, who shared with Deleuze and Guattari an ensemble of dense conceptual terms, like multiplicity, perspective, dividual, and fractality, is in more than a few ways the most "molecular" author of the three.[54] In Latour's case, finally, the connections are actual and

54. Marilyn Strathern will of course find it quite strange to see her portrait painted in Deleuzian terms. But we should recall Deleuze's comment about his method of reading philosophers as an art of portraiture: "It is not a matter of making [something] lifelike." (Deleuze and Guattari 1996: 55).

explicit, or "molar," and constitute one of the chief materials of the theoretical infrastructure of his work. Yet at the same time, significant portions of it are quite foreign to Deleuze's philosophy (without for that being unstimulating).

No coincidence, then, that these three are among the few anthropologists who could be accurately labeled post-structuralists, rather than postmodernists: each managed to take on board the insights of structuralism and then set off in their own direction, rather than signing up for the bad, retrograde theoretical trips that so many of their contemporaries did: the sentimental pseudo-immanentism of lived worlds, existential dwellings, and bodily practices that this generation subscribed to, when they had not opted for sociobiological, or political-economic/World-Systems or neo-diffusionist-"invention of tradition" macho-positivist Theories of Everything. By the same token, Deleuze's thought, at least from *Difference and Repetition* and *The Logic of Sense* on, can be taken as an extreme effort to deterritorialize structuralism, a movement or style from which he extracted (some would say, into which he introduced) its most radically novel insights so as to pursue, on their basis, other, often quite different itineraries (Maniglier 2006: 468-469).[55] In effect, in the course of elaborating the most realized philosophical expression of structuralism, both books entered into a violent theoretical tension with it that verged on rupture. The rupture became manifest in *Anti-Oedipus*, a book that furnished one of the principle axes for the crystallization of post-structuralism, in its proper sense of a style of thought radicalizing the revolutionary aspects of structuralism against the *statu quo ante*, and thus was a tumultuous rejection (sometimes too much so, even I will admit) of its most conservative aspects.

The anthropologist who decides to read or reread Deleuze and Guattari after years of immersion in her own discipline's literature can only have the curious feeling of a reverse déjà vu, of something that has already been written in the future.... A number of theoretical perspectives and descriptive techniques have only recently lost the whiff of scandal that once surrounded them in anthropology, and are now forming a rhizome with the

---

55. See Deleuze's 2004[1972] article, which inspired a good deal of the breakthroughs internal to structuralism, like those of Petitot.

Deleuzo-Guattarian corpus from 20 or 30 years ago.[56] A precise account of the importance of their texts to the discipline would require tracing in detail the network of forces social anthropology is currently enmeshed in—a task beyond the scope of the present essay. If I can put things generally, however, it will not be difficult to establish the role these two thinkers played in sedimenting a certain contemporary conceptual aesthetic.

For some time, as is often noted, there has been a displacement of the center of human-scientific interest toward semiotic processes like metonymy, indexicality, and literality, each of which is a way of refusing metaphor and representation (metaphor as the essence of representation), of privileging pragmatics over semantics, and of choosing coordination rather than subordination. The linguistic turn that served, during the last century, as the virtual point of convergence of diverse philosophical temperaments, projects, and systems seems to have begun to turn elsewhere—away from linguistics and, to a certain extent, from language qua anthropological macroparadigm: the displacements just indicated show how the lines of flight leading away from language-as-model were drawn from the very interior of that model of language.

Even the sign itself seems to have become separated from language. The sense that there is a discontinuity between sign and referent, or language and world, that guarantees the reality of the first and the intelligibility of the second is becoming metaphysically obsolete, at least when put in the terms in which it has been traditionally expressed; *this* is where we are beginning to not be modern or, rather, where we are beginning to have never been modern.[57] On the side of the world (a side no longer having another side since there is now only an indefinite plurality of "sides"), the

56. "Perhaps that sense of *déjà vu* is also a sense of habitation within a cultural matrix" (Strathern 2004: xxv). The reader may recall that Deleuze saw *Difference and Repetition* as an expression of the spirit of the intellectual era achieved by realizing the latter's full philosophical consequences (Deleuze 1994: 1). Inversely, she could end up surprised at the scant references made to either volume of *Capitalism and Schizophrenia* in French anthropology. A recent, notable example is Descola's *Beyond Nature and Culture*, which contains several unanticipated analogies with the developments of Chapter Three of *Anti-Oedipus* and Chapter Five of *A Thousand Plateaus*, but in which the name of Deleuze appears just once.

57. I have not here completely accounted for (because I have not yet absorbed all its implications) the reopening of Saussurean semiology Maniglier is undertaking—a conceptual labor that involves redefining the sign in terms of "an ontology of becomings and multiplicities" (2006: 27, 465).

corresponding displacement has led to the preference for the differential-fractal instead of the unitary-whole-combinatory, the perception of flat multiplicities in place of hierarchical totalities, the interest in trans-categorical connections between heterogeneous elements over correspondences between intrinsically homogeneous series, and the accent on a wavelike or topological continuity of forces rather than a geometric, corpuscular discontinuity of forms. The molar discontinuity between, on the one hand, the two conceptually homogeneous series of signifier and signified, (which are themselves in a relation of structural discontinuity) and, on the other, the phenomenologically continuous series of the real resolves into molecular discontinuities—which reveal continuity, in other words, to be intrinsically differential and heterogeneous (the distinction between the continuous and the undifferentiated is absolutely crucial here). A flat ontology, to use DeLanda's term (2002), prevails, in which the real emerges as a dynamic, immanent multiplicity in a state of continuous variation, a metasystem far from equilibrium, rather than a combinatory manifestation or grammatical implementation of transcendent principles or rules, and as a differentiating relation, which is to say, as a heterogeneous disjunctive synthesis instead of a dialectical (horizontal) conjunction or hierarchical (vertical) totalization of contraries. And to this ontological flattening corresponds a "symmetric" epistemology (Latour 1993): rigorously put, we are witnessing the collapse of the distinction between epistemology (language) and ontology (world) and the progressive emergence of a "practical ontology" (Jensen 2004) in which knowing is no longer a way of representing the unknown but of interacting with it, i.e., a way of creating rather than contemplating, reflecting, or communicating (see Deleuze and Guattari 1991). The task of knowledge is no longer to unify diversity through representation but, as Latour again puts it, of "multiplying the agents and agencies populating our world" (1996: 5). (The Deleuzian harmonics are audible.)[58]

---

58. The notion of a flat ontology returns us to the "univocity of being," the medieval theme recycled by Deleuze: "Univocity is the immediate synthesis of the multiple: the one is only said of the multiple, in lieu of the latter's subordination to the one as to a superior, common genre capable of encompassing it." (Zourabichvili, 2003: 82). "The correlate," as Zourabichvili continues, "of this immediate synthesis of the multiple is the distribution of all things on one plane of common equality: here 'common' does not have the sense of a generic identity, but of a transversal, nonhierarchical communication between beings that are only different. Measure (or hierarchy) also changes its meaning: it is no longer the external measure of being to a standard, but the measure internal to each in relation

So a new image of thought that is at once nomadological and multinaturalist.

The subsequent chapter takes up only one dimension of this contemporary eido-aesthetic. More an example than anything, two possible directions for deepening the dialogue between Deleuze and Guattari's schizophilosophy and social anthropology will be pursued. First, some schematic parallels between Deleuzian concepts and analytic themes in current anthropology will be drawn. After that, we will examine the effect exercised by an aspect of classic social anthropology—the theory of kinship—on the Deleuzo-Guattarian conception of the primitive territorial machine, a.k.a. pre-signifying semiotics.

---

to its own limits." The idea of a flat ontology is extensively commented on in DeLanda, 2002; he develops it in its own direction In DeLanda, 2006. Jensen (2004) raises in an excellent analysis the theoretico-political (whether well-developed or not) repercussions of these ontologies, most particularly in the case of Latour. The latter insists, in *Reassembling the Social*, on the methodological imperative of "keeping the social flat" that is proper to actor-network theory—whose other name, we discover, is "the ontology of the actant-rhizome." (Latour 2005: 9) The conceptual analysis specific to this theory—its method of *obviation*, as Wagner would say—consists in a hierarchical dis-encompassment of the socius in a way that liberates the intensive differences that traverse and detotalize it—an operation radically different from recapitulating in the face of "individualism," contrary to what the retroprophets of the old holist testament claim.

Chapter Six

An Anti-Sociology of Multiplicities

In *Anti-Oedipus*, as is well known, Deleuze and Guattari overthrow the temple of psychoanalysis by knocking out its central pillar—the reactionary conception of desire as lack—and then replace it with the theory of desiring machines, sheer positive productivity that must be coded by the socius, the social production machine. This theory runs through a vast panorama of universal history, which is painted in the book's central chapter in a quaintly archaic style that could make the anthropological reader wince. Not only does it employ the venerable savagery-barbarism-civilization triad, but the proliferating ethnographic references are treated in a seemingly cavalier way that the same reader might be tempted to call "uncontrolled comparison." Yet if that reader stops to think for a moment, she may very well conclude that the traditional three-stage *topos* is submitted to an interpretation that is anything but traditional, and that this impression of erratic comparison derives from the fact that the controls used by the authors are not the usual ones—they are differentiating rather than collectivizing, as Wagner would put it. *Anti-Oedipus* is indeed the result of a "prodigious effort to think differently" (Donzelot 1977: 28), its purpose being not merely to denounce the repressive paralogisms of psychoanalysis but to establish a true "anti-sociology" (id.: 37).[59] An obviational project like this should certainly appeal to contemporary anthropology; or at least to that anthropology

59. In *Anti-Oedipus*, "the reversal of psychoanalysis [is] the primary condition for a shakeup of a completely different scope [...] on the scale of the whole of the human sciences; there is an attempt at subversion on the general order of what Laing and Cooper had carried out solely on the terrain of psychiatry" (Donzelot op. cit.: 27).

107

that does not consider itself to be an exotic, inoffensive branch of sociology, but rather regards the latter as a somewhat confused, almost inevitably normative branch of "auto-anthropology."[60]

The second book of the diptych, *A Thousand Plateaus*, distances itself from *Anti-Oedipus'* psychoanalytic concerns. The project of writing a "universal history of contingency" (D. 2006: 309) is carried out in a decidedly nonlinear fashion in which the authors cross different "plateaus" of intensity (a notion, it should be remembered, inspired by Bateson) corresponding to diverse material-semiotic formations and peopled by a disconcerting quantity of new concepts. The book puts forward and illustrates a theory of multiplicities—the Deleuzian theme that has carried the greatest repercussions in and for contemporary anthropology.

For many, Deleuzian multiplicity has seemed the concept best suited for characterizing not only the new practices of knowledge peculiar to anthropology but also the phenomena they take up, and its effect has been liberating. It has opened a line of flight between those two dualisms that have functioned as the walls of its epistemological prison from the time of its origins in the darkness of the 18th and 19th centuries: Nature and Culture and the Individual and Society, those "ultimate mental frameworks of the discipline" that ostensibly could never be false, since it is by means of them that we think the true and false. But could that really be all? Frameworks change, and the possibilities of thought change with them (the ideas of what thinking and the thinkable are change, and the very idea of a framework changes as the framework of ideas does). The concept of multiplicity may have only become thinkable—and therefore thinkable by anthropology—because we are currently entering a nonmerologic, postplural world where we have never been modern; a world that, more through disinterest than any *Aufhebung*, is leaving in the dust the old infernal distinction between the One and the Multiple that governed so many dualisms, the anthropological pairs and many others as well.[61]

Multiplicity is thus a meta-concept that defines a new type of entity, and the well-known (by name at least) "rhizome" is its

60. See L.-S. 1978[1964]; Strathern 1987; Viveiros de Castro 2003.

61. On the mereological model, see Strathern, 1992a. On the idea of a postplural world, see Strathern 1991, XVI; 1992a: 3-4, 184 et passim; 1992b: 92. The expression "infernal distinction" has been borrowed from Pignarre and Stengers, 2005.

concrete image.[62] The sources of the Deleuzian idea of multiplicity lie in Riemann's geometry and Bergson's philosophy (Deleuze 1966: ch. 2), and its creation aims at dethroning the classical metaphysical notions of essence and type (DeLanda 2002).[63] It is the main tool of a "prodigious effort" to imagine thought as an activity other than that of identification (recognition) and classification (categorization), and to determine what there is to think as intensive singularity rather than as substance or subject. The politico-philosophical intentions of this decision are clear: the transformation of multiplicity into a concept and the concept into a multiplicity is aimed at severing the primordial link between the concept and power, i.e., between philosophy and the state. Which is the meaning of Deleuze's celebrated call "to invert Platonism" (D. 1990: 253). Thinking through multiplicities is thinking against the State.[64]

A multiplicity is different from an essence. The dimensions composing it are neither constitutive properties nor criteria for classificatory inclusion. A chief component of the concept of multiplicity is, on the contrary, the notion of individuation as non-taxonomical differentiation; the process of the actualization of a virtual different from the realization of the possible through limitation and refractory to the typological categories of similitude, opposition, analogy, and identity. Multiplicity is the mode of existence of pure intensive difference—"irreducible inequality that forms the condition of the world (Deleuze 1994: 222).[65]

---

62. I say meta-concept because every concept is a multiplicity in its own right, though not every multiplicity is conceptual (D. G. 1994: 21ff).

63. DeLanda (2002: 9-10, 38-40, et passim) is a detailed exposition of the mathematical origins and implications of the Deleuzian concept of multiplicity; also evoked in Plotnitsky 2003, and Duffy, Smith, Durie, and Plotinsky in Duffy 2006. Zourabichvili 2003 (pp. 51-54), in turn, is the best overview of the concept's properly philosophical connections and its place in Deleuze's work.

64. In memory of Pierre Clastres (1974). Clastres was (and remains) one of the rare French anthropologists who knew how to make something out of *Anti-Oedipus*' ideas, besides being one of the inspirations for the theory of the war machine developed in Plateaus 12 and 13 of *A Thousand Plateaus*.

65. Cf. Lévi-Strauss when he states, beyond just these passages, that "[d]isequilibrium is always given"(1966: 222), and that "[the] being of the world consists of a disparity. It cannot be said purely and simply of the world that it is; it has the form of an initial asymmetry" (1971: 539). Here we are faced with two of the chief themes of structuralism, through which it communicates with its posterity: a nature necessarily in disequilibrium on account of structure, and the constitutive asymmetry of the real.

The notions of type and entity, in fact, are entirely inadequate for defining rhizomatic multiplicities. If there is "no entity without identity," as Quine famously alliterated, one must conclude that multiplicities do not qualify for that enviable status. A rhizome does not behave as an entity, nor does it instantiate a type; it is an acentric reticular system constituted by intensive relations ("becomings") between heterogeneous singularities that correspond to events, or extrasubstantive individuations ("haecceities"). Hence a rhizomatic multiplicity is not truly a *being* but an assemblage of becomings, a *"between"*: a *difference engine*, or rather, the intensive diagram of its functioning. Bruno Latour, who in his recent book on actor-network theory indicates how much it owes to the rhizome concept, is particularly emphatic: a network is not a thing because anything can be described as a network (2005: 129-31). A network is a *perspective*, a way of inscribing and describing "the registered movement of a thing as it associates with many other elements" (Jensen 2003: 227). Yet this perspective is internal or immanent; the different associations of the "thing" make it differ from itself—"it is the thing itself that has been allowed to be deployed as multiple" (Latour 2005: 116). In short, and the point goes back to Leibniz, there are no points of view *on* things—it is things and beings that are the points of view (Deleuze 1994: 49; 1990d: 173-174). If there is no entity without identity, then there is no multiplicity without perspective.

A rhizome is not truly *one* being, either. Nor can it be several. Multiplicity is not something like a larger unity, a superior plurality or unity; rather it is a *less than one* obtained by subtraction (hence the importance of the ideas of the minor, minority, and minoritization in Deleuze). Multiplicities are constituted by the absence of any extrinsic coordination imposed by a supplementary dimension—n+1: n and its "principle" or "context," for example. The immanence of multiplicities implies autoposition, anterior to context itself; and being congenitally devoid of unity, they constantly differ from themselves. Multiplicities are, in sum, tautegorically anterior to their own "contexts"; like Roy Wagner's (1986) symbols that stand for themselves, they possess their own internal measure and represent themselves. Multiplicities are systems at n-1 dimensions (D. G. 1987: 6, 17, 21) where the One operates only as what should be subtracted to produce the multiple, which thus turns out to have been created by "detranscendence"; they evince an immanent organization "belonging to the many as such, and which has no need whatsoever of unity in order to form a system" (D. 1968: 236).[66]

This turns them into systems whose complexity is "lateral," that is, resistant to hierarchy or to any other type of transcendent unification—a complexity of alliance rather than descent, to anticipate an argument that will be examined below. Emerging when and where open intensive lines (lines of force, not lines of contour; cf. ATP: 549) connect heterogeneous elements, rhizomes project, again, a radically fractal ontology that ignores the distinctions between "part" and "whole."[67] A baroque instead of a romantic conception of complexity, as Kwa (2002) persuasively argued. Indeed, multiplicity is the quasi-object that substitutes for the Romantic organic totalities and Enlightenment atomic associations that were once thought to exhaust the conceptual possibilities available to anthropology. In that way, multiplicity calls for a completely different interpretation of the emblematic megaconcepts of the discipline, Culture and Society, to the point of rendering them "theoretically obsolete" (Strathern 1996).

Wagner's fractal person, Strathern's partial connections, Callon and Latour's socio-technical networks are some well-known anthropological examples of flat multiplicities. "A fractal person is never a unit standing in relation to an aggregate, or an aggregate standing in relation to a unit, but always an entity with relationship integrally implied" (Wagner 1991: 163, my emphasis). The mutual implication of the concepts of multiplicity, intensity and implication is in fact a point elaborated at length by Deleuze (1994: ch. VI). François Zourabichvili, one the most perceptive

---

66. A multiplicity or a rhizome is a system, one must notice, and not a sum of "fragments." It is simply another concept of system, which differs from the arborescent system as an immanent process differs from a transcendent model (ATP: 22). We are not talking post-modernism here.

67. "We believe only in totalities that are lateral." The whole not only coexists with all the parts; it is contiguous to them, it exists as a product that is produced apart from them and yet at the same time is related to them (AOE: 42, 43-4). About the heterogeneity of the elements connected in a rhizome, it is important to notice that it does not concern a previous ontological condition, or essence of the terms (what counts as heterogeneous, in this sense, depends on the observer's "cultural predispositions"—Strathern 1996: 525), but an effect of its capture by a multiplicity, which renders the terms that it connects heterogeneous by making them operate as tautegorical singularities.

commentators on the philosopher, observes that "implication is the fundamental logical movement in Deleuze's philosophy" (2004[1994]: 82); elsewhere, he underscores that Deleuzian pluralism supposes a "primacy of relations." The philosophy of difference is a philosophy of relation.

Yet not *every* relation will do. Multiplicity is a system defined by a modality of relational synthesis different from a connection or conjunction of terms. Deleuze calls it *disjunctive synthesis* or *inclusive disjunction*, a relational mode that does not have similarity or identity as its (formal or final) cause, but divergence or distance; another name for this relational mode is "becoming." Disjunctive synthesis or becoming is "the main operator of Deleuze's philosophy" (Zourabichvili 2003: 81), being that it is the movement of difference as such—the centrifugal movement through which difference escapes the powerful circular attractor of dialectical contradiction and sublation. A difference that is positive rather than oppositional, an indiscernibility of the heterogeneous rather than a conciliation of contraries, disjunctive synthesis takes disjunction as "the very nature of relation" (id. 2004[1994]: 99), and relation as a movement of "reciprocal asymmetric implication" (id. 2003: 79) between the terms or perspectives connected by the synthesis, which is not resolved either into equivalence or into a superior identity:

> Deleuze's most profound insight is perhaps this: that difference is also communication and contagion between heterogeneities; in other words, that a divergence never arises without reciprocal contamination of points of view [...] To connect is always to communicate across a distance, through the very heterogeneity of the terms. (Zourabichvili 2004[1994]: 99)

Coming back to the parallels with contemporary anthropological theory, it is worth recalling that the theme of separation as relation is emblematic of Wagnerian and Strathernian anthropology. The conception of relation as "comprising disjunction and connection together" (Strathern 1995: 165; my emphasis) is the basis of the theory of differential relations, the idea that "[r]elations make a difference between persons" (id. 1999: 126; cf. also 1996: 525, and naturally, 1988: ch. 8). To compress an otherwise long point, let us say that the celebrated "system M" (Gell 1999), the

Strathernian description of Melanesian sociality both as an exchange of perspectives and a process of relational implication-explication, is a symmetrical-anthropological theory of disjunctive synthesis.[68]

From a "metatheoretical" perspective, in turn, it is possible to observe that the subtractive rather than additive multiplicity of rhizomes turns the latter into a nonmerological, postplural "figure" capable of tracing a line of flight from the dilemma of the one and the many that Strathern, with her characteristically remarkable perspicacity, identifies as anthropology's characteristic analytical trap:

> [A]nthropologists by and large have been encouraged to think [that] the alternative to one is many. Consequently, we either deal with ones, namely single societies or attributes, or else with a multiplicity of ones. [...] A world obsessed with ones and the multiplications and divisions of ones creates problems for the conceptualization of relationships. (Strathern 1991: 52-53)

A dis-obsessing conceptual therapy therefore proves necessary. To compare multiplicities is different than making particularities converge around generalities, as is the habit of those anthropological analyses that perceive substantial similarity underneath every "accidental" difference: "in every human society...." This refers us to an observation of Albert Lautmann (Deleuze's author of choice as far as mathematics is concerned):

> The constitution, by Gauss and Riemann, of a differential geometry that studies the intrinsic properties of a variety, independent of any space into which this variety would be plunged, eliminates any reference to a universal container or to a center of privileged coordinates. (*apud* Smith 2006: 167, n. 39)

---

68. This theory has for a chief reference Wagner's fundamental article (1977) on "analogical kinship" in Melanesia, whose language of "flux" and "break" strangely evokes *Anti-Oedipus* (which the author does not cite and probably did not know). Among the recent works that could be inscribed in the movement of ideas of Wagner and Strathern is Rupert Stasch's (2009) monograph on the relational imagination of the Korowai of Western New Guinea, a defense and illustration of the self-problematizing power of savage thought, an exposition of the astonishing Korowai theory of relation qua disjunctive and heterogenetic multiplicity.

Substitute anthropology for geometry here, and the consequences become evident. How such variety could be of service to anthropology is not very difficult to imagine, as everything ordinarily denounced in the discipline as scandalous contradiction suddenly becomes conceivable: how variations can be described or compared without presupposing an invariable ground, where the universals lie, and what then happens to the biological constitution of the species, symbolic laws, and the principles of political economy, not to speak of the famed "external reality" (all of which, rest assured, were previously supposed to have been readily conceivable *in potentia* but not in act).... Whatever difficulties arise, we gain from the right to speculate on these issues. It could even be said such an anthropology would be trading in exotic, contraband intellectual goods, much like differential geometry; but they would be no more exotic than those that nourish the anthropological orthodoxy about comparison and generalization, tributary that the discipline is to our metaphysics—the same metaphysics, it will be recalled, that was so proud to not admit into its walls anything that was not geometry.

But comparing multiplicities is something different than establishing correlational invariants by means of formal analogies between extensive differences, as is exactly the case with classic structuralist comparisons where "it is not the resemblances, but the differences, which resemble each other" (Lévi-Strauss 1963: 77). To compare multiplicities—which are systems of comparisons in and by themselves—is to determine their characteristic mode of divergence, their internal and external difference; here, comparative analysis amounts to separative synthesis. Where multiplicities are concerned, there are not relations that vary but variations that relate: differences that differ. [69] As that molecular sociologist Gabriel Tarde wrote more than a century ago:

> The truth is that differences go differing, and changes go changing, and that, as they take themselves thus as their own finality, change and difference bear out their necessary and absolute character. (1999 [1895]: 69)

Chunglin Kwa has observed concerning this point that "the fundamental difference is between the romantic conception of

---

69. This would, moreover, be an acceptable gloss of Lévi-Strauss' canonical formula.

society as an organism and the baroque conception of the organism as a society" (2002: 26). While he does not furnish names, this is a perfect description of the difference between the sociologies of Durkheim and Tarde. Against the *sui generis* character of social facts espoused by the former, "the universal sociological point of view," the latter asserts that "everything is a society, every phenomenon is a social fact" (Tarde 1999[1895]: 58, 67). This position refuses all validity to the distinction between the individual and society, part and whole, just as it remains innocent of those drawn between human and nonhuman, animate and inanimate, and person and thing. Tarde's fractal ontology ("to exist is to differ") and borderless sociology even achieves a "universal psychomorphism": all things are persons, or "little persons" (ibid 43), persons in persons, and so on—persons all the way down.

Intensive difference, difference of perspective, difference of differences. Nietzsche remarked that the point of view of health concerning illness differs from the point of view of illness concerning health. [70] For difference is never the same; *the way is not the same in both directions*:

> A meditation on Nietzschean perspectivism gives positive consistence to the disjunction: *distance* between *points of view*, at once undecomposable and unequal with itself, since the way is indeed not the same in the two directions (Zourabichvili 2003).

The comparison of multiplicities—in other words, comparison as "the invention of multiplicities" (a.k.a. Deleuze meets Wagner)—is disjunctive synthesis, as are the relations that it relates.

Deleuze's texts create the impression of a philosopher reveling in conceptual dyads, with the list of them being long and colorful: difference and repetition, intensive and extensive, nomadic and sedentary, virtual and actual, flows and quanta, code and axiomatic, deterritorialization and reterritorialization, minor and major, molecular and molar, supple and rigid, smooth and striated, and so on. Owing to this stylistic "signature," Deleuze has sometimes

---

70. D., 1969 d: 202-203. In the same way, it is the slave of the Master-Slave dialectic that is dialectical, not the master. (D. 1983: 10).

been classified as a dualist (Jameson 1997)—a rather premature interpretation, to put it politely.[71]

A slightly attentive reading, in fact, is all it takes to show that the rapid pace of exposition in the two *Capitalism and Schizophrenia* books, in which dualities abound, is constantly interrupted by provisos, qualifications, involutions, subdivisions and other argumentative displacements of the dual (or other) distinctions that had just been proposed by the authors themselves. Such methodical interruptions are exactly this, a question of method and not a pang of regret following a little indulgence in the binary sin; they are perfectly determined moments of conceptual construction.[72] Neither principle nor result, the Deleuzian dyads—one might wish to call them, after Strathern (2005) "conceptual duplexes"— are means to arrive elsewhere. The exemplary case here is, once again, the distinction between root-tree and canal-rhizome:

> The important point is that the root-tree and the canal-rhizome are not two opposed models; the first operates as a transcendent model and tracing, even if it engenders its own escapes; the second operates as an immanent process that overturns the model and outlines a map, even if it constitutes its own hierarchies, even if it gives rise to a despotic channel. It is not a question of this or that place on earth,

---

71. For a subtler interpretation of Deleuze as a philosopher of "immediate or nondialectical duality," see Lawlor 2003.

72. This the case with the duality between arborescence and rhizome ("have we not … reverted to a simple dualism?" ATP: 14), two schemes that do not cease to interfere with each other; with the two types of multiplicity, molar and molecular, which always operate at the same time and in the same assemblage such that there is no dualism of multiplicities but only "multiplicities of multiplicities" (ATP: 38); with the distinction between form of expression and form of content, in which there is neither parallelism nor representation but "a manner in which expressions are inserted into contents, (…) in which signs are at work in things themselves just as things extend into or are deployed through signs" (ATP: 96); with the opposition between the segmentary and the centralized, which must be replaced by a distinction between two different but inseparable segmentations, the supple and the rigid—"they overlap, they are entangled" (ATP: 231, 234); and with, finally, smooth (nomadic, war-machinic) and striated (sedentary, state-like) spaces, whose difference is said to be complex both because "the successive terms of the oppositions fail to coincide entirely"—that is, smooth versus striated is not exactly the same thing as nomadic versus sedentary etc.—and because "the two spaces in fact exist only in mixture" (ATP: 524). To summarize, soon after distinguishing two poles, processes or tendencies, the Deleuzian analysis, on the one hand, unfolds the polarity into further polarities, asymmetrically embedded in the first (thus bringing about a "mixture" *de jure*), and on the other, it indicates the *de facto* mixture of the initial poles. And the typical conclusion is: "All of this happens at the same time" (ATP: 246).

or of a given moment in history, still less of this or that category of thought. It is a question of a model that is perpetually in construction or collapsing, and of a process that is perpetually prolonging itself, breaking off and standing up again. No, this is not a new or different dualism. [...] We invoke one dualism only in order to challenge another. We employ a dualism of models only in order to arrive at a process that challenges all models. Each time, mental correctives are necessary to undo the dualisms we had no wish to construct but through which we must pass. Arrive at the magic formula we all seek—PLURALISM=MONISM—via all the dualisms that are the enemy, an entirely necessary enemy, the furniture we are constantly rearranging (D. G. 1987: 22-23).

Along with brushing off the readings that reduce their philosophy to another Great Divide Theory,[73] the authors illustrate two characteristic procedures. First, there is treatment of concepts in a "minor" or pragmatic key, as tools, bridges, or vehicles rather than as ultimate objects, meanings or destinations—the philosopher as *penseur sauvage*. Whence the authors warily realistic attitude toward the dualistic propensities of inertial thinking. In *Anti-Oedipus*, they expound a monist conception of desiring production; in *A Thousand Plateaus*, they develop a "post-plural" theory of multiplicities—two pointedly non-dualistic enterprises. Yet they do not suppose that dualisms are a surmountable obstacle through the sheer power of wishful (un-) thinking, like those who fancy that it is enough to call someone else a dualist to stop being one themselves. Dualisms are real and not imaginary; they are not a mere ideological mirage but the *modus operandi* of an implacable abstract machine of overcoding. It is necessary to undo dualisms precisely because they were made. Moreover, it is possible to undo them for the same reason: the authors do not think that dualisms are the event horizon of Western metaphysics, the absolute boundary that can only be exposed—deconstructed—but never crossed by the prisoners in the Cave. There are many other possible abstract machines. In order to undo them, however, the

---

73. Anthropologists are in general predisposed to this type of knee-jerk deconstruction. See Rival 1998 and Rumsey 2001 for two pertinent examples: both authors protest against a supposed great divide between The West = arborescence and The Rest = rhizome. These two critics show a certain naiveté as they imagine a certain naiveté on the part of the criticized, who knew perfectly well what they were (not) doing: "[W]e are on the wrong track with all these geographic distributions. An impasse. So much the better." (ATP: 22).

circular trap of negating or contradicting them must be avoided: they have to be exited, in "a calculated way," which is to say always through a tangent—by a line of flight.

This takes us to the second procedure. Deleuzian dualities are constructed and transformed according to a recurrent pattern, which determines them as *minimal multiplicities*—partial dualities, one might say. Every conceptual distinction begins with the establishment of an extensive-actual pole and an intensive-virtual one. The subsequent analysis consists in showing how the duality changes its nature as it is taken from the standpoint of one pole and then the other. From the standpoint of the extensive (arborescent, molar, rigid, striated, etc.) pole, the relation that distinguishes it from the second pole is typically an opposition: an exclusive disjunction and a limitative synthesis; that is, an extensive, molar and actual relation itself. From the standpoint of the other (rhizomatic, molecular, supple, smooth, etc.) pole, however, there is no opposition but intensive difference, implication or disjunctive inclusion of the extensive pole in the intensive or virtual pole; the duality posed by the first pole reveals itself as the molar echo of a molecular multiplicity at the other.[74] It is as if each pole apprehends its relation with the other according to its own nature; or, in other words, as if the relation between the poles belongs, necessarily and alternatively, to the regime of one or the other pole, either the regime of contradiction or of the line of flight; it cannot be drawn from outside, from a third, encompassing pole. Perspectivism—duality as multiplicity—is what dialectics—duality as unity—has to negate in order to impose itself as universal law.[75]

---

74. "[A]n alternative, an exclusive disjunction is defined in terms of a principle which, however, constitutes its two terms or underlying wholes, and where the principle itself enters into the alternative (a completely different case from what happens when the disjunction is inclusive)" (D. G. 1983: 80). This pattern appears early in the Deleuzian corpus: see his comments on the Bergsonian division between duration and space, which cannot be simply defined as a difference in nature: the division is rather between duration, which supports and conveys all the differences in nature, while space presents only differences in degree. "There is thus no difference in nature between the two halves of the division: the difference in nature is wholly on one side" (Deleuze 1966: 23).

75. For an Americanist anthropologist, this duality of dualities irresistibly recalls the central argument of *The Story of Lynx* (Lévi-Strauss 1991) about the contrasting conceptions of twinhood in the respective mythologies of the Old and New Word. We will see later what its importance is here.

118

The two poles or aspects are always said to be present and active in every phenomenon or process. Their relation is typically one of "reciprocal presupposition," a notion advanced many times in *A Thousand Plateaus* (1987: 49-50, 73, 97, 235, 554) in lieu of notions of causality (linear or dialectical), micro-macro reduction (ontological or epistemological), and expressivity (hylomorphic or signifying). From an anthropological perspective, it is tempting to relate reciprocal presupposition to the Wagnerian double semiotics of invention and convention, in which each mode of symbolization precipitates or "counter-invents" the other, according to a "figure-ground reversal scheme" (Wagner 1981: ch. 3; 1986).[76] Or still, to the behavior of certain central analytical duplexes in *The Gender of the Gift* (Strathern 1988), such as those that preside over the economy of gender or the logic of exchange in Melanesia, in which one pole—cross-sex/same-sex, mediated/unmediated exchange—is always described as a version or transformation of the other, "each providing the context and grounding for the other," as Strathern summarized apropos a quite different (precisely!) context (1991: 72).[77] The crucial point here is that reciprocal presupposition entails that both poles of any duality are equally necessary, (they are mutually conditioning), but does not thereby make them symmetrical or equivalent. Inter-presupposition is *asymmetric* reciprocal implication: once more, "the way is not the same in both directions...." Hence when Deleuze and Guattari distinguish rhizomatic maps from arborescent tracings, they observe that the maps are constantly being totalized, unified and stabilized by the tracings, which are in turn subject to all sorts of anarchic deformations induced by rhizomatic processes. Yet, at the end of the day, "the tracing should always be put back on the

76. Wagner qualifies the reciprocal co-production between cultural convention and invention as "dialectical" (1981: 52; the term is widely used in Wagner 1986), which could confuse a Deleuzian reader. Yet the characterization of this dialectics, besides being explicitly non-Hegelian, makes it very evocative of Deleuzian reciprocal presupposition and disjunctive synthesis: "a tension or dialogue-like alternation between two conceptions or viewpoints that are simultaneously contradictory and supportive of each other" (Wagner 1981: 52). In sum, a "dialectic" with neither resolution nor conciliation: a Batesonian schismogenesis rather than a Hegelian *Aufhebung*. The work of Bateson is the transversal connection between the aparallel conceptual evolutions of Roy Wagner and Deleuze and Guattari.

77. In the Melanesian gender-kinship model, "each relation can come only from the other," and "... conjugal and parent-child relations are metaphors for one another, and hence a source of internal reflection" (Strathern 2001: 240).

map. This operation and the previous one are not at all symmetrical" (D. G. 1987: 14). They are not symmetrical because the latter operation of tracing works contrary to the process of desire (and "becoming is the process of desire"—D. G. 1987: 334) whereas the other advances it.[78]

This asymmetrical relation between processes and models in reciprocal presupposition (in which the rhizome is process, and the tree model) reminds one very much of the distinction between difference and negation developed in *Difference and Repetition* (D. 1994: 302-ff): negation is real but its reality is purely negative; it is only inverted, extended, limited and reduced difference. So although Deleuze and Guattari more than once caution that they are not establishing an axiological contrast between rhizome and tree, the molecular and the molar, and so on (D. G. 1987: 22, 237), the fact remains that there is always a tendency and a counter-tendency, two entirely different movements: the actualization and the counter-effectuation (or "crystallization") of the virtual (D. G. 1994: 147-52). The first movement consists in a decline in differences of potential or intensity as these are explicated in extension and incarnated as empirical things, while the second is the creator or "implicator" of difference as such, a process of return/reverse causality (D. G. 1987: 476) or "creative involution" (ibid: 203). But this does not prevent it from being strictly contemporaneous with the first movement, as its transcendental and therefore non-annullable condition. This latter movement is the Event or the Becoming, a pure reserve of intensity—the part, in everything that occurs, that escapes its own actualization (D. G. 1994: 147).

Once again, it seems natural to approximate this asymmetry of inter-implicated processes to certain aspects of Wagnerian semiotics (1981: 51-53, 116, 121-22). The "dialectical" or obviational nature of the relation between the two modes of symbolization belongs as such to one of the modes, that of invention-differentiation, whereas the contrast between the two modes is, by itself, the result of the other mode's operation, the

---

78. In the article cited in the previous note, Strathern makes the following observation: "cross-sex relations both alternate with same-sex relations, and contain an inherent premise of alternation within" (Strathern 2001: 227). This would be an example of reciprocal asymmetric presupposition: the relation between same-sex and cross-sex relations is, itself, of the cross-sex variety. This is yet another way of illustrating the Lévi-Straussian premise that identity is only a particular case of difference.

conventionalization-collectivization one. Moreover, although the two modes operate simultaneously and reciprocally in every act of symbolization (they operate upon each other, since there is nothing "outside" them), there is "all the difference in the world" (op. cit.: 51) between those cultures whose controlling context—in the terms of ATP, the dominant form of territorialisation—is the conventional mode, and those in which the control rests with the differentiating mode. If the contrast between the modes is not in itself axiological, the culture that favors conventional and collectivizing symbolization—the culture that engendered the theory of culture as "collective representation"—is firmly territorialized on tracing mechanisms, thereby blocking or repressing the dialectics of invention; it must for that reason, in the final analysis, "be put back on the map." This, according to Wagner, is what anthropologists do, or rather, "counter-do." Similarly, the contrast advanced in *The Gender of the Gift* between gift-based and commodity-based "socialities" is explicitly assumed to be internal to the commodity pole (op. cit.: 16, 136, 343), but at the same time it is as if the commodity form were a unilateral transformation of the gift instead of the opposite, insofar as the analysis of gift-based sociality forces the anthropologist to recognize the contingency of the cultural presuppositions of anthropology itself and thus displace its commodity-based metaphors (op. cit.: 309). The point of view of the gift on the commodity is not the same as the point of view of the commodity on the gift. Reciprocal asymmetric implication.[79]

---

79. The same strategy of evoking one dualism only in order to challenge another is employed, for example, by Latour in his counter-critical booklet on "factishes": "The double repertoire of the Moderns does not reside in their distinction of facts from fetishes, but, rather, in the [...] subtler distinction between the theoretical separation of facts from fetishes, on the one hand, and an entirely different practice, on the other hand" (Latour 1996: 42-43).

Chapter Seven

Everything is Production: Intensive Filiation

If there is indeed an implicative asymmetry that could be taken as being primary in the Deleuzian conceptual system, it resides in the distinction between the intensive (or virtual) and the extensive (or actual). What interests me here is the bearing this distinction played in *Capitalism and Schizophrenia*'s rereading of the two chief categories of classical kinship theory, alliance and filiation. The choice is justifiable in the first place because Deleuze and Guattari's treatment of these two notions expresses with particular clarity an important displacement that takes place between *Anti-Oedipus* and *A Thousand Plateaus*. Second, the choice also suggests the possibility of a transformation of the anthropology of kinship that would align it with "nonhumanist developments" (Jensen 2004) occurring in several other areas of research. For the question is, in effect, that of the possibility of the conversion of the notions of alliance and filiation, classically considered the coordinates of hominization qua what is effectuated in and by kinship, into modalities opening onto the extrahuman. If the human is no longer an essence, what are the implications for an anthropology of kinship?

After having played a quasi-totemic role in the discipline between 1950 and 1970, when they synechdochally identified two diametrically opposed conceptions of kinship (Dumont 2006), alliance and filiation, following the general destiny of the Morganian paradigm they belonged to, suddenly lost their synoptic value and immediately assumed the function of simple analytic conventions (and this when they had not even reached that retirement age for ideas that involves passing from use to mention). The pages that follow will propose a reflexive interruption of this movement by suggesting that certain parts of the classic theory can be recycled. This is not, however, to propose a backward intellectual development, whether by reproducing the often empty formalisms of "prescriptive alliance" that were frequently erected against *The Elementary Structures of Kinship* or by returning to the substantialist metaphysics of filiation groups, which was the trademark of the (Durkheim-inspired) British school of Radcliffe-Brown, Meyer Fortes, and Jack Goody. It is, on the contrary, a matter of imagining the possible contours of a rhizomatic conception of kinship capable of extracting all the consequences of the premise that "persons have relations integral to them" (Strathern 1992b: 101). If the theory of filiation groups had for its archetype the ideas of substance and identity (the group as metaphysical individual) and the theory of marriage alliance's was opposition and integration (society as dialectical totality), the perspective offered here draws some elements for a theory of kinship qua difference and multiplicity from Deleuze and Guattari—of relation as disjunctive inclusion.

Social anthropology occupies pride of place in *Capitalism and Schizophrenia*. Starting with Bachofen, Morgan, Engels and Freud and then coming to Lévi-Strauss and Leach, the diptyque's first book completely rewrites the theory of the primitive socius. Its principal interlocutor is the structuralism of Lévi-Strauss, on the basis of and also often against which a plethora of theoretical and ethnographic references are mobilized, which range from the functionalism of Malinowski to the juralism of Fortes, the ethnographic experimentation of Griaule and Dieterlen to the ethno-Marxism of Meillassoux and Terray, and the relational segmentarity of Evans-Pritchard to the social dramaturgy of Victor Turner.[80] The Lévi-Straussian conception of kinship, founded on the transcendental deduction of the incest prohibition as the

---

80. Deleuze and Guattari's ethnological library included an ample "Africanist" section, a fact that reflects the conditions of the French milieu at the time, when Africanism was the most widespread subspeciality as well as the one most refractory to the influence of structuralism.

condition of sociality as such, is rejected by Deleuze and Guattari for being what they regard as an anthropological generalization of Oedipus. Our authors then unfavorably compare Mauss' *Essay on The Gift* to Nietzsche's *The Genealogy of Morals*, which they suggest should be anthropologists' real bedside reading (D. G. 1983: 189 et seq.).

◊ The difference Deleuze and Guattari make between Mauss and Nietzsche seems a bit exaggerated to me. The "exchange"/"debt" distinction does not correspond to any recognizable Maussian development and is not always as obvious as the authors suggest.[81] After all, what gets exchanged in the Potlatch and with the Kula are debts: the primary aim of agonistic gift exchange in the first case is to "kill" the other, sometimes literally, with debt. In *Anti-Oedipus*, the notion of exchange is often conflated with market exchange or the social contract, ideas that are doubtlessly present in *The Gift* but which are, I think, clearly subordinated to the more profound idea of obligation, which is conceived by Mauss less as a transcendental norm than as a division internal to the subject, its dependence in the face of an immanent alterity. The Nietzschean theory, furthermore, of the proto-historical repression of "biological memory" as indispensable to the creation of "social memory" is not so incompatible with the hominizing paradigm common to both the Maussian and structuralist theories of exchange. I believe that it is only when the Deleuze and Guattari of *A Thousand Plateaus* (D. G. 1987: 264) clearly define becoming as anti-memory that the terms of the problem can be said to have decisively changed.

The Mauss/Nietzsche contrast in *Anti-Oedipus* comes down to a polemical backdrop on which the names of Hegel, Kojève, Bataille, the Collège de Sociologie and, much closer to us, Lévi-Strauss, Lacan, and Baudrillard appear. The "general economy" Bataille deduced from the Nietzschean reading of Essay on the Gift is only rarely mentioned in Anti-Oedipus (D. G. 1987: 4, 190). The contempt Deleuze and Guattari show the Bataillean category of transgression (the observation is Lyotard's) partially explains this quasi-silence. That being said, in his essay on Klossowski included in *The Logic of Sense*, Deleuze draws a contrast between, on the one hand, exchange, generality (equivalence), and false repetition, and, on the other, gift, singularity (difference), and authentic repetition. Even while anticipating the theses of *Anti-Oedipus* on exchange (as well as those from the start of *Difference and Repetition*– D. 1994: 1), the contrast is here correctly associated with Bataille: Théodor, the hero of one of Klossowski's novels, "knows that the true repetition is

---

81. The distinction already appears in *Nietzsche and Philosophy* (D. 1983: 135).

in the gift, in the economy of the gift which is opposed to the mercantile economy of exchange (... homage to Georges Bataille)" (D. 1990c: 288).

Against the theme of exchange as a sociogenetic synthesis of contradictory interests, *Anti-Oedipus* advances the postulate that the social machine responds to the problematic of the flux of desire. Deleuze and Guattari propose a conception that is at once inscriptionist—"the socius is inscriptive," it is what marks the body, circulation being only a secondary activity (D. G. 1983: 184 et seq.)—and productionist: "Everything is production" (D. 1983: 4). In the best style of the *Grundrisse*, production, distribution, and consumption are conceived as moments of production qua universal process. Inscription is the moment of the recording or codification of production that counter-effectuates the socius fetishized as an instance of a natural or divine Given, the magical surface of inscription or element of anti-production (the "Body without Organs").

But on the whole, all this never undoes the impression that the schizoanalytic demolition of kinship undertaken in *Anti-Oedipus* remains incomplete, mostly because it remains a critique. Note carefully the exaggerated, even parodic Kantianism of the book's language: transcendental illusion, illegitimate use of the syntheses of the unconscious, the four paralogisms of Oedipus.... *Anti-Oedipus* remains in this way within Oedipus: it is a book that is necessarily, or worse dialectically, Oedipal.[82] It is fed by an anthropocentric conception of sociality: its problem continues to be "hominization," the passage from Nature to Culture. Obviously the shortcomings of this approach are only raised to a radically anti-Oedipal perspective in the second volume of *Capitalism and Schizophrenia*. In truth, it would be absurd to imagine the authors of *A Thousand Plateaus* saying, if their previous book is taken into account, that every "anthropological" kind of inquiry about the distinctiveness of the species or the human condition, about the cause or sign of its election (or malediction), is irremediably compromised by Oedipus. The fault is not in the response, but in the question.

These limitations of *Anti-Oedipus'* approach explain the interpretation of alliance as what transmits the Oedipal triangle, an argument that puts parenthood prior to conjugality (the first is "prolonged" in the second) and treats it as the simple instrument of filiation (D. G. 1983: 71-2). In other words, the critique of the exchangeist conceptions of *Anti-Oedipus* depends on a counter-

---

82. "The ambition of *Anti-Oedipus* was Kantian in spirit" (D. 2006: 309).

theory of Oedipus in which it is filiation and production that are primordial, not exchange and alliance. In this sense (as well as in others), *Anti-Oedipus* is very much an anti-structuralist book. But if Deleuze and Guattari distanced themselves in this way from Lévi-Strauss' *evaluation* of the structure of human kinship, they first had to accept the *terms* by which he had formulated the question. They seem to believe, for example, that alliance is a matter of kinship, and that kinship is a matter of society. For once, they prove too prudent.

Chapter Three, "Savages, Barbarians, and Civilized Men," the central, longest part of *Anti-Oedipus*, begins with an exposition of "the primitive territorial machine" and its "declension" of alliance and filiation (D. G. 1983: 146). The fundamental hypothesis behind the text's alternative theory of structuralism consists in *making filiation appear twice over*. Alliance only appears as an extensive moment; its function is precisely to code kinship, to carry out the transition from intensive to extensive kinship.

The authors postulate the primordial existence of a precosmological filiation that is intense, disjunctive, nocturnal, and ambiguous, a "germinal implex or influx" (D. G. 1983: 162) that is the first state of inscription marked on the full, unengendered body of the earth: "a pure force of filiation or genealogy, Numen" (D. G. 1983: 154). This analysis depends almost exclusively on an interpretation of narratives collected in West Africa by Marcel Griaule and his team, most notably on the great origin myth of the Dogon published in *The Pale Fox* (Griaule and Dieterlen 1986): the cosmic egg of Amma, the Earth placenta, the incestuous trickster Yuruggu, the Nommo, and the hermaphroditic, anthropo-ophidiomorphic "twins."

The place the tale holds in the general argument is revealed to be of high theoretical importance: it functions as "the reference anti-myth" of *Anti-Oedipus*.[83] In Chapter Two ("Psychoanalysis and Familialism"), the authors establish a contrast between dramatic-expressive and machinic-productive conceptions of the unconscious, which leads them to frequently pose the impatient question, "Why return to myth?" (D. G. 1983: 67, 83-84, 113), which refers to psychoanalysis' emblematic use of Greek myth. But when, in the following chapter (D. G. 1983: 154-66), they reach the culmination of their anthropological reconstruction of kinship, it is they themselves who return to myth. This is to say that Deleuze and Guattari do not introduce the Dogon material without passing to a radical re-evaluation of the concept of myth:

> [R]esorting to myth is indispensable, not because myth would be a transposed or even an inverse representation of real relations in extension, but because only myth can determine the intensive conditions of the system (the system of production included) in conformity with indigenous thought and practice. (DG 1977: 157)

These apparently discordant evaluations of the recourse to myth, at the very heart of *Anti-Oedipus*, demand a far more profound reflection than I am presently capable of. Speculatively put, we could say that what is being observed in these references to Oedipus' tragedy and the cycle of *The Pale Fox* is less a difference in the author's attitude toward myth than a difference internal to what we call myth: the story of Oedipus belongs to the barbarian or Oriental regime of despotic signification, while the Dogon tale instead belongs to the savage regime of primitive or "presignifying" semiotics (in Deleuze and Guattari's sense, D. G. 1987: 117 et seq.). At issue, then, is not one and the same myth, or even another genre of the same *logos*; rather, there would be myth, and then there would be *myth*, in the same way that there would be figure and then *figure*, to evoke a key geophilosophical concept (the concept, in a certain sense, of the almost-concept; see D. G.

---

83. Cartry and Adler's article on the Dogon myth is at the origin of the attribution of such a role to this particular ethnographic material; it is cited in some crucial moments of the analysis. These two anthropologists, along with A. Zempléni, attentively read the third chapter of the manuscript of *Anti-Oedipus* (cf Nadaud 2004: 17-18). Furthermore, Deleuze and Guattari's ideas in turn had a concrete influence on Cartry and Adler's study (1971: 37, n.1).

1994: 90 et seq.). An entirely different question of meaning is raised by mythic enunciation when we leave behind the prephilosophical "Masters of Truth" (Detienne, 1996[1967]) and their monarchical regime of enunciation—the classical world of the Hellenist and the historian of philosophy—and enter the extraphilosophical world of "societies against the state," the world of *la pensée sauvage* and radical anthropological alterity…. A question, alas, that has not yet received the analysis worthy of it.[84]

But the Dogon metamyth is not any old thought emerging from the mind of some generic savage thought. It is a cosmogenic myth from West Africa, a region where a culture of kinship profoundly marked by the ideas of ancestrality and descent flourishes, and which is thus also characterized by the presence of political groups constituted on the basis of common parental origin (lineages). So it should not be surprising that this myth allows the authors of *Anti-Oedipus* to seize on filiation as the original relational dimension of kinship, and see alliance as an adventitious dimension whose function would be to distinguish lineage-based affiliations. We are the heart of a universe of structuralist-functional kinship that is quite Fortesian (Fortes 1969, 1983). What is intense and primordial are these ambiguous, involuted, implicative, and (pre-) incestuous filiative lineages that lose their inclusive and unlimited usage to the extent that, being the object of a "nocturnal and biocosmic memory," they "suffer repression" exercised by alliance in order to be explicated and actualized in the physical space of the socius (D. G. 1983: 155).

Everything nevertheless plays out as if the system of the Dogon, who are synechdochially savages at that point in *Anti-Oedipus*, express the theory of filiation on the virtual/intensive plane and the theory of alliance on the actual/extensive plane. This is because the authors thoroughly account for Leach and Fortes' criticisms of "complementary filiation," (100) even as they conclude, in a crucial passage on Lévi-Strauss' views on the logic of cross-cousin marriage (L.-S. 1969: 129-132), that "alliances never derive from filiations, nor can they be deduced from them," and that "in this system in extension there is no primary filiation, nor is there a

84. The debate between Lévi-Strauss and Ricoeur on the subject of the structural analysis of myth has its roots in this difference. See "La pensée sauvage et le structuralisme," *Esprit, 322*, November 1963. Richir (1994) offers some interesting suggestions about different regimes of myth; see also page 141 here.

first generation or an initial exchange, but there are always and already alliances" (D. G. 1983: 155-57).[85] In the extensive order, filiation takes on an *a posteriori*, "administrative and hierarchical" character, while alliance, which is primary there, is "political and economic" (D. G. 1983: 146). The affine, the ally of marriage qua sociopolitical persona, is there from the beginning to render familial relations coextensive with the social field (D. G. 1983: 160). But something is there before the beginning. In the order of metaphysical genesis—from the mythic perspective, in other words (D. G. 1983: 157)—alliance comes afterward: "The system in extension is born of the intensive conditions that make it possible, but it reacts on them, cancels them, represses them, and allows them no more than a mythical expression" (D. G. 1977: 160). The question that remains, obviously, is what this mythic expression (in the nontrivial sense) is, since myth "does not express but conditions" (D. G. 1983: 157).

The field of kinship subsequent to the incest prohibition is thus organized by alliance and filiation into a relation of reciprocal presupposition actually ordered by the first, and virtually by the second. The intensive plane of myth is peopled with preincestuous filiations that ignore alliance. Myth is intensive because it is (pre-) incestuous, and vice versa: alliance is "really" the principle of society, and the end of myth. It would be difficult to not recall here the final paragraph of The Elementary Structures of Kinship, where Lévi-Strauss observes that in both the myths of the Golden Age and beyond, "mankind has always dreamed of seizing and fixing that fleeting moment when it was permissible to believe that the law of exchange could be evaded, that one could gain without losing, enjoy without sharing," and that total happiness, "eternally denied to social man" would consist in "keeping to oneself" (L.-S. 1969: 496-97).

To recast the problem in terms of the conceptual economy of *Anti-Oedipus*, it would seem that the decisive aspect of the analysis of the Dogon myth is the determination, on the one

---

85. Cf. as well this piece of typically structuralist reasoning: "First of all, when considering kinship structures, it is difficult not to proceed as though the alliances derived from the lines of filiation and their relationships, although the lateral alliances and the blocks of debt condition the extended filiations in the system in extension, and not the opposite" (DG 1977: 187).

hand, of (intensive) filiation as the operator of the disjunctive synthesis of inscription—the Nomo who is/are at once one and two, man and human, human and ophidian, or *The Pale Fox*, who is simultaneously son, brother, and spouse of the Earth, etc.—and, on the other, of alliance as the operator of the conjunctive synthesis.

> Such is alliance, the second characteristic of inscription: alliance imposes on the productive connections the extensive form of a pairing of persons, compatible with the disjunctions of inscription, but inversely reacts on inscription by determining an exclusive and restrictive use of these same disjunctions. It is therefore inevitable that alliance be mythically represented as supervening at a certain moment in the filiative lines (although in another sense it is already there from time immemorial). (D. G. 1983: 155)

We saw above that disjunctive synthesis is the relational regime characteristic of multiplicities. As one can read just after the above passage, the problem is not how to get from filiations to alliances, but how to "pass from an intensive energetic order to an extensive system." And in this sense,

> nothing is changed by the fact that the primary energy of the intensive order [...] is an energy of filiation, for this intense filiation is not yet extended, and does not as yet comprise any distinction of persons, nor even a distinction of sexes, but only prepersonal variations in intensity.... (D. G. 1983: 155-56)

It would be necessary to add here that if this intensive order knows neither distinctions of person nor sex, it should no more allow for distinctions of species, especially not of humans and nonhumans. In myth, all actants occupy a unique interactional field that is at the same time ontologically heterogeneous and sociologically continuous. Once again, when everything is human, the human is an entirely different thing....

The following question thus naturally emerges: if "nothing is changed" by the fact that the primary energy is filiative, is it possible to determine an intensive order in which it would be alliance that is primary? Is it truly *necessary* for alliance to always exclusively arrange, distinguish, render discrete, and police an anterior pre-incestuous filiation? Is it *possible* to conceive of an intensive,

131

anOedipal alliance including "prepersonal variations in intensity?" In short, the problem consists in constructing a concept of alliance qua disjunctive synthesis.

Yet to do this, significant distance would have to be taken from *Anti-Oedipus'* account of the sociocosmology of Lévi-Strauss, while the concept of exchange would have to be submitted to a *perversive* Deleuzian interpretation. And to that end, one would simultaneously and reciprocally have to admit, once and for all, that the Lévi-Straussian theory of matrimonial exchange continues to be, once everything is accounted for, an infinitely more sophisticated anthropological construction than the juralist doctrine of filiation groups. In a certain sense, *The Elementary Structures of Kinship* was the first *Anti-Oedipus* inasmuch as it forced a break with the family-centric, parenthood-dominated image of kinship. Or, to put things slightly differently, the relation between *Anti-Oedipus* and *The Elementary Structures* is analogous to that between the latter and *Totem and Taboo*.

At the very least, a reprise of structuralist kinship discourse in an anti-Oedipal key requires abandoning the description of the "atom of kinship" as an exclusive alternative—this woman is either my sister or spouse, that man is either my father or my maternal uncle—and then reformulating it in terms of an inclusive, nonrestrictive disjunction: "my sister and/or my spouse." The difference between sister and spouse or brother and brother-in-law should be taken as an internal difference, "nondecomposable and unequal with itself"; what Deleuze and Guattari say about schizophrenia and the masculine/feminine and dead/living disjunctions would also be valuable in our case: a given woman is in fact either my sister or my sister-in-law but "belongs precisely to both sides"—as a sister on the side of sisters (and brothers) and as a wife on the side of wives (and husbands). Not both at once for me but "each of the two as a terminal point of the distance over which [she] glides. [...][The] one at the end of the other, like the two ends of a stick in a nondecomposable space" (D. G. 1983: 76).

This point can be reformulated in language that every anthropologist will recognize. My sister is my sister *because* she is someone else's wife. Sisters are not born sisters without at the same time being born as wives; the sister exists *in order* that there will be a wife; every "woman" is a term—a metarelation—constituted by the assymetrical relation between "sisterly" and "wifely" relations (with the same things obviously applying to "men"). The consanguinity of the sister, like its molar sexual affectation, is not given—there never is a "basic biological given" (Héritier 1981)—but rather instituted, not only in the way the affinity of the wife is but also by its intermediary (formal causality inside out). The opposed sexual relation between my sister/wife and I is what engenders my relation with my brother-in-law. Opposed sexual relations engender not only relations of the same sex but also communicate their own internal differential potential (Strathern 1988, 2001). Two brothers-in-law are linked in the same way as the cross-sex dyads that founds their relation (brother/sister—husband/wife), and this not despite their difference but because of it. One of the brothers-in-law sees the conjugal face of his sister in her husband, and the other sees the sororal side of his wife in her brother. They both see the other as defined by the link with the opposite sex that differentiates them: each sees himself as having "the same sex" as the other inasmuch as the latter is seen as being "like" the opposite sex, and reciprocally. The two faces of the relational term thereby create a division internal to the terms thereby connected. Everyone becomes double, simultaneously "man" and "woman"; connecter and connected are revealed to be permutable without thereby becoming redundant; each point of the triangle of affinity includes the other two as *versions of itself.*

◊ We should return here to Wagner's (1977) analysis of matrimonial exchange among the Melanesian Daribi: the giving patrilineal clan sees its women as an efferent flux of its own masculine substance; but the receiving clan will see that same flux as constituted by a feminine substance. When patrimonial prestations follow the reverse track, the perspective, too, is reversed: "What might be described as exchange or reciprocity is in fact an [...] intermeshing of two views of a single thing" (1977: 628). This interpretation of the exchange of Melanesian gifts as intentionally definable in terms of exchanges of perspective (in which, it should be noted, the notion of perspectivism is what conceptually determines exchange and not the opposite) was extended by Marilyn Strathern to a very high level of sophistication in *The Gender of the Gift* (1988), which is probably the most influential anthropological study of the last quarter century. This aspect of Wagner and Strathern's work thus represents an "anticipatory transformation" of the theme of the relations between cosmological perspectivism and potential/virtual affinity, which was merely sketchy in Amazonian ethnology at that moment. A synergistic interpretation took place only much later (Strathern 1999: 246 and 2005: 135-162; Viveiros de Castro 1998, 2008a).

About the anteriority of "wife" to "sister," I would advise the reader to refer to a paragraph from the manuscript of *The Savage Mind* excised from the 1962 version, but recently restored by Frédéric Keck in the critical edition included in the Pleiade *OEuvres*:

> The speculative foundation of alimentary prohibitions and exogamic rules therefore consists in repugnance toward conjoining terms that could be from a general point of view (every woman is "copulable" in the same way every kind of food is edible) but between which the mind has posed a relation of similarity in a particular case (woman, animal, my clan).... [W]hy is this accumulation of conjunctions [...] taken as harmful? The only possible response [...] *is that the similar is initially not given as a fact but promulgated as a law [...]. Assimilating what is similar under a new relation would be to contradict the law allowing for the similar to be a means of creating the different. Indeed, similarity is the means of difference, and nothing other than that [...].*
> (Lévi-Strauss 2008: 1834-35, n. 14, my emphasis.)

This remarkable passage was certainly not suppressed for contradicting Lévi-Strauss' general ideas about similarity and difference. On the contrary, it was a development anticipating the formula, already mentioned, that will appear later, in *The Naked Man* ("resemblance does not exist in itself; it is only a particular case of difference") and that in any case is nothing else but a more abstract articulation of the argument about the impossible Amerindian twinhood found in *The Story of Lynx*. The passage seems, on the contrary, quite elegant in its diacritical value: it allows one to measure the distance separating the structuralist concept of matrimonial exchange from principles such as that of the "nonaccumulation of the identical" proposed by François Héritier, a principle that has resemblance following from itself, according to a substantialist prejudice (in the double sense) entirely foreign to the Lévi-Strauss' ontology of difference. For structuralism, in effect, an idea like the nonaccumulation of the identical is of the same order, if I can be allowed the oxymoron, as a secondary principle.

Yet the complex duplication created by exchange (in which there are, it should be noted in passing, two triangles, one for each sex taken as "connector") is explicitly described by Deleuze and Guattari in their commentary on the analogy Proust makes between homosexuality and vegetable reproduction in *Sodom and*

Gomorrah. Something of the order of an "atom of genre/gender" can be glimpsed here:

> [The] vegetal theme [...] brings us yet another message and another code: everyone is bisexual, everyone has two sexes, but partitioned, noncommunicating; the man is merely the one in whom the male part, and the woman the one in whom the female part, dominates statistically. So that at the level of elementary combinations, at least two men and two women must be made to intervene to constitute the multiplicity in which transverse communications are established-connections of partial objects and flows: the male part of a man can communicate with the female part of a woman, but also with the male part of a woman, or with the female part of another man, or yet again with the male part of the other man, etc. (D. G.: 1983: 69)

"At least two men and two women...." If they are connected by an "exchange of sisters," a matrimonial arrangement, in other words, between two pairs of siblings of the opposite sex (two bisexual dividuals), we end up with an extensive, canonically structuralist version of multiplicity-gender. But clearly, "everything must be interpreted in intensity" (D. G. 1983: 158). Such is the work the little "etc." at the end of the passage would seem to be doing. Have we passed from exchange to becoming?

PART THREE

Demonic Alliance

Chapter Eight

The Metaphysics of Predation

The contrariwise reading of structuralism proposed below will first require some digression into intellectual autobiography. I beg the reader's indulgence, as the story concerns my experience as an Americanist ethnologist in its bearing on the issues.

In *Totemism Today* and *The Savage Mind*, the two transitional works where the prestructuralism of *The Elementary Structures of Kinship* gives way to the post-structuralism of the *Mythologiques*,[86] Lévi-Strauss establishes a paradigmatic contrast between totemism and sacrifice that for me had a status that could be described as properly mythic, allowing me to more distinctly formulate what I had previously only confusedly perceived as the limits of structural anthropology. These were as much limits in the geometric sense—the perimeter of the jurisdiction of Lévi-Strauss' method—as they were mathematico-dynamic: the attractor toward which its virtualities tended. The totemism/sacrifice contrast was crucial for my reevaluation of Amazonian ethnography in light of the fieldwork I had done among the Araweté (a people, again, of the Tupi language of the Eastern Amazon), the main resource in my attempt to rethink the meaning of warrior cannibalism and shamanism, both of which are central (or rather "de-central") cosmopolitical institutions of Tupi and other Amerindian societies.

---

86. See Viveiros de Castro 2008c.

The question of the existence of "sacrificial" rites in indigenous Amazonia raised certain problems about the historical and typological relations between the cultures of the South American lowlands and the state-based formation of the Andes and Mesoamerica, for which sacrifice is a key theologico-political *dispositif*. Behind this problem, in turn, lay an even larger one concerning the emergence of the state in primitive societies. Amazonianists interested in the question tended to focus on shamanism, since the region appeared to yield no counter-examples to the literature's portrait of the shaman as a proto-sacerdotal delegate of transcendence. But the Americanist consensus was that the classic, French sociological definition taken from Hubert and Mauss (1964) (which remained the chief reference in the discipline) failed to satisfactorily account for the South American shamanic complex.

Yet the link between Araweté ethnography and the problem of sacrifice was directly suggested to me not by their shamanic practices but by their eschatology. Araweté cosmology reserves a special place of honor for posthumous cannibalism. The celestial divinities, known as the Mai, devour the souls of the dead upon their arrival in the heavens, in a prelude to the metamorphosis of the latter into immortal beings like those eating them. I argued in my monograph on the Araweté that this mystico-funerary cannibalism is a structural transformation of the bellico-sociological cannibalism of another group, the Tupinambá, who inhabited the Brazilian coast in the 17th century, and who were the most important tribe speaking the Tupi language, which prevailed at the time all the way from Rio de Janeiro to Bahia.

It will be necessary to spell out the basic features of Tupinambá cannibalism, which was a very elaborate system for the capture, execution, and ceremonial consumption of their enemies. Captives of war, who frequently shared both the language and the customs of their captors, lived for long periods among the latter before being subjected to solemn, formal execution in the village center. During that time, they were well treated, living in freedom under the watch of their captors while the long preparations for the execution ritual were being undertaken. In fact, the captor's custom was to give the victims women from their group as spouses, thereby transforming them into brothers-in-law—the same term, *tojavar*, meant in ancient Tupi both "brother-in-law" and "enemy," its literal sense having been "opponent"—which shows us how Amerindian predation is implicated, as Lévi-Strauss observed, in the problem of affinity. The ritual cycle culminated in the event of the captive's killing, an act that held an initiatic value for the executioner-officiant (who thereby received a new name, commemorative scarifications, the right to marry and have children, access to paradise, etc.) and was followed by the ingestion of his body by those in attendance—guests from neighboring villages as much as their hosts—with the sole exception of the officiant. Not only would he not eat the captive, but afterward he would also enter into a funerary confinement, a period of mourning. He entered, in other words, into a process of identification with this "opponent" whose life he had just taken.

This Tupinambán anthropophagy was often interpreted as a form of human sacrifice, whether figuratively, per the authors of the first colonial chronicles, or conceptually, as Forestan Fernades, one of the founding fathers of Brazilian sociology, did in applying Hubert and Mauss' schema to the 16th century materials. To do this, however, Fernandes had to postulate a detail that nowhere appeared in his sources: a supernatural entity supposed to be the recipient of the sacrifice. According to him, the sacrifice was intended for the spirits of the dead of the group, who were avenged and honored by the captive's execution and ingestion.

In my study on the Araweté, I contested the idea that supernatural entities were somehow involved in Tupi cannibalism, and that their propitiation had been the reason for the rite. Although it is true that the Araweté case (but it alone) sees certain "supernatural entities" occupying the active pole in the cannibal relation, reading their eschatology through the Tupinambá sociology showed this to be of little importance. My argument was that the Araweté *Mai* /gods held the place otherwise occupied by the group functioning as the subject in the Tupinambá rite—the group of the killer and his allies, those ingesting the captive—while the position of the object of the sacrifice, the captive in the Tupinambá ritual, was held by the Araweté dead. The living Araweté, finally, occupied the position of the "cosubjects" that was held in the Tupinambá case by the enemy group from which the victim had been taken.[87] In short, the transformation imposed on divine Araweté cannibalism by Tupinambá human cannibalism bore not on the symbolic content or social function of the former practice but instead consisted in a pragmatic sliding, a twist or translation of perspective that affected the values and functions of subject and object, means and ends, and self and other.

From there, I concluded that the notion of a coordinated change of perspectives was much more than a description of the relation between the Araweté and Tupinambá versions of the cannibal motif. It manifests a property of Tupi cannibalism itself qua actantal schema, which I defined as a process for the transmutation of perspectives whereby the "I" is determined as other through the act of incorporating this other, who in turn becomes an "I" ... but only ever *in* the other—literally, that is, *through* the other. Such a definition seemed to resolve a simple but quite insistent question: what was really eaten in this enemy? The answer could not be his matter or substance, since this was a ritual form of cannibalism where the consumption of (a quantity of) the victim's flesh was effectively insignificant; the extant sources, moreover, only rarely offer testimony that a physical or metaphysical virtue was attributed to the victim's body and are, at any rate, far from conclusive. The "thing" eaten, then, could not be a "thing" if it were at the same time—and this is essential—a body. This body, nevertheless, was a sign with a purely positional value. What was eaten was the enemy's relation to those who consumed him; in other words, *his condition as enemy*. In other words, what was assimilated from the victim was the signs of his alterity, the aim being to reach his alterity as point of view on the Self. Cannibalism and the peculiar form of war with which it is bound up involve

87. Insofar as ceremonial death was considered a *kalos thánatos* (a good/beautiful death), the relation between enemy groups was endowed with an essential positivity. Not only did it give access to individual immortality, but it also allowed for collective vengeance, which was the motor and leitmotif of Tupinambá life. Soares de Souza offered this lapidary formula: "As the Tupinambá are very warlike, all their guiding principles consist in knowing how to make war with their opponents" (1972: 320). As for the dialectic between the death of the individual and the life of the group, see this passage from Thevet: "And do not think that the prisoner surprised to receive this news [that he will be executed and quickly devoured] thus is of the opinion that his death is honorable and that he would much prefer to die thusly than in his home through some contagious death: for (they say) one cannot avenge death, which offends and kills men, but one avenges those who have been slain and massacred in war" (1953[1575]).

a paradoxical movement of reciprocal self-determination through the point of view of the enemy.

I was obviously proposing with this thesis a counter-interpretation of certain classic precepts of the discipline. If the goal of multiculturalist European anthropology was to describe human life as it is experienced from the indigenous point of view, indigenous multinaturalist anthropophagy presumed as a vital condition of its self-description the "semiophysical" prehension—taking life through eating—of the point of view of the enemy. Anthropophagy as anthropology.[88]

All this first dawned on me while pondering Araweté war songs, where the warrior, through a complex, anaphoric use of deixis, speaks of himself from the point of view of his slain enemy: the victim, who is in both senses the subject of the song, speaks of the Araweté he has killed, and speaks of his own killer—the one who "speaks" by singing the words of his deceased enemy—as a cannibal enemy (although among the Araweté, it is words alone that one eats). *Through* his enemy, that is, the Araweté doing the killing sees himself *as* the enemy. He apprehends himself as a subject at the moment that he sees himself through the gaze of his victim, or, to put it differently, when he declares his singularity to himself through the voice of the latter. Perspectivism.

Tupi warrior semiophagy was not at all a marginal development in Amerindian territories. The notion that there exists an indigenous philosophy of cannibalism that is also a political philosophy was extensively outlined by Clastres is his theorization of war (Clastres 2010; see Clastres and Sebag, 1963; Clastres, 1968 and 1972 for the theory's inception). Yet its ethnographic generality and complexity were only starting to be recognized at the time I was first working on the Tupi materials.[89] The work of

---

88. Or, in the vein of the ferocious humor of the author of the celebrated 1928 *Cannibal Manifesto*, Oswald Andrade: odontology as ontology (de Andrade 1997).

89. Several of them deserve special mention: Bruce Albert's (1985) thesis on the war/funerary complex of the Yanomami, the articles Patrick Menget (1985a) edited for a special issue of *The Journal of The Society of Americanists*, Anne-Christine Taylor's extremely fine articles on Jivaro headhunting as an apparatus of capture for the virtualities of persons (1985), Chaumeil's (1985) on the cosmological economy of war of the Yagua, Menget's works (1985b, 1988) on the "adoption" of enemy women and children by the Ikpeng, Eriksons' (1986) concerning the cannibal ethnosociology of Pano language peoples, and, finally, those of Overing (1986) on images of cannibalism in Piaroa cosmology. In the years that followed, the studies only proliferated, so that the works of Philippe Descola, B.

several Amazonianist colleagues was suggesting that an economy of predatory alterity might be something like the basal metabolism of Amazonian sociality: the idea, in brief, was that the interiority of the social body is integrally constituted through the capture of symbolic resources—names and souls, persons and trophies, words and memories—from the exterior. By taking for its principle this movement of the incorporation of the enemy's attributes, the Amerindian socius had to "define" itself with these same attributes. We can see that this was at work in the great Tupinambá ritual event of the putting to death of the captive, where the place of honor was reserved for the twin figures of the killer and his victim, who reflect each other and reverberate to infinity. These, in the end, are the essentials of the "metaphysics of predation" Lévi-Strauss spoke of: primitive society is a society lacking an interior that only comes to be "itself" *outside itself.* Its immanence coincides with its transcendence.

So it was less through shamanism than war and cannibalism that I first encountered the problem of sacrifice. Yet if the Maussian definition felt inappropriate—neither the sacred nor a recipient were present—the notion Lévi-Strauss had forwarded in his discussion of totemism seemed to cast the Tupi anthropology in a new light.

The contrast Lévi-Strauss draws between totemism and sacrifice is first presented in the form of the orthogonal opposition between the Ojibwa *totem* and *mandido* systems discussed in the initial chapters of *Totemism Today* (L.-S. 1963a: 22-23). This opposition is then generalized, reworked (L.-S. 1966: 225), and systematized in the seventh chapter of *The Savage Mind* along the following lines:

> Totemism postulates the existence of a homology between two parallel series—natural species and social groups—and does so by establishing a formal, reversible correlation between them qua two systems of globally isomorphic differences.

Keifenheim, I. Combés, A, Vilaça, Carlos Fausto, Alexadre Surralès, Dmitri Kardinas, and Tanya Stolze-Lima should also be cited.

1. Sacrifice postulates the existence of a single, at once continuous and directional series through which a real, irreversible mediation between two opposed, nonhomologous terms (humans and divinities) is carried out; the contiguity between the series is established through identification or successive analogical approximations.

2. Totemism is metaphoric, and sacrifice metonymic, the first being "an interpretive system of references," and the second "a technical system of operations." One belongs to language, and the other to speech.

From this definition it can be deduced that sacrifice actualizes processes that are, at first glance, quite different from the proportional equivalences at work in both totemism and the other "systems of transformation" taken up in *The Savage Mind*. The logical transformations of totemism are established between terms whose reciprocal positions are modified by permutations, inversions, chiasms, and other combinatory, extensive redistributions—totemism is a *topos* for discontinuity. Sacrificial transformations, on the other hand, activate intensive relations that modify the nature of the terms themselves; something passes between them. Transformation is here less a permutation than a *transduction*, in Gilbert Simondon's sense, requiring an energetics of the continuous. If the objective of totemism is to set up a resemblance between two series of given differences discrete unto themselves, the goal of sacrifice is to induce a zone or moment of indiscernibility between two poles presumed to be self-identical, which thus approaches difference entirely differently (from the inside rather than the outside, so to speak). Resorting to a mathematical analogy, we could say that the model for totemic structural transformations could be said to be combinatory analysis, while the instrument for exploring what Lévi-Strauss dubbed the "kingdom of continuity" of sacrifice's intensive metamorphoses directs us, instead, to differential calculus. Imagine the death of the victim as the path of a tangent, the best approximation of the curve of divinity....

So while Lévi-Strauss defines totemism as a system of forms, his conception of sacrifice suggests a system of forces. A veritable fluid mechanics, in fact: he characterizes sacrifice in terms of a schema of communicating vases, referring, for example, to a "continuous solution" between "reservoirs," a "deficit of contiguity" refilled "automatically," and other, similar formulas. All of which irresistibly evokes the key idea that a *difference of potential* would be the principle of sacrifice.

◊ The same hydraulic-energetic language reappears in the analysis, in the "Finale" of *The Naked Man*, of laughter and aesthetic emotion as a discharge of accumulated symbolic energy. Lévi-Strauss had further recourse to it in his celebrated reference to "hot," historical societies that struggle against entropy by using the difference of potential contained in class inequalities or the exploitation of other peoples to engender becoming and energy (L.-S. and Charbonnier, 1969: 38-42). The notion of difference of potential plays a decisive role, however little remarked on, in the construction of the concept of *mana* in *The Outline of a General Theory of Magic*. Hubert and Mauss argue that *mana* is the idea of the differential value of things and beings ("in magic it is always a matter of the respective values recognized by a society") and thus of their hierarchical arrangement, and that this hierarchical difference of value (Mauss with Nietzsche!) is coherent with the translation of *mana, orenda*, etc. by Hewitt as "magical potential." "What we call," they conclude, "the relative position or respective value of things could also be called a difference in potential, since it is due to such differences that they are able to affect one another. [...] [T]he idea of *mana* is none other than the idea of these relative values and the idea of these differences in potential. Here we come face to face with the whole idea on which magic is founded, in fact with magic itself" (Mauss 2001: 148-49). Lévi-Strauss' interpretation of *mana* in terms of a lack of adequation between signifier and signified (L.-S. 1987a: 62), then, is a compromise between an explanation that could be called totemic, insofar as it appeals to a model of differences between a signifying and signified series, and a sacrificial account that registers a perpetual disadjustment (the absence of a péréquation) between the two series, a disequilibrium that very much resembles Hubert and Mauss' "difference of potential."

In sum, two different images of difference—one extensive, the other intensive (form and force). Images that are different enough to be "incompatible," suggests the author (L.-S. 1966: 223), a judgment I will take the liberty of interpreting as an indication that they are *complementary* in the sense given the term by Niels Bohr, whom Lévi-Strauss frequently cited.[90] But in this case,

90. See, for example, L.-S. 1963c: 296; 1963d: 364; 2004: 42; L.-S. and Charbonnier 1969: 18, 23.

totemism and sacrifice designate not two distinct systems but rather two necessary yet mutually exclusive descriptions of the same phenomenon: sense or semiosis as the articulation of heterogeneous series.

Yet this complementarity, at least where Lévi-Strauss is concerned, is clearly asymmetrical. In his inaugural lecture at the Collège de France, he affirms that structural anthropology should, in contrast with history, "adopt a *transformational* rather than a *fluxional* method" (L.-S. 1978c: 18) and thereby suggests an algebra of groups rather than a differential dynamic. It should be recalled that "method of fluxions" was the name Newton gave to what subsequently came to be known as differential calculus. And in fact everything happened as if structural method in anthropology—perhaps the interpretive habits of this method would be better—had been conceived in order to account for form rather than force, the combinatory and the corpuscular over the differential and the wavelike, and language and categorization to the detriment of speech and action.[91] As a consequence, those aspects that appeared resistant to structural analysis were habitually treated by Lévi-Strauss as minor semiotic (or even ontological) modes—the invocation of a "minor anthropology" at the outset of the present work was no coincidence—either because they would have attested to the limits of the thinkable, or foregrounded the asignificant, or else expressed certain illusory powers. Thus, as we know, sacrifice is deemed imaginary and false, and totemism as objective and true (L.-S. 1978a: 256-57), a judgment repeated and generalized when myth is counter-posed to ritual at the close of *The Naked Man* (L.-S. 1981: 667-75)—a judgment,

---

91. That said, Deleuze had, in 1972, already observed the following about the mathematics of structuralism: "Sometimes the origins of structuralism are sought in the area of axiomatics, and it is true that Bourbaki, for example, uses the word "structure." But this use, it seems to me, is in a very different sense [...] The mathematical origin of structuralism must be sought rather in the domain of differential calculus, specifically in the interpretation which Weierstrass and Russell gave to it, a *static and ordinal* interpretation, which definitively liberates calculus from all reference to the infinitely small, and integrates it into a pure logic of relations" (D. 2004: 176).

I am tempted to say, that teaches us more about the cosmology of Lévi-Strauss than that of the peoples he so effectively studied.[92]

Totemism today finds itself dissolved into the general classificatory activity of the savage mind,[93] with sacrifice awaiting a comparable constructive dissolution. The story of how totemism was unmade by Lévi-Strauss is well known: it ceased to be an institution to become a method of classification and system of signification referring to natural and contingent series. Would it be possible to rethink sacrifice along similar lines? Would it be possible, in short, to see the divinities functioning as the terms of the sacrificial relation as being as contingent as the natural species of totemism? What would a generic schema of sacrifice resemble if its typical institutional crystallizations are only one of its particular cases? Or, to formulate the problem in language more sacrificial than totemic, what would a field of dynamic virtualities be if sacrifice was just a singular actualization of it? What forces are mobilized by sacrifice?

Whatever judgments could be made here about Lévi-Strauss aside, the contrasts he established between metaphoric discontinuity and metonymic continuity, positional quantity and vectoral quality, and paradigmatic reference and syntagmatic operation were all extremely clarifying in that they led me to inscribe Tupi ritual cannibalism in the column (the paradigm!) of sacrifice. Being a veritable anti-totemic operator, cannibalism realizes a transformation that is potentially reciprocal—the imperative of vengeance that gives it meaning in Tupinambá society—but really irreversible in relation to the terms it connects through these acts of supreme contiguity and "discontiguity" (the violent physical contact of execution, the decapitation and consumption of the body of the victim) which involve a movement of indefinition and the creation of a zone of indiscernibility between killers and victims, eater and eaten. There is no need to postulate the existence of supernatural entities in order to account for the fact

92. The opposition between myth and ritual made in *The Naked Man* was a huge impediment to structuralism's posterity, as witnessed by the numerous attempts at its modalization, reformulation, or outright rejection (and with it, whole swathes of the Lévi-Straussian problematic). Americanist ethnology in particular was forced to reckon with the opposition in at least two of the chief studies of Amazonian ritual systems (Hugh-Jones 1979, Albert 1985).

93. With the important exception, already noted, of the work of Philippe Descola, for whom the typical cases of totemism are to be found in aboriginal Australia.

that one is in the presence of sacrifice. In the tripolar interpretation of Tupinambá ritual developed in my ethnography on the Araweté, the actants are the consuming group, the dual person of the executioner/victim, and the enemy group. The "death" is only a vicarious function alternately and successively assumed by these three poles of the ritual; but it is nonetheless what drives the forces circulating in the process.

All that is well and good. But does the concept of "sacrifice," in this new Lévi-Straussian sense, truly account for what occurs in ritual cannibalism? There is nothing imaginary or even false in Tupi cannibalism. Not even vengeance, which is rigorously impossible, would be imaginary, as it was above all a schematism of social *poiesis* or mechanism for the ritual production of collective temporality (the interminable cycle of vengeance) through the installation of a perpetual disequilibrium between enemy groups.[94] And in any case, if it is always necessary to imagine an enemy—to construct the other as such—the objective is to *really* eat it … in order to construct the Self as other. Something indeed does not pass through the concept of sacrifice, even if more things do than through totemism.

94. "Perpetual disequilibrium" is a key concept in *The Story of Lynx* (L.-S. 1995) and was elaborated, as if by chance, on the basis of an analysis the Tupinambá twin myth gathered by Thevet circa 1554.

Chapter Nine

Transversal Shamanism

We have circled back to shamanism, which was dealt with above in our summary of perspectivist theory. On account of their capacity to see other species as the humans that these species see themselves as, Amazonian shamans play the role of cosmopolitical diplomats in an arena where diverse socionatural interests are forced to confront each other. In this sense, the function of the shaman is not entirely different from that of a warrior. Both are "commuters" or conductors of perspective, the first operating in a zone of interspecificity and the second in an interhuman or intersocietal one.[95] These zones are in a relation more of intensive superposition than of horizontal adjacency or vertical encompassment. Amazonian shamanism, as is often remarked, is the continuation of war by other means. This has nothing to do, however, with violence as such[96] but with communication, a transversal communication between incommunicables, a dangerous, delicate comparison between perspectives in which the position of the human is in constant dispute. And what, exactly, does that human position come down to? That is the question raised when an individual finds itself face to face with allogenic bundles of affections and agentivity, such as an animal or unknown being in the forest, a parent long absent from one's village, or a deceased person in a dream. The universal humanity of beings—the "cosmic background

95. It should not be forgotten that each species has its own shamans, and that the relations human shamans develop with the latter primarily occur with the species they ally themselves with.

96. Shamans nonetheless are frequently indispensable auxiliaries in war, whether as oracles or invisible warriors.

humanity" that makes every species of being a reflexive genre of humanity—is subject to a principle of complementarity, given that it is defined by the fact that two different species that are each necessarily human in their own eyes can never simultaneously be so in the other's.

It would be equally correct to say that war is the continuation of shamanism by other means: in Amazonia, shamanism is as violent as war is supernatural. Both retain a link with hunting as the model of perspectival agonism, configuring a transhuman ethogram that manifests an entirely metaphysical attraction to danger (Rodgers 2002) and that remains marked by the profound conviction that every vital activity is a form of predatory expansion.[97]

If cast in terms of the opposition Lévi-Strauss draws between totemism and sacrifice, shamanism would certainly end up on the side of the latter. Shamanic activity certainly consists, it is true, in establishing correlations and/or translations between the respective worlds of each natural species, and this through finding active homologies or equivalences between the perspectives in confrontation (Carneiro da Cunha 1998). But the shaman himself is nevertheless a real relater, not a formal correlater: he must always move from one point of view to another, transform into an animal in order to transform that animal into a human (and vice versa). The shaman utilizes—"substantiates" and incarnates, establishes a rapport (a relation) and report [*rapporte*] (a narration) between—the differences of potential inherent in the divergences of perspective that constitute the cosmos: his power as much as its limits derive from these differences.

Here at last is where the Maussian theory of sacrifice begins to yield some returns. We can imagine the sacrificial schema constituting a complete or saturated mediating structure that joins the polarity between the agent of the sacrifice (who offers the sacrifice and reaps its benefits) and the recipient by means of the double intermediation of the sacrificer (the officiant/executioner) and the victim. The two Amazonian "sacrificial" figures can be imagined as degenerations of the Maussian schema in the same sense that

97. This is why the supposed importance Amerindians attribute to the values of "conviviality" and "tranquility"—a subject recent Amazonianist literature has spilled enormous amounts of ink and moral tears on—seems to me a comically equivocal interpretation of the ambiguous powers of predatory alterity assumed by indigenous thought qua universal ontological horizon.

Lévi-Strauss said restricted exchange is a mathematically degenerated case of general exchange.

A distinctive characteristic of Amazonian shamanism is that the shaman is *simultaneously* the officiant and the vehicle of sacrifice. It is in him that the "deficit of contiguity" is realized—the void created by the separation of body and soul, the subtractive externalization of the parts of the person of the shaman—which can release a beneficial semiotic flux passing between humans and nonhumans. And it is the shaman himself that passes to the other side of the mirror; he does not send delegates or representatives in the form of victims but is himself the victim: he is "condemned" (so to speak) to death, as in the case of the Araweté shaman, whose people's cannibal divinities hail him, during his celestial voyages, as "our future sustenance"—the same expression employed five centuries prior by the Tupinambá to mock their captives.[98] The threshold to another sociocosmic regime is crossed when the shaman switches to sacrificing the other—when he becomes, for example, an executioner of human victims or an administrator of the sacrifices of the powerful, someone who sanctions movements that he alone can supervise. This is where the shadow of the priest looms behind the shaman.

The opposition should of course not be taken as absolute. "Amazonian shamanism" is a term that contains an important difference, identified by Hugh-Jones (1996), between "horizontal" and "vertical" shamanism. The contrast is particularly salient apropos the Bororo of central Brazil or the Tukano and the Arawak of Rio Negro, who all distinguish between two categories of mystical mediators. Those shamans that Hugh-Jones classes as horizontal are specialists whose powers derive from their inspiration and charisma, and whose actions, which are directed outside the socius, do not preclude aggression and moral ambiguity; their chief interlocutors are animal spirits, who are perhaps the most

---

98. It is through this Araweté shortcut that we encounter cannibalism again, which is an even more dramatic reduction of sacrificial schema: not only is the sacrificer-executor identified with the victim (mourning, symbolic death, interdiction of the manducation of the enemy), but the sacrificing group (those who devour the victim) coincides with the recipient of the sacrifice. Simultaneously, following a characteristic twist, the schema doubles, and the group the enemy comes from, driven to ritual vengeance, becomes on the one hand co-sacrificing—those who seem to "offer" the victim—while also, on the other, getting defined as a future recipient, the holder of the title to a warrior vengeance that will be fatally exercised against the devouring group.

153

frequent cause of illness in indigenous Amazonia (illness is frequently conceived as a case of cannibal vengeance on the part of animals who have been consumed). As for the vertical shamans, these comprise the master-chanters and ceremonial specialists, the peaceful guardians of an esoteric knowledge indispensable if reproduction and internal group relations (birth, initiation, naming, funerals, etc.) are to come off properly.

The shaman I term the "sacrificer-victim" is the horizontal kind; this particular specialist, as Hugh-Jones observes, is typical of those Amazonian societies having an egalitarian, bellicose ethos. The vertical shaman, on the other hand, is present only in hierarchical, pacific societies, and verges on being a priest-figure. Yet it should be noted that nowhere is there to be found an Amazonian society in which vertical shamans alone preside; wherever only one kind of shaman can be perceived, the tendency is for it to take on the functions of the two types of the Bororo and Tukano but with the attributes and responsibilities of the horizontal clearly predominating.

Hugh-Jones acknowledges the contrast to be a highly simplified, schematic ideal type. But by no means does that undermine its analytic relevance, which is, from where I stand, entirely justified by the ethnography. The division of cosmopolitical mediational labor between the two types has an important comparative dimension when placed in the series of mediatory divisions enumerated by Lévi-Strauss in "The Structural Study of Myth": "messiah > dioscuri > trickster > bisexual being > sibling pair > married couple > grandmother-grandchild > four-term group > triad" (L.-S. 1963[1955]: 226). For this reason, the asymmetric duality of shamans points to a characteristic property of Amerindian cosmological structures—the "dualism in perpetual disequilibrium" treated in *The Story of Lynx*. But before opening that box, it should be noted that messianism, the first term of the series, is effectively a central component of the problem Hugh-Jones elaborates apropos the distinction between the two shamans. The numerous millenarian movements that have emerged in the Northwest Amazon from the mid-19th century on were all led, Hugh-Jones stresses, by shaman-prophets fitting the horizontal profile. What this suggests is that the distinction has less to do with two types of specialists, the shaman *stricto sensu*

154

(or shaman-warrior) and the shaman priest, than two possible trajectories of the shamanic function: sacerdotal transformation and prophetic transformation. Prophetism would result, in that event, from the historical warming of shamanism, and the emergence of the sacerdotal function so defined from its political cooling—its subsumption by social power.

Another way of formulating this hypothesis would be to say that sacerdotal transformation—its differentiation of a baseline shamanism—is bound up with the constitution of social interiority qua the appearance of values of ancestrality, which express diachronic continuity between the living and the dead, and of political hierarchy, which establish and consecrate synchronic discontinuities between the living. In effect, if the horizontal shaman's archetypal Other is theriomorphic, the Other of vertical shamanism tends to assume the anthropomorphic traits of the ancestor.

Horizontal Amerindian shamanism is situated in a cosmological economy where the difference between living and dead humans is of less importance than the resemblance shared by dead humans and living nonhumans. The world of the dead counts no animals among its inhabitants, as Conklin (2001) remarked of the Western Amazonian Wari's cosmology, and this is because the dead are themselves animals—animals in their game version—having been transformed into the quintessential meat, wild boars, and thus food. Other people turn at death into jaguars, who constitute the other pole of animality, a hunter- or cannibal-version.[99] Just as animals were human in the beginning, so humans will be animals when they meet their end such that the eschatology of (dis-) individuation rejoins the mythology of prespeciation. The ghosts of the dead are, in the realm of ontogenesis, like animals are in the order of phylogenesis. ("In the beginning, all animals were humans....") No surprise, then, that the dead, being images defined by their disjunctive relation to the human body, are attracted to the bodies of animals. This is why death in Amazonia involves being transformed into an animal: if the souls of animals are conceived as possessing a primordial human corporeal

99. We are reminded of the "Caititu Rondo" of *The Raw and The Cooked*, in which pigs and jaguars are presented as two opposed animal archetypes of affinity (the bad and the good affine, respectively), which is to say of humanity as structured by alterity; and we also recall, with Carneiro da Cunha (1978) that the dead and affines are basically the same.

form, then it is logical that human souls would be conceived as having the posthumous form of a primordial animal, or as entering a body that will eventually be killed and eaten by the living.

The emergence of vertical shamanism can thus be linked to the separation of the dead and animals into two distinct positions of alterity. At a certain moment (precisely when it happens, I must admit, eludes me), dead humans begin to be seen more as humans than as dead, and this opens the symmetric possibility of a more realized "objectification" of nonhumans. In sum, the separation of humans from nonhumans, the projection outward of a generic figure of animality qua the Other of humanity, is a function of this prior separation of the dead from animals, which accompanies the emergence of a generic figure of humanity objectified in the form of the ancestor. The basic eschatological fact that the dead become animals, then, simultaneously humanized animals and altered the dead. Once the split between the dead and animals was achieved, the former remained humans (or even became superhuman) and the latter slowly ceased to be, drifting into sub- or anti-humanity.

To summarize several aspects of Hugh-Jones' dichotomy, we could say that horizontal shamanism is exopractical while vertical shamanism is endopractical. Let me suggest that in indigenous Amazonia, exopraxis is logically, chronologically, and cosmologically anterior to endopraxis and that it furthermore always remains operational as a residue blocking the constitution of chiefdoms or states having a realized metaphysical interiority (and this applies even to more hierarchical formations, such as those of the Northwest Amazon). The dead never cease to be partially animal, since every dead individual, to the extent that it has a body, engenders a ghost; and to that extent, while some are born aristocrats, no one immediately dies an ancestor; if we are in the precosmological, precorporeal plane of myth and not the space time of the inside, then there are no pure ancestors, for humans and animals communicate directly among themselves there. On the other hand, animals, plants, and other Amazonian categories of beings never cease to be completely human; their post-mythic transformation into animals, etc., counter-effectuates an original humanity, which is the foundation of the access to shamanic logopraxis enjoyed by their actual representatives. All of the dead

156

continue to be somewhat beast, and every beast continues to be somewhat human. Humanity remains immanent by largely reabsorbing the pockets of transcendence that flicker on and off in the dense, teeming forest that is the Amazonian socius.

The horizontal shaman's omnipresence in the region indicates that it is impossible for political power and cosmopolitical force to coincide, which makes the elaboration of a classical sacrificial system quite difficult. The institution of sacrifice by the so-called "high cultures" of the Andes and Mesoamerica would thus involve a sort of capture of shamanism by the State that puts an end to the former's cosmological *bricolage* while at the same time initiating the theological engineering of the priest.[100]

The distinction between horizontal and vertical shamanism has sometimes been coupled with that between transcendence and immanence (Pedersen 2001; Holbraad and Willerslev 2007). As with the perspectivism that makes up its backdrop, Amazonian shamanism is effectively a practice of immanence. However, this does not at all imply that the humans and extrahumans shamanism connects are "equal in status," an inference sometimes made when immanence is confused with equality (as often happens in the Amazonianist literature). On the contrary, there is instead an absence of a fixed point of view between beings. Amazonian perspectivism should not be interpreted as a hierarchical scale of perspectives that progressively include each other along a "chain of ontological dignity"[101] and even less as some kind of "point of view of everything." Shamanism's *raison d'être* is the differences of transformative potential between existents, but no point of view contains another in a unilateral way. Every point of view is "total," and no point of view knows

100. I am casting this distinction between the shaman and the priest in terms of the opposition Lévi-Strauss draws between the bricoleur and the engineer; it also corresponds, furthermore, to the one made in *A Thousand Plateaus* between the presignifying or primitive semiotics of segmentarity, multidimensionality, and anthropophagy and a signifying or despotic semiotics of interpretosis, infinite debt, and faciality (D. G. 1987: 111 et seq.). In Descola's terms, the contrast would be between animism and analogism.

101. What I am suggesting here is that Eduardo Kohn's (2002, 2005) discrepant remarks about the Ávila Runa should be interpreted as manifestations of a tendency, which is probably quite old, toward "verticilization" among forest Quechua people. See on this point Taylor (2009) on the Jivaro Achuar: "Neither the classes of spiritual beings nor the forms of interaction that humans develop with them are ordered according to a scale of dignity or power, and neither sex exclusively benefits from a capacity to enter into relations with nonhumans."

its like or equivalent. Horizontal shamanism is therefore not truly horizontal but *transversal*. The relation between points of view (the relation that is a point of view qua multiplicity) is of the order of a disjunctive synthesis or immanent exclusion, and not of a transcendent inclusion. In sum, the perspectivist system is in perpetual disequilibrium, to once again invoke Lévi-Strauss' characterization of Amerindian cosmologies.

If all this is indeed the case, then the interpretation of (horizontal) Amazonian shamanism as a structural reduction of the Maussian schema proves, in the end, inadequate. Shamanism escapes the presumedly exhaustive division between totemic logic and sacrificial practice. The shaman is not a larval, inchoate priest; shamanism is a low-impact prophetism instead of a quasi-sacerdotal religion. Shamanic operations, if we do not allow them to be reduced to the symbolic play of totemic classifications, can no longer be said to endeavor to produce the fusional continuum sought in the imaginary interseriality of sacrifice. Exemplars of a third form of relation, they dramatize the communication that occurs between the heterogeneous terms constituting preindividual, intensive multiplicities: the blood/beer, to return to our example, implied in every becoming-jaguar.

Through this—by way of becoming—we find ourselves back with Deleuze and Guattari. And it is not at all by chance that we meet them again in *A Thousand Plateaus*, at the very point in the book where they propose a reinterpretation of the opposition between totemism and sacrifice.

Chapter Ten

Production Is Not Everything: Becomings

It was emphasized above that the double author of *Anti-Oedipus* argued that "nothing is changed" by the fact that the primordial energy is one of affiliation—in other words, it would just be a contingent fact. We then asked whether it would not be legitimate to conceive of another intensive order where the primary energy would be an "energy of alliance." The problem, we concluded, was to determine the conditions for the construction of a concept of alliance qua disjunctive synthesis.

The possibility of an intensive interpretation of alliance only becomes intelligible with *A Thousand Plateaus*, in the long chapter on becomings. The notion of becoming was central to Deleuze beginning with his studies on Bergson and Nietzsche, and occupies a well-known role in *The Logic of Sense*. But beginning with the co-authored essay on Kafka (D. G. 1986), it acquired a singular conceptual inflection and intensity that only reached a truly evasive speed in one of the plateaus, "1730: Becoming-Intense, Becoming-Animal, Becoming-Imperceptible." Becoming is that which literally evades, flees, and escapes *mimesis*, whether imitative or reproductive ("Mimicry is a very bad concept"),[102] as much as *memesis*, both mnemonic and historical. Becoming is amnesic, prehistorical, aniconic, and sterile: it is difference in practice.

---

102. D. G. 1987: 11.

◎ ◎ ◎

Chapter 10 of *A Thousand Plateaus* gets underway with a treatment of the opposition Lévi-Strauss makes between serial-sacrificial and totemic-structural logic: the imaginary identification between human and animal, on the one hand, and the symbolic correlation of social and natural differences on the other. Between the two analogical models of series and structure, Deleuze and Guattari introduce the Bergsonian motif of becoming, a type of relation irreducible to serial resemblance as much as to structural correspondence. The concept of becoming describes a relation whose apprehension is, at first glance, difficult for the analytic framework of structuralism, where relations function as molar logical objects, essentially apprehended in extension (oppositions, contradictions, mediations). Becoming is a real relation, molecular and intensive, that operates on another register than that of the still-too morphological relationality of structuralism. The disjunctive synthesis of becoming is, according to the rules of the combinatory play of formal structures, not possible; it operates in areas far from equilibrium and that are inhabited by real multiplicities (DeLanda 2002: 75). "Becoming and multiplicity are the same thing…."[103]

If serial resemblances are imaginary and structural correlations symbolic, becomings are real. Neither metaphor nor metamorphosis, a becoming is a movement that deterritorializes the two terms of the relation it creates, by extracting them from the relations defining them in order to link them via a new "partial connection." In this sense, the verb to become designates neither a predicative operation nor a transitive action: being implicated in a becoming-jaguar is not the same thing as becoming a jaguar. The "totemic" jaguar, whereby a man is "sacrificially" transformed, is imaginary, but the transformation itself is real. It is the becoming itself that is feline; in a becoming-jaguar, the "jaguar" is an immanent aspect of the action and not its transcendent object, for becoming is an intransitive verb.[104] From the moment a human becomes jaguar, the jaguar is no longer there (which is why we

---

103. D. G. 1987: 249.

104. And hyperdefective, given that its only mode is the infinitive, the mode of extrahistorical instantaneousness.

appealed to the formula "human/jaguar" above to designate that specific disjunctive multiplicity of becoming). As the authors say, while citing, significantly, certain Amerindian myths:

> Lévi-Strauss is always encountering these rapid acts by which a human becomes animal at the same time as the animal becomes.... ("Becomes what? Human, or something else?"). (D. G. 1987: 237)

Becoming, they continue, is a verb having a consistency unto itself; it is not to imitate, to appear, to be, or to correspond. And—surprise—becoming "is not producing, producing a filiation or producing through filiation" (D. G. 1987: 292). Neither production nor filiation. As Dorothy would have said to Toto: "I don't think we're in *Anti-Oedipus* anymore."

"Intensive thinking in general is about production," Manuel DeLanda affirms (2003). Well, perhaps things are not as "in general" as that.... The concept of becoming effectively plays the same axial cosmological role in *A Thousand Plateaus* as production does in *Anti-Oedipus*. Not because "everything is becoming"—that would be a solecism—nor because the book does not contain other interesting ideas, but because the consummate anti-representative *dispositif* of *A Thousand Plateaus*, the one that blocks the work of representation, is the concept of becoming—just as production was *Anti-Oedipus'* anti-representative *dispositif.* Production and becoming are two distinct movements. Certainly, both bear on nature, and both are intensive and prerepresentational; in a certain sense, they are two names for the same movement: becoming is the process of desire, desire is production of the real, becoming and multiplicity are one and the same thing, becoming is a rhizome, and the rhizome is a process of unconscious production. But in another sense, they are definitely not the same movement: the way between production and becoming, as we saw Zourabichvili put it, "is not the same in both directions." Production is a process that realizes the identity of the human and nature and that reveals nature to be a process of production ("the human essence of nature and the natural essence of man become one within nature in the form of production or industry" [D. G. 1983: 4]), while becoming, on the contrary, is a "counter-natural" participation of the human and nature; it is an instantaneous movement of capture, symbiosis, and transversal connection

161

between heterogeneities (D. G. 1987: 240). "That is the only way Nature operates—against itself. This is a far cry from filiative production or hereditary reproduction" (D. G. 1987: 242). Becoming is the other side of the mirror of production: the inverse of an identity. An identity "with the opponent." or opposite, to recall the Tupinambá word for enemy.

"The Universe does not function by filiation" (D. G. 1987: 242); read: the universe in all its states, the intensive-virtual as much as the extensive-actual. But if it does not work through *filiation*, and not anything whatsoever, then we could be tempted to believe it possible that it functions by *alliance*. And in effect, we can read in the first plateau that "the tree is filiation, but the rhizome is alliance, uniquely alliance" (D. G. 1987: 25). And now, we also find that

> becoming is not an evolution, at least not an evolution by descent and filiation. Becoming produces nothing by filiation; all filiation is imaginary. Becoming is always of a different order than filiation. It concerns alliance. (D. G. 1987: 238)

Very well then. What exactly happened between *Anti-Oedipus'* affirmation of the intensive, ambiguous, and nocturnal filiation of the Dogon myth and *A Thousand Plateaus'* refusal to attribute any positive role to the same relational mode? How could an affiliation that was *intensive* become *imaginary*?

The change, I think, reflects a major shift of focus from an intraspecific to an interspecific horizon: from a human economy of desire—a world-historical desire, no doubt, that was racial and sociopolitical and not familial, personological, and Oedipal, but a *human* desire all the same—to an economy of trans-specific affects ignorant of the natural order of species and their limiting synthesis, connecting us, through inclusive disjunction, to the plane of immanence. From the perspective of the desiring economy of *Anti-Oedipus*, extensive alliance limits intensive, molecular filiation by actualizing it in the molar form of a filiation group; but from the perspective of the cosmic economy of affect—of desire as *inhuman force*—it is now filiation that limits, through its imaginary identifications, an alliance between heterogeneous beings that is as real as it is counter-natural: "If evolution includes any veritable becomings, it is in the domain of symbioses that bring into play beings of totally different scales and kingdoms, with no possible filiation" (D. G. 1987: 238).

What follows is the favored example of the wasp and the orchid, an assemblage [*agencement*] "from which no wasp-orchid can ever descend"—and, without which, they add, no known wasp or orchid could descend, for the natural filiation at the heart of each species depends on this counter-natural alliance between the two species.

The conceptual deterritorialization of sexuality set in motion in *Anti-Oedipus* is achieved here: the binary organization of sexes, including bisexuality (cf. "the atom of gender" on page 135) gives way to "n sexes," which in turn connects with "n species" on the molecular plane: "*Sexuality proceeds by way of the becoming-woman of the man and the becoming-animal of the human*: an emission of particles" (D. G. 1987: 278-79). And if every animal implicated in a becoming-animal is a multiplicity ("What we are saying is that every animal is fundamentally a band, a pack" [D. G. 1987: 239]), it is because it defines a multiple, lateral, heterogenetic, extrafiliative, and extrareproductive sociality that pulls human sociality into a universal demonic metonymy:

> We oppose epidemic to filiation, contagion to heredity, peopling by contagion to sexual reproduction, sexual production. [...] Unnatural participations or nuptials are the true Nature spanning the kingdoms of nature. (D. G. 1987: 241)

Alliance, perhaps ... but not *every* alliance. As we have seen, the first volume of *Capitalism and Schizophrenia* postulates two filiations: an intensive and germinal one, and another that is extensive and somatic, with the latter being counterposed to alliance, the extensive principle that plays the role of the "repressing representation" of the representative of desire or germinal impulse. Now in *A Thousand Plateaus*, we find two alliances: the one dissected in *Anti-Oedipus*, which is internal to the socius and even to the masculine gender (primary collective homosexuality), and another, immanent to becoming, that is as irreducible to production and imaginary metamorphosis (mythic genealogy, animal filiation) as to exchange and symbolic classification (exogamic alliance, totemism).

163

Every becoming is an alliance. Which does not mean, once again, that every alliance is a becoming. There is extensive, cultural, and sociopolitical alliance, and intensive, counter-natural, and cosmopolitical alliance. If the first distinguishes filiations, the second confuses species or, better yet, counter-effectuates by implicative synthesis the continuous differences that are actualized in the other direction (the way is not the same ...) through the limiting synthesis of discontinuous speciation. When a shaman activates a becoming-jaguar, he neither "produces" a jaguar nor "affiliates" with a reproductive line of jaguars: he *adopts* and *coopts* a jaguar—establishes a feline alliance:

> Rather, a zone of indistinction, of indiscernibility, or of ambiguity seems to be established between two terms, as if they had reached the point immediately preceding their respective differentiation: not a similitude, but a slippage, an extreme proximity, and absolute contiguity; not a natural filiation, but an unnatural alliance. (D. 1997: 78)

We can observe the way this definition of becoming (for that is exactly what is at stake here) transversally sets up a paradigmatic dualism: {filiation, metonymic continuity, serial resemblance} vs. {alliance, discontinuity, oppositional difference}. The "absolute contiguity" of the tangential-differential kind established by counter-natural alliance is certainly different from the absolute, contrastive "discontiguity" between filiative lineages that is established by symbolico-cultural alliance (exogamy). But at the same time, needless to say, it does not come down to an imaginary identification or nondifferentiation between "two terms." It is not a matter of opposing, as classical structuralism did, natural filiation and cultural alliance. The counter-naturality of intensive alliance is equally counter-cultural or counter-social.[105] What we are discussing is an included third, or another relation—a "new alliance":

> "Alliance" is a good and a bad word. Every word is good if it can be used to cross the boundary between people and things. So alliance is

---

105. Counter-social to the extent, we could say, that human sociality is necessarily counter-intensive, once it is engendered as the extensification of the "primary energy of the intensive order."

a good word if you use it for a microbe. Force is a good word if you use it for a human. (Latour 1993: 263)

There is no need to leave Africanist territory to find a first example of such a transborder alliance, this affinity (affine=*ad-finis*) between humans and nonhumans. In a section of the second plateau entitled "Memories of a Sorcerer II," Deleuze and Guattari evoke animal-men, such as the "sacred deflowerers," studied by Pierre Gordon, or the hyena-men of certain Sudanese traditions that G. Calame-Griaule described. Both of them stimulated a commentary that I take as decisive:

> [T]he hyena-man lives on the fringes of the village, or between two villages, and can keep a lookout in both directions. A hero, or even two heroes with a fiancée in each other's village, triumphs over the man-animal. It is as though it were necessary to distinguish two very different states of alliance: a demonic alliance that imposes itself from without, and imposes its law upon all of the filiations (a forced alliance with the monster, with the man-animal), and a consensual alliance, which is on the contrary in conformity with the law of filiations and is established after the men of the villages have defeated the monster and have organized their own relations. This question of incest can thus be modified. For it is not enough to say that the prohibition against incest results from the positive requirements of alliance in general. There is instead a kind of alliance that is so foreign and hostile to filiation that it necessarily takes the position of incest (the man-animal always has a relation to incest). The second kind of alliance prohibits incest because it can subordinate itself to the rights of filiation only by lodging itself, precisely, between two distinct filiations. Incest appears twice, once as a monstrous power of alliance when alliance overturns filiation, and again as a prohibited power of filiation when filiation subordinates alliance and must distribute it among distinct lineages. (D. G. 1987: 540, n.21)

"The question of incest can thus be modified...." The authors would seem to be alluding here to the theory of *The Elementary Structures of Kinship*, but the observation equally applies to the way the question was treated in *Anti-Oedipus*. Because now it is the notion of alliance that appears twice over; it is not only "sexuality as a process of filiation" but also "a power of alliance inspiring illicit unions or abominable loves," and its goal is not just to manage but also "to prevent procreation" (D. G. 1987: 246): an anti-filiative alliance, an alliance against filiation. Even the exchangeist, repressing alliance productive of filiation from *Anti-Oedipus* starts here to exhibit certain savage and obscure powers—as if it had been contaminated by the other, "demonic" alliance.[106] "It is true that the relations between alliance and filiation come to be regulated by laws of marriage, but even then alliance retains a dangerous and contagious power. Leach was able to demonstrate [...]" (D. G. 1987: 246).[107] We can see that the word "power" [*puissance*] insistently qualifies alliance in general in this key chapter of *A Thousand Plateaus*. Alliance ceases to designate an institution—a structure—and begins to function as a power and potential; a becoming. From alliance as form to alliance as force, by way of a leap over filiation qua substance? This is why we are no longer in the mystical-serial element of sacrifice or the mythical-structural one of totemism but in the magical-real element of becoming.

Neither are we, moreover, in the element of the social contract. "Desire knows nothing of exchange, *it knows only theft and gift* [...]" (D. G. 1983: 186). But as with the case of alliance, there is exchange, and then there is exchange. There is an exchange that cannot be called "exchangeist" in the market/capitalist sense of the term, since it belongs to the category of theft and gift: the exchange, precisely, characteristic of so-called gift economies— the alliance established by the exchange of gifts, the perpetual, alternating movement of double capture in which the partners commute (counter-alienate) invisible perspectives through the circulation of visible things: it is "theft" that realizes the immediate disjunctive synthesis of the "three moments" of giving,

---

106. "[The] potential wild beast which, in social terms, is what a brother-in-law amounts to, since he has taken away your sister" (L.-S. 1981: 485). As the author himself cautions us, one must know how to take such mythical equivalences literally, via "a meaning which transcends the distinction between the real and the imaginary: a complete meaning of which we can now hardly do more than evoke the ghost in the reduced setting of figurative language" (L.-S. 1966: 265).

107. The reference here is to Leach's "Rethinking Anthropology," in which it is observed (1961: 20) that there is a general "metaphysical influence" exercised between allies by marriage. For a recent commentary on this, see Viveiros de Castro 2008a.

receiving, and returning.[108] Because even though gifts can be reciprocal, that does not make exchange any less of a violent movement; the whole purpose of the act of giving is to force the recipient to act, to provoke a gesture or response: in short, to steal his soul (alliance as the reciprocal soul theft). And in this sense, that category of social action called gift exchange does not exist; every action is social as and *only as* action on action or reaction on reaction. Here, *reciprocity* simply means *recursivity*. No insinuation of sociability, and still less of altruism. Life is theft.[109]

◎ ◎ ◎

The allusion to African sorcerers, naturally, is not accidental. Deleuze and Guattari link becomings to sorcery as both practice and discourse (magical tales), opposing them, on the one hand, to the clear and distinct world of myths and totemic institutions and, on the other, to the obscure and confused world of the priest and sacrificial technology. Their observation is of major importance, as transversal Amazonian shamanism belongs to the "obscure and distinct" world of magic, sorcery, and becoming.

There is something here that will require subsequent reflection and about which I will only suggest some leads, inspired by an article of Goldman's (Goldman 2005). Where Mauss is concerned, it would obviously be necessary to return, if shamanism is to be understood, to the study of magic, not the text on sacrifice—to the dated, despised *Outline of a Theory of Magic* that he drafted with Hubert, and that contains *in potentia* the entirety of the celebrated *Essay on the Gift*, in which case the *Essay*'s *hau*, which lies at the origin of the principle of reciprocity of *The Elementary*

---

108. On exchange and perspective, see Strathern, 1988: 230, 271, 327; 1991: *passim*; 1992a: 96-100; 1999: 249-56; Munn, 1992/1986: 16; Gregory, 1982: 19, and on the notion of double capture, see Deleuze and Parnet 1987: 1-3; Stengers 2010 [1996]: 266, n. 11.

109. "Language can work against the user of it. [...] Sociality is frequently understood as implying sociability, reciprocity as altruism and relationship as solidarity" (Strathern 1999: 18). "Action on action" is one of those formulas to which Foucault had recourse, as we know, to describe power (there are only forces applied to forces, as Deleuze's Nietzsche would say), and "reaction to reaction" is the way Bateson explained the concept of schizmogenesis, which was of as much importance to Lévi-Straussian structural analysis as to Deleuzo-Guattarian schizoanalysis. As for the theft that is life, see Alfred North Whitehead: "Life is robbery, and the robber requires a justification" (*apud* Stengers 2011: 31). Shall we call this justification "the gift?"

Structures, is but an exchangeist version of the *Outline's mana*, which in turn is the preconcept of "the floating signifier" (L.-S. 1987a: 63).[110] In Lévi-Strauss, in turn, the relevant text is less "The Sorcerer and His Magic" than a rather mysterious commentary found in the third volume of the *Mythologiques* (1979: 117-22), which will be adumbrated here.

Just after the summary of M60, "The Misadventures of Cimidyuë," Lévi-Strauss mentions, in almost one breath, the existence of mythic narrations having a serial form and their unique oneric atmosphere, in which meetings with deceiving spirits who induce conceptual distortions and perceptual equivocations abound, as do cryptic allusions to sorcery practices—hence their association with rituals for the ingestion of hallucinatory drugs that induce "identifications" with animals.

For a brief instant this commentary allows us to glimpse *another* Amerindian mythopraxis running alongside, sometimes even as its counter-current (like one of those bidirectional rivers the book evokes), the etiological mythology that Lévi-Strauss privileges: the stories of transformation or, as Deleuze and Guattari call them, "sorcery tales" in which variations of perspective affecting the characters ("these rapid acts") are the narrative focus. *Perspectivism directly refers us to the becoming-sorcerer of Amerindian mythology.*

Not so much a novelized linear historical involution of myth (as Lévi-Strauss imagines things in the chapter of *The Origin of Table Manners* concerning it), this would be a lateral becoming internal to myth that causes it to enter into the regime of multiplicity, in which the fragments of an infinite, scattered rhapsody on *quasi-events* glistens.[111] Anecdotes, rumors, gossip, family and village folklore—the "small tradition" of Redfield—as well as humorous anecdotes, hunting incidents, visitations of spirits, bad dreams, sudden frights, and precognitions ... such are the elements of *minor myth*, myth when it is the register and instrument of simulacra, hallucinations, and lies. And if the myth of "the great tradition" (myth submitted to a major use by the philosophies and religions of the world: Ricoeurian Near Eastern myth)

110. The condition of the relational potentialization the incest prohibition institutes, which comes, as we know, from Lévi-Strauss's reading of Essay on *The Gift*, and is fundamentally linked to the perpetual disequilibrium between signifier and signified that he discussed in the *Outline*.

111. On the notion of "quasi-events," see Rodgers 2004 and Viveiros de Castro 2008b.

is the bearer of dogma and faith, of *credo quia absurdum*, Lévi-Strauss' minor myth (Amerindian myth in its becoming-sorcerer) illustrates instead the doubly inverted maxim of Henri Michaux: "This is false, even if it is true."[112] As we can still witness today in the Science Wars, the distance between religion and magic is far greater than the one that separates religion from science.

In the end, neither sacrifice nor totemism will suffice. "People say, 'It's either this or that,' and it's always something else" (Lévi-Strauss and Éribon 1991: 125). The conclusion will have to be that *The Savage Mind*'s concept of sacrifice confuses two *faux amis* by fusing two operations—interserial resemblance and extraserial becoming—into one. Moreover, it would be necessary to further conclude that the other operation of the savage series, totemism, is in the end not the best model for difference; or rather, it is precisely a *model*, and thus does not provide us with all the *processes* of difference. We must not let ourselves be hypnotized by the proportional analogies, Klein groups, and permutation tables; instead, we have to drop correlational homology for transformational staggering (Maniglier 2000: note 26).

According to the formula of the 1962 books, totemism is a system of classificatory relations in which nothing happens between correlative series: a model, apparently, of perfect equilibrium. The totemic "differences of potential" are internal to each series, and incapable of producing effects on the alternate one. Becoming, on the contrary, affirms relation as pure exteriority, and the extraction of terms from the series they belong to—their insertion into rhizomes. It calls not for a theory of relations locked inside terms but a theory of terms open to relations. To some extent, becoming, as we saw, constitutes not a third *type* of relation but a third *concept* of it, one through which sacrifice

112. The *Mythologiques* warn us several times that they do not include in their itinerary the stories associated with esoteric doctrines, learned brotherhoods, and theological elaborations (they thus exclude the mythology of the continent's Highlands, along with a part of the mythologies of the Northwest Amazon and the North American Southwest). As if Amerindian mythology—etiological structural myth—constantly anticipates the bifurcation of its trajectory: the becoming-sorcerer of minor myth, which transforms it into tales of transformation—myth as rhizomatic multiplicity—and the arborescent drift toward cosmogony and theology, toward monarchic *logos*: the myth of the state. Might there be here a possible analogy with the double trajectory of Amazonian shamanism toward both prophetism and priesthood? For it is true that from the point of view, for example, of someone like Paul Ricoeur, *the whole* of the Amerindian mythology analyzed by Lévi-Strauss belongs to minor myth.

as much as totemism should be read: that is, as secondary re-territorializations of a primary relational difference, as alternative ways of actualizing becoming as universal intensive multiplicity. Actualized simultaneously in totemic sacrifices and sacrificial mixtures (or: Latour's purification and mediation), becoming is endlessly counter-effectuated at the margins of sacrificial devices and in the intervals of totemic taxonomies—at the peripheries of "religion" and the borders of "science."

◊ That said, one must all the same grasp the consequences of the fact that the analogical schema of totemism, with the symmetrical corre-spondence it makes between natural and social differences, is based on an asymmetry that is its *raison d'être*, which is the fact that totemic spe-cies are endopractical—bears marry bears, lynxes marry lynxes—which makes them suitable for signifying exopractical social species, in which the bear and the lynx marry. External differences become internal dif-ferences, distinctions become relations, and terms becomes functions. A canonical formula lies in wait behind totemism, and it transforms, as the fourth chapter of The Savage Mind shows, the totemic dispositif into one of castes. It would seem significant that it would be exactly here, in his demonstration of the limits of symmetry (L.-S. 1966: 126) between the functional specialization of endogamous castes and the functional homogeneity of exogamous clans, that Lévi-Strauss describes totemism with terms like "imaginary," "illusion," "empty form," "deceitful usur-pation…." If totemism will later in the book be declared fundamentally true, in opposition to the pure power of the false of sacrifice, the analysis of caste in this chapter shows that illusion and truth are not so simply distributed: "castes naturalize a true culture falsely, totemic groups cul-turalize a false nature truly" (L.-S. 1966: 127). Which is to say that it is as if nature and culture were in perpetual disequilibrium, as if there could be no parity between them, and as if "truth" in the one series cor-responded to "illusion" in the other. This motif, which could be called the principle of complementarity of sense, accompanies Lévi-Strauss everywhere in his thought, from "Introduction to the Work of Marcel Mauss" to *The Story of Lynx*.

In summary, it could in all modesty be said that the future of the master concept of anthropology—relation—depends on how much attention the discipline will end up lending to the concepts of difference and multiplicity, becoming and disjunctive synthesis. A poststructural theory of relationality, by which I mean a theory respecting the "unfounded" compromise between structuralism and relational ontology, cannot ignore the *series* Gilles Deleuze's philosophy constructs: the country populated by the figures of Leibniz, Spinoza, Hume, Nietzsche, Butler, Whitehead, Bergson, and Tarde and thus also by the ideas of perspective, force, affect, habit, event, process, prehension, transversality, becoming, and difference. Such is the lineage of a minor structuralism, from which an essential articulation or mediation would have been subtracted—a character even more strategic than the transcendental subject Lévi-Strauss so memorably eliminated from his own Kantianism. A structuralism with a little something less; a structuralism, then—and yet we will have to say it with all the necessary circumspection—that would not obsessively revolve around Kant.

This has to be said not only with circumspection but a sure sense of direction, because the point is not to abandon Kantian anthropology only to step backwards into the arms of a "Cartesian anthropology," with or without dualisms (or brackets); not to replace a Kantianism without a transcendental subject with a "Kantianism" with an empirical subject—with a cognitive innateism, with or without modularity. And it is equally crucial to resist (to follow the Deleuzian projective tangent) another prestructuralism, sometimes presented as the future of anthropology, that favors, in a strange reaction to the notion of relation, the reproliferation of identities, substances, essences, transcendences, consciousnesses, and (especially) agencies. Even the "materiality" of bodies and signs is currently being recruited for the lame tasks of reincarnating the mystery of incarnation, and celebrating the miracle of agency…. When the chase is not on for "substance," as it has been for a certain French analysis of kinship. *That* anthropology has spent more than twenty years enthusiastically applying itself to undermining the exchangeist—in other words, relational—foundations of structuralism, an episode that has seen it establishing innate ideas and joining them to corporeal fluid Substance on substance.

Chapter Eleven

The System's Intensive Conditions

We will return once more to the passage from Lévi-Strauss already cited several times in these pages, the one where the dean of the Americanists connects "critical analyses" of the notion of affinity (which Brazilian ethnologists led the way in[113]) to the uncovering of an indigenous philosophical problematic. All of this derives, at the end of the day, from Lévi-Strauss himself, and I think that he knew it perfectly well. That South American affinity is indeed not a sociological category but a philosophical idea was something Lévi-Strauss had observed in a premonitory way in one of his very first works, some years before he reduced this idea of cosmological reason, in *The Elementary Structures of Kinship*, to a category of sociological understanding, while making the latter, in turn, subordinate to the ur-schematism of kinship—but not without something of the idea's power of deterritorialization being conserved in the process. Thus in the article from *American Anthropologist* in which he compares the ancient Tupinambá to the Nambikwara that he came to know some years prior, he observes that

> a certain kinship tie, the brother-in-law relationship, once possessed a meaning among many South American tribes far transcending a simple expression of [kin] relationship" (L.-S. 1943: 398).

---

113. With the more than decisive help of colleagues of other nationalities, notably Peter Rivière, Joanna Overing, Bruce Albert, Anne-Christine Taylor, and Peter Gow.

Everything is there. Perhaps it should be specified that the word choice indicates the truly transcendental rather than transcendent nature of the meaning of this Amerindian cosmopolitics: it is the condition of kinship and, as such, its dimension of immanent exteriority.

The difference between the two kinds of alliance proposed in *A Thousand Plateaus* seems to forcefully impose itself, as a kind of typical trait (ethnologically speaking), when the West African landscape is left in order to forge into indigenous America. It closely corresponds to a contrast that ethnographers of the region established between, on the one hand, an intensive or "potential" cosmological and mytho-ritual affinity that can be perfectly qualified as "ambiguous, disjunctive, nocturnal, and demonic," and, on the other, an extensive or actual affinity subordinate to consanguinity. Since I have already treated this subject in a number of works on Amazonian kinship, I will be merely allusive.[114]

As a general rule, matrimonial affinity is conceived in Amazonian societies as a particularly delicate relation, in every sense: dangerous, fragile, awkward, embarrassing, and precious. It is morally ambivalent, affectively strained, politically strategic, and economically fundamental. Consequently, relations of affinity become the object of a collective disinvestment that allows relations of consanguinity (siblinghood and filiation) to camouflage it. Terminological affines (those *a priori* affines whose presence defines "elementary systems of kinship") are conceived as types of cognates—in this case, cousins and cross-cousins—rather than as affines; true affines are treated consanguinally in both reference and address (my brother-in-law becomes my maternal uncle and so on); the specific terms of affinity are avoided in favor of consanguinal euphemisms or technonyms that express a transitive cognation ("maternal uncle and my son" rather than

114. See for example Viveiros de Castro 1992/1986, 2001b, 2002b, 2008a. What I have most often called "potential affinity" should be rechristened "virtual affinity"—a suggestion that Taylor had also made (2000: 312: n. 6)—so as to render the affinity with the Deleuzian theory of the virtual more consistent. On this subject, see Viveiros de Castro 2002b: 412-13 and Taylor 2009. The direct sources for the notion of potential affinity are Overing 1983 and 1984, Albert 1985, Taylor 1993, and also my own work on the Tupi (Viveiros de Castro 1992[1986]).

"brother-in-law," and so on again); conjoints become *una caro*, a single flesh that cuts across sex and neighbor…. As Peter Rivière (1984: 70) observed apropos the typical case of the Guyanes, where a strong atmosphere of village or cognatic endogamy prevails, "within the ideal village, affinity does not exist."

But if affinity does not exist in the ideal village, it is going to have to exist somewhere else. At the interior of every real village, to begin with, but more so in its exterior—in other words, as intensive or virtual affinity. For as soon as one leaves the village, whether real or ideal, the camouflage is inverted, and affinity becomes the non-marked form of social relation, one all the stronger when generic, and more explicit because less actual: the perfect brother-in-law is the sibling of the sister to whom I am not married, or who is not married to my sister.[115] Affines are enemies, and enemies are thus affines. When affines are not enemies but parents and coresidents—the "ideal" case—then they must *not* be treated as affines; when enemies are not affines, it is because they are in fact enemies, meaning that they should be treated *as* affines.

Supralocal relations in the Amazon tend in this way to be strongly connoted by affinity: locally exogamous alliances that are rare, but politically strategic; diverse ritualized bonds of friendship or commercial partnership; and ambivalent intercommunity ceremoniality that is the inverse of a permanent state of physical or spiritual war (whether latent or manifest) between local groups. And, to make a fundamental point, this intensive affinity crosses the borders between species: animals, plants, spirits, and other tribes whose humanity is uncertain are all found to be implicated in such synthetic-disjunctive relations with humans.[116] In the first place, and also most often in the last, others are all affines,

115. For example, it was to the Tupinambá prisoner—the enemy/brother-in-law (see above) destined to be put to death in the village center, to whom a woman from the group was given for the length of his captivity, in a simulacrum of affinity so real that this woman was, ideally, a sister of the future executioner.

116. We will insist on the fact that this *a priori* affinitization of the other takes place despite the fact that effectively matrimonial alliances are realized in the majority of Amazonian regimes in the interior of the local group. In truth, alliances cannot not be concentrated in the local group when it is precisely this concentration that defines the "local" dimension—village, endogamous nexus, or multicommunity ensemble. In the same way, the situation does not significantly change when Amazonian regimes that encourage or prescribe village exogamy or filiation groups are considered. Potential affinity and its cosmological harmonics continue to set the tone for generic relations with nonallied groups: whites, enemies, animals, spirits.

partners obliged in the cosmic play of theft and gift—or of an "exchange" that should be understood as a particular case of theft and gift in which the difference of potential between partners tends toward zero "but is never completely annulled." Even at the heart of the ideal village of the Guyanes, a certain coefficient of alterity is necessary between the partners of a matrimonial union, seeing that the sister always remains unmarriageable; the union of a man with the daughter of his sister being what most approaches this incestuous ideal (the union with the uterine niece is the preferential marriage of diverse Amazonian tribes). This is to say that if the analysis is taken far enough, the affinity "that does not exist" will be found in the ideal village. And in any case, incest, as we know, is impossible[117]; every actual endogamy is the inferior limit of a virtual exogamy. As Lévi-Strauss himself said, similarity is a particular case of difference, and sociality the inferior limit of predation.

The relation of pure virtual affinity or meta-affinity, the generic Amazonian schematization of alterity, doubtlessly belongs to that "second type of alliance" from *A Thousand Plateaus*. It is hostile to filiation because it appears precisely where marriage is not an option, disappears where the latter is realized, and has a productivity of a non-procreative kind. Or rather, it subordinates every internal procreation to a demonic alliance with the exterior. Not a mode of *production* (of homogenetic filiation) but a mode of *predation* (of heterogenetic cooptation), "reproduction" by semiotic capture and by ontological "re-predation": the cannibal internalization of the other as condition of the externalization of the self, a self that sees itself, in a certain way, "self-determined" by the enemy, which is to say *as* the enemy (see above page 143). Such is the becoming-other intrinsic to Amazonian cosmopraxis. Virtual affinity is linked more to war than to kinship; it takes part in a war machine anterior and exterior to kinship as such. An alliance against affiliation, then: not because it is the "repressing representation" of a primordial intensive filiation, but because it prevents filiation from functioning as the germ of a transcendence (the mythical origin, the foundational ancestor, the identitiarian

---

117. See Wagner (1972) on the tautological character of the notion of the incest prohibition—a sister is not forbidden because she is a sister, but is a sister at the same time that she is forbidden. See, equally, a very similar argument of Deleuze and Guattari's (1983: 162) on the impossibility of "enjoying the person and the name at the same time."

filiation group). Every filiation is imaginary, is what the authors of *A Thousand Plateaus* tell us. And we could add: every filiation projects a State, is a State filiation. We could further say, in homage to Pierre Clastres, that Amazonian intensive alliance is an alliance against the State.

Intensive or primordial alliance is one of the diacritical signs of Amazonian sociality, and perhaps of the continent as a whole; here we touch the "bedrock" of American mythology (L.-S. 1995: 222). Consider the continental complex tracked in the *Mythologiques*: if Amerindian myths are compared to our own mythology of culture, a certain difference stands out, which is that of the pre-eminence of relations of matrimonial alliance in the first, and of kinship relations in the second. The central figures of Amerindian myth are canonically linked as affines; a celebrated character of these stories, to take an example, is the cannibal brother-in-law, the nonhuman master of cultural goods, who submits his son-in-law to a series of trials with the intention of murdering him; the young man survives them (most often thanks to the intervention of other nonhumans who take pity on him) and then returns to the center of his human community bearing the precious spoils of culture. The content of this archemyth (L.-S. 1981: 562) is not altogether different from the Promethean scenario: present are both sky and earth, with a hero trapped in between, as well as civilizing fire, the "gift" of women, and the origin of human mortality. But the antagonists of the human heroes of the Amerindian myth are fathers-in-law or brothers-in-law and not paternal or filial figures like those that dominate the mythologies of the Old World, be they Greek, Near Eastern, African, or Freudian. To put it succinctly, we will say that in the Old World, humans had to steal fire from a divine father, while Amerindians either had to take it from a father-in-law or receive it as a gift from a brother-in-law, both of whom were animals.

What we call "mythology" is a discourse—of certain others, as a general rule—about the given (Wagner 1978); it is myths that give, once and for all, what will be taken as the given: the primordial conditions from and against which humans will be defined or constructed; this discourse establishes the terms and limits (where they exist) of this ontological debt. If that is the case, then the Amerindian debt is not to filiation and kinship—the basic

177

genealogical given—but to marriage and affinity; the Other, as we have seen, is above all an affine. It should be noted that the reference here is not to the trivial fact that indigenous myths treat relations of affinity as always already there—they do the same with consanguinal relations, or they imagine worlds in which pre-humans are ignorant of matrimonial prohibitions, etc.—but rather to the fact that affinity constitutes the "armature," in the sense the *Mythologiques* give the term, of the myth. This armature, or framework, contains a great variety of entities; more precisely, it is replete with animal affines. It is indispensable that they be animals or, in general, nonhumans, whether vegetable, astronomical, meteorological, or artifactual (in truth, future nonhumans: in myth, the whole world is partially human, actual humans included, even if the way is not the same in the two directions). For it is precisely this alliance with the nonhuman that defines "the system's intensive conditions" in Amazonia.

Amerindian myths certainly contain Oedipal incest, conflicts between fathers and sons, and everything else one might imagine. *The Jealous Potter* dwells, for reasons that are known, on a "Jivaro Totem and Taboo" (L.-S. 1988: ch. 14). But it is clear enough that for Lévi-Strauss, the mythology of the continent, particularly the part of it that treats the origin of culture, turns around affinity and exchange and not kinship and procreation; just as the incest characteristic of the Amerindian imaginary that Lévi-Strauss places at the foundation of *The Elementary Structures of Kinship* is brother-sister incest, or "alliance incest," rather than the effectively Freudian "filiation incest" between parents and children. It will be recalled that the most vastly diffused myth in the New World (L.-S. 1979: 42, 91-99; 1981: 211-13) places the origin of both sun and moon in incest between a brother and a sister. This is the story that the author will call "the American Vulgate" (L.-S. 1982: 192) and that constitutes the fundamental cell of M1, the Bororo reference myth in which arche-Oedipal mother-son incest and the mortal combat with the father that ensues are transcribed by Lévi-Strauss as, respectively, incest between "*germains*" (some structural-anthropological humor there) and a conflict between "affines": in Bororo society, which is organized into exogamous matrilineal clans, every individual belongs to his mother's clan, while his father is an affine, the member of a clan allied through

178

marriage. From the father's perspective, the son is like one of his wife's brothers. This Lévi-Straussian displacement of the problematic of incest is deftly employed in *Anti-Oedipus'* commentary on the Dogon myth: "Incest with the sister is not a substitute for incest with the mother, but on the contrary the intensive model of incest as a manifestation of the germinal lineage" (D. G. 1983: 159).

But on the intensive plane, there cannot at all be a clear opposition (it would have to be extensive) between alliance and filiation. Or better, if there are two alliances, there must also be two filiations. Even if every production is filiative, every filiation is not necessarily (re)productive; if reproductive and administrative filiations exist (representatives of the State), there are also contagious, monstrous filiations that result from counter-natural alliances and becomings, i.e., incestuous or transpecific unions.[118]

Endogamy and exofiliation: these are the elementary structures of anti-kinship. If exogamous affinity does not exist in the ideal Guyane village, it is endofiliative consanguinity that does not exist in other ideal Amerindian villages; since the majority of the children of the group are of enemy origin, as in the "ideal" case of the Caduevo described in *Tristes Tropiques*:

> What we call "natural" sentiments were held in great disfavor in their society: for instance, the idea of procreation filled them with disgust. Abortion and infanticide were so common as to be almost normal— to the extent, in fact, that it was by adoption, rather than by procreation, that the group ensured its continuance. (L.-S. 1974: 162)

Another example of perverse deviation of structuralist doctrine can be found by returning to the Tupinambá, who while preferring to marry the daughters of their sisters, at the same time enthusiastically abandon themselves to capturing brother-in-laws

---

118. There are Amazonian mythologies that project a precosmic setting much like the situation of intensive filiation Deleuze and Guattari perceive in the Dogon myth. The myths of the Tukano and Arawak people of the Northwest Amazon are the most notable here, despite the fact that, as G. Andrello (2006) notes, they arrive back at the same schema of intensive affinity that constitutes the basic state—the plane of immanence—of the Amazonian precosmos.

from the outside, enemies to whom they give their own sisters as temporary spouses before ceremonially executing and devouring them. A nearly incestuous hyperendogamy is doubled by a cannibal hyperexogamy. According to the ostentatious schematism of myth: copulate with a sister, and adopt a small animal.... But also, in a double twist of that schema: marry a star, and carry its sisters in one's intestines.[119]

On the whole, the question is less of knowing if there are one or two kinds of both alliance and filiation, or if the myths recognize primordial filiation or not, than of determining *where intensity comes from*. In the end, the question is to know if the exterior is born from the interior—if alliance descends from and depends on affiliation—or if, on the contrary, the interior is the repetition of the exterior: if filiation and consanguinity are a particular case of alliance and affinity, the case in which difference qua intensive disjunction tends toward zero ... without ever being annulled, of course.[120]

It is precisely this zone of "indistinction, indiscernibility, and ambiguity" between affinity and consanguinity[121]—less their nondifferentiation than their infinite reverberation and internal redoubling, the fractal involution that puts each in the other— that is stressed by the importance to Amerindian mythology of the figure of twinhood, which, after being only quickly evoked in "The Structure of Myths," gradually takes shape and continues to become more developed in the *Mythologiques* (foremost in the myths of the sun and the moon) until it is transformed into "the key to the whole system" in *The Story of Lynx* (L.-S. 1995: 222). For far from representing the prototype of similarity or of consanguinal identity, Amerindian twinhood—provisional, incomplete, semi-meditative, divergent, in disequilibrium, and tinted by incestuous antagonism—is the internal repetition of potential affinity; the unequal twins are the mythical personification of "the unavoidable dissymmetry" (1979: 489) that forms the condition of the world. Consanguinity as the metonymy of affinity, and

119. See L.-S. 1981: 262-64, 309-11 for the sisters the Coyote lodges in his intestines and whom he regularly excretes in order to solicit their advice.

120. As we know, "intensive quantity [...] has a relation to zero, with which it is consubstantial" (D. 1983).

121. This zone is also internal to the latter, rendering filiation and siblinghood indistinct: cf. the mother-sister of M1.

twinhood as the metaphor for difference: you have to be a bit Leibnizian to relish the irony.

◊ Differential twinhood begins by separating the person from itself, in revealing itself an intensive category: as the chapter on the "fateful sentence" in *The Story of Lynx* so beautifully puts things ("If it's a girl/boy, I'll rear her/him, if it's a boy/girl I'll kill him/her"), a child still in its mother's womb is the "twin to itself" (L.-S. 1995: 60 et seq.) since it carries a virtual double of the opposite sex that disappears when the new unisexual individual is finally born. (The paradox of Schrödinger's cat could be viewed as a transformation of this mythic theme, which perhaps becomes most visible for Lévi-Strauss under the form of the quantum cat itself—evoked, moreover, on page xii of *The Story of Lynx*). It will be noted that the book concentrates on the pair of masculine twins common in Amerindian mythology (to better contrast them, moreover, to the Dioscures), but in *The Naked Man*, the author advances the argument that twins of the same sex are a transformational state "derived" from and "subsidiary" to an armature formed by (incestuous) twins of the opposite sex (L.-S. 1981: 216-18). The disparity between Amerindian twins of the same sex would thus derive, inter alia, from its "origin" in a pair of twins of the opposite sex. Which suggests not, as Françoise Héritier once claimed (1981: 39), that every difference derives from sexual difference, but exactly the opposite: every sexuality is differential, just like every system of signs (Maniglier 2000, Viveiros de Castro 1990). To paraphrase Lévi-Strauss again (1981: 603), the experience constitutive of kinship is not the opposition between the sexes, but the other apprehended as opposition. See above, pages 133-134, for the Strathernian version of this profound structuralist intuition.

We can conclude this brief evocation with a reaffirmation of the idea of potential affinity as a foundational indigenous Amazonian cosmological category that constitutes, from the point of view of its theoretical and ethnographic frame of reference, a break with the "exchangeist" image of the socius. Hence the importance of the notions of predation or prehension—theft and gift, cannibalism and becoming-enemy—that have always accompanied it. Both are attempts to capture the movement of a power of alliance that would be something like the fundamental state of indigenous metaphysics, a cosmopolitical power irreducible to the domestic-public affinity of classical kinship theories (i.e., the "domestic domain" and the "public sphere"), whether structural-functionalist, structuralist, or Marxist. Theft, gift, contagion, expenditure, becoming: *that* is the exchange in question. Potential alliance is the becoming-other circumscribing and subordinating Amazonian kinship. It was by means of this idea that the ethnology of these peoples, faithful to the *Mythologiques* well before *The Elementary Structures of Kinship* (so as to be all the more faithful to the latter!) anticipated an incisive observation of Patricė Maniglier:

> Kinship is essentially not social; it neither exclusively operates through the latter nor primordially regulates and determines the relations of humans with each other but rather ensures what could be called the political economy of the universe, the circulation of things of this world in which we take part. (Maniglier 2005b: 768).

PART FOUR

The Cannibal *Cogito*

The philosopher must become nonphilosopher so that nonphilosophy becomes the earth and the people of philosophy…. The people is internal to the thinker because it is a "becoming-people," just as the thinker is internal to the people….

—*What Is Philosophy?*

Chapter Twelve

The Enemy in the Concept

Anti-Narcissus—the book that I would have liked to write but that I only managed to outline in the previous chapters—would have been a thought experiment [*une expérience de pensée*], an exercise in anthropological fiction. A "thought experiment" not in the usual sense of thought (imaginarily) entering experience but, rather, of the entry into thought of (real) experience. Not the imagining of an experiment, but an experimentation with the imagination or an "experimentation with thought itself."[122] In the present case, the accumulated experience is that of a generation of ethnographers of indigenous Amazonia, and the experiment is a fiction whose controls lie in this experience. The fiction, then, would be anthropological, but the anthropology is not fictional.

The fiction consists in treating indigenous ideas as concepts and then following the consequences of this decision: defining the preconceptual ground or plane of immanence the concepts presuppose, the conceptual persona they conjure into existence, and the matter of the real that they suppose. Treating these ideas as concepts does not involve objectively determining them as something other than what they are, such as another kind of actual object. Casting them in terms of default anthropological "concepts"—individual cognitions, collective representations, propositional attitudes, cosmological beliefs, unconscious schemas, textual complexes, embodied dispositions, and so on—would be to make mere anthropological fictions of them.

---

122. This reading of the notion of *Gedakenexperiment* was used by T. Marchaisse to describe François Jullien's work on China (Jullien and Marchaisse 2000: 71).

Anti-Narcissus, then, cannot be said to be either a study in "primitive mentality" or an analysis of indigenous "cognitive processes": its object is less the mode of indigenous thought than the objects of this thought—the possible world projected by its concepts. Nor is it an ethnosociological essay about a particular worldview. This is, first of all, because there is no pre-prepared world to be seen; no world before vision, or better, no world prior to the division between the visible and the invisible that would institute the horizon of thought. But this is also because treating ideas as concepts is to decline to explicate them in terms of that very transcendent notion of (ecological, economic, political, or whatever) context in order, instead, to privilege the immanent notion of the problem. Finally, there is no question here of an interpretation of Amerindian thinking; this is, again, an experimentation with it, and thus also with our own. To recall Roy Wagner one last time: "Every understanding of another culture is an experiment with one's own."

Let's be clear: I do not (necessarily …) think that the minds of Amerindians are the collective scene of "cognitive processes" different from those of whichever other humans. We have no need to imagine Indians as being endowed with a particular neurophysiology that takes up sheer diversity in its own way. For my part, I think they think exactly "like us." But I also think that they think, by which I mean that the concepts they have elaborated are very different from our own, and that the world these describe is therefore likewise very different from ours.[123] Where the Indians themselves are concerned, I think that they think that all humans, and, beyond them, many other nonhuman subjects think exactly "like them." But they also think that, instead of expressing a universal referential convergence, this is precisely the reason for divergences of perspective.

The image of savage thought that I am endeavoring to define is aimed neither at indigenous knowledge and its more or less true representations of reality—the "traditional knowledges" so lusted after in the global market of representations—nor at its mental categories, the "representationality" of which the cognitive sciences endlessly go on about; neither at representations,

---

123. See François Jullien on the difference between affirming the existence of different "modes of orientation in thought" and affirming the operation of "another logic" (Jullien and Marchaisse 2000: 205-207).

whether individual or collective or rational or less rational, that partially express states of things anterior and exterior to themselves, nor at cognitive processes and categories, whether universal or particular or innate or acquired, manifesting properties of a thing in the world, be it mind or society. The "objects" whose existence is being affirmed here are indigenous concepts, the worlds these constitute (and that thus express them), and the virtual ground from which they emerge.

Treating indigenous ideas as concepts entails regarding them as carrying a philosophical meaning or a potential philosophical use. It will be said, of course, that this is a thoroughly irresponsible decision, and all the more so because the Indians are not the only ones in the story who are not philosophers: the author himself, as I will emphatically stress, is not really one either. How can the notion of the concept be applied, for example, to a thinking that has apparently never deemed it necessary to peer into itself, and that instead redirects us to the fluent, multicolored schematism of symbol, figure, and collective representation rather than the rigorous architecture of conceptual reason? Doesn't a widely recognized psychological and historical abyss prevent it, a "decisive rupture" between, on the one hand, the *bricoleur* and his signs and, on the other, the engineer and his concepts? (L.-S. 1966) Between generic human mythopoesis and the particular universe of Occidental rationality (Vernant 1996[1966]: 229), or the paradigmatic transcendence of the figure and the syntagmatic immanence of the concept (D. G. 1994)?

I retain serious doubts about all these contrasts, which more or less emanate from Hegel. Moreover, there are certain internal, nonphilosophical reasons that provided me the impetus to speak of the concept. The first stems from my decision to put indigenous ideas on the same plane as anthropological ideas.

This book began with the declaration that anthropological theories are in strict continuity with the intellectual pragmatics of the collectives such theories take as their object. The experiment proposed here thus begins by affirming the equivalence, in principle, of anthropological and indigenous discourse, with the same going for their "reciprocal presupposition" of each other, which accede as such to existence only by entering into relation with knowledge. Anthropological concepts actualize this relation, which is why they are entirely relational—but more in their expression than in their content. They are not, per the cognitivist dream, veridical reflections of indigenous culture; nor are they illusory projections of the culture of the anthropologist, as per the constructionist nightmare. What these concepts reflect is a certain relation of intelligibility between two cultures, and what they project is two cultures as their specific presuppositions. In this, they are doubly uprooting: they are like vectors that always point toward the other side, transcontextual interfaces whose function is to represent, in the diplomatic sense of the term, the Other at the core of the Same ... here as much as there.

The origin and relational function of anthropological concepts are usually indicated by the exotic words attached to them: *mana*, *totem*, *kula*, *potlatch*, *tabu*, *gumsa/gumlao*, and so on. Other, no less authentic concepts instead bear the etymological signature of the analogies the discipline has drawn between the discipline's own tradition and those that have been its objects; in this case, gift, sacrifice, kinship, person, and so on. A last group, finally, are the neologisms invented either as attempts to generalize the conceptual apparatuses of certain peoples—animism, opposition, segmentarity, restricted exchange, shizmogenesis—or, inversely and more problematically, that turn them, within the interior of a certain theoretical economy, into diffuse notions in our own tradition, and thus universalizes them: gender, the incest prohibition, the symbol, culture, etc.[124]

In the end, doesn't the inventiveness of anthropology reside there, in this relational synergy between the conceptions and practices of the worlds of its "subject" and "object?" Recognizing that might, among other things, go some way toward alleviating the inferiority complex the discipline manifests before the hard sciences. "The description of the *kula*," as Latour remarked,

is on a par with that of the black holes. The complex systems of social alliances are as imaginative as the complex evolutionary scenarios conceived for the selfish genes. Understanding the theology of Australian Aborigines is as important as charting the great undersea rifts. The Trobriand land tenure system is as interesting a scientific objective as polar icecap drilling. If we talk about what matters in a

124. On the signatures particular to philosophical and scientific ideas, and the baptism of concepts, see D. G. 1994: 8, 23-24.

definition of a science—innovation in the agencies that furnish our world—anthropology may very well be near the top of the disciplinary pecking order. (1996: 5)

The analogy drawn here between indigenous concepts and the objects of the natural sciences is not only possible, but even necessary: we should be capable of producing a scientific description of indigenous practices as though they were objects in the world, or, even better, so that they could be objects of the world. (The scientific objects of Latour are everything but indifferent entities that patiently await our description.) Another possible strategy would be to compare, as Horton has, indigenous conceptions and scientific theories by means of what he calls the "similarity thesis" (1993: 348-354). Yet another is the one I am proposing here. It seems to me that anthropology has always been far too obsessed with its relation to "Science"—is it, could it be, and should it be science?—but also, more profoundly (and herein lies the real problem) in relation to the conceptions of the people it studies, whether in order to disqualify them as errors, dreams, or illusions and then offer a scientific explanation of why those "others" were never able to account for themselves scientifically, or to dignify them by making them basically assimilable to science, the fruits of one and the same will to knowledge consubstantial with all humanity, in which case we are back to Horton's similarity thesis or Lévi-Strauss' science of the concrete (Latour 1993: 97-98). Yet this image of science as the gold standard of thought is not the only ground on which to conceive our relationship with the intellectual activity of peoples foreign to the Western tradition.

We need to imagine a different analogy than Latour's, along with a similarity other than Horton's. An analogy that, in lieu of considering indigenous conceptions as entities similar to black holes or tectonic plates, would make them something of the order of the Cogito or the monad. We could say in this respect that the Melanesian concept of the person as a "dividual" (Strathern 1988) is just as imaginative as Locke's possessive individualism, that deciphering "the philosophy of Indian chiefdom" (Clastres 1987[1962]) is of as much importance as understanding the Hegelian doctrine of the state, that Māori cosmology is comparable to the Eleatic paradoxes and Kantian antinomies (Schrempp 2002), and Amazonian perspectivism a philosophical objective as

191

interesting as Leibniz's system…. And if the question is to know exactly what is important to evaluate in a philosophy—its capacity to create new concepts—then anthropology, without at all pretending to replace philosophy, proves itself to be a powerful philosophical instrument capable of expanding the still excessively ethnocentric horizons of "our" philosophy, and liberating us, in the same move, from so-called "philosophical" anthropology. Let's not forget Tim Ingold's powerful definition (1992: 696) of anthropology as "philosophy with the people in." Although what Ingold means here is "ordinary people" (everyday people or common mortals), he is also playing on the political sense of a "people." A philosophy, then, with all the people(s) in: the possibility of philosophical activity maintaining a relationship with the "non-philosophy"—the life—of the other peoples inhabiting the planet and not just our own, and where the "uncommon" people are those outside our sphere of "commun-ication." If real philosophy abounds in imaginary savages, anthropological geophilosophy makes imaginary philosophy with real savages—"imaginary gardens with real toads in them," as Marianne Moore once said. And toads, as we know, often turn out to be princes. But you had better know how to kiss them….

Note the incisive displacement occurring in this paraphrase. What concerns us is not, or not only, the anthropological description of the *kula*—of the Melanesian form of sociality—but the *kula* as a Melanesian description, of "sociality" as an anthropological form. Or it would be a matter, to take another example, of understanding "Australian theology," but in this case as something that itself constitutes a *dispositif* of understanding. In this way, the complex systems of alliance or of possessing the earth would be regarded as inventions issuing from the indigenous sociological imagination. Of course the *kula* will always have to be described as a description, Aboriginal religion understood as an understanding, and the indigenous imagination imagined: such conceptions must be transformed into concepts, by extracting concepts from them and then presenting these. And a concept is a complex relation between conceptions, an assemblage [*agencement*] of preconceptual intuitions. Where anthropology is concerned, the conceptions thereby related comprise, before all else, those of the anthropologist and the indigenous such that there is a relation of relations. Indigenous concepts are the concepts of the anthropologist. And by design, quite naturally.

If cannibalism is an image of thought and the enemy a conceptual persona, all that remains is to write a chapter of Deleuzo-Guattarian geophilosophy. A prototypical expression of the other in the Occidental tradition is the figure of *the friend*. The friend is an other, but the other as a moment of the self. If I were to define myself as the friend of the friend, this would only be because the friend, per Aristotle's well-known definition, is another oneself. Ego is there from the outset, with the friend being the Other-condition retroactively projected onto the conditioned form of the subject. As François Wolff has observed, this definition implies a theory where "every relation to the other, and consequently every form of friendship, has its foundation in the relation of each man with himself" (2000: 169). The social bond presumes self-relation as its origin and model.

But the Friend does not only found a certain anthropology. When the historico-political conditions of the constitution of Greek philosophy are considered, the Friend turns out to be indissociable from a certain relationship to truth: it is "a presence that is intrinsic to thought, a condition of possibility of thought itself, a living category, a transcendental lived reality" (D. G. 1995: 3). The Friend is, in short, what Deleuze and Guattari call a conceptual persona, the schematism of the Other proper to the concept. Philosophy requires the friend, and *philia* is the element of knowledge.

Yet the liminal problem raised by every attempt at identifying an Amerindian equivalent to "our philosophy" is that of knowing how to think a world constituted by the Enemy as transcendental determination. Not the friend-rival of Greek philosophy but *the immanence of the enemy* specific to Amerindian cosmopraxis, where intimacy is not the simple privative complement of friendship (or some negative facticity) but a *de jure* structure of thought that defines another relation to knowledge and another regime of truth: cannibalism, perspectivism, multinaturalism. If the Deleuzian Other is the very concept of the point of view, what would a world constituted by the point of view of the enemy as transcendental determination be? Animism taken to its final conclusion—as only the Indians know how to do—is not only a perspectivism but an "enemyism."

All this brings us back to the following "impossible" question: what happens when one takes indigenous thought seriously? When the anthropologist's goal ceases to be its explanation, interpretation, contextualization, or rationalization and shifts to using it, drawing out its consequences, and verifying the effects it can produce in our own thought? What is it that indigenous thought thinks? Think, I mean, without thinking that what (we think) the other thinks is "only apparently irrational" or, worse still, naturally reasonable, but to think this other thought outside those alternatives, as something entirely foreign to that old game.

To start with, taking it seriously means not neutralizing it—it means bracketing, for example, the question of whether and how such thought might illustrate human cognitive universals, explain modes of transmission of socially-determined knowledge, express a culturally particular worldview, functionally validate a given distribution of political power, or confirm other of the myriad ways that the others' thought is neutralized. It means suspending such questions or at least avoiding isolating anthropology by means of them; it means deciding, for example, to simply think the other's thought as an actualization of unsuspected virtualities of thought.[125]

Would taking it seriously mean, then, "believing" what the Indians say, or regarding their thought as the expression of some truth about the world? Here we have yet another poorly formulated question. To believe or not believe in a body of thought first requires taking it as a system of beliefs. But those problems that are truly anthropological are posed neither in the psychological terms of belief nor the logical terms of truth; alien thought should be taken neither for an opinion, which is the only possible object of belief or disbelief, nor as a group of propositions, the

---

125. This is basically what Godfrey Lienhardt said about the exercise, incumbent on anthropology, of mediating between indigenous "habits of thought" and those of our own society: "in doing [this], it is not finally some mysterious 'primitive philosophy' that we are exploring, but the further potentialities of our thought and language" (Asad 1986: 158-159).

equivalent for judgments about truth. We are quite familiar with all the damage anthropology does by conceiving indigenous people's relation to their discourse in terms of belief—culture becomes, in that event, a species of theological dogmatism—and by treating it as an opinion or a body of propositions, which makes it the object of an epistemic teratology obsessed with error, madness, illusion, and ideology. "Belief," as Latour observed, "is not a state of mind but a result of relationships among people; we have known this since Montaigne." (2010: 2)

If Amerindian indigenous thought is not to be described as belief, it should no more be related to in the mode of belief, whether by suggesting with goodwill that it contains a "wealth of allegorical truth" (an allegory that would be social for the Durkheimians, and natural for the old American school of cultural materialism) or, even worse, by imagining it to be the bearer of some inborn esoteric science divining the inner, ultimate essence of things. "An anthropology that [...] reduces meaning to belief, dogma, and certainty, is forced into the trap of having to believe either the native meanings or our own" (Wagner 1981: 30). The plane of "meaning"—sense, signification, significance—is not populated with psychological beliefs or logical propositions, and there is only a "wealth" of something other than truths. Neither a form of *doxa* nor a figure of logic (neither an opinion nor a proposition), indigenous thought should be taken—it we truly want to take it *seriously*—as a practice of sense: as a self-reflexive apparatus for the production of concepts, of "symbols that represent themselves."

Refusing to put the question in terms of belief seems to me a crucial aspect of the anthropological decision. In order to emphasize it, we will resume our discussion of the Deleuzian Other (D. 1990a; D. G. 1994). The other is the expression of a possible world, but this world must always, in the ordinary course of social interaction, be actualized by Ego: the implication of the possible in the other is explicated by an "I." This entails the possible passing through a process of verification that dissipates its structure in entropic fashion. When I develop a world expressed by the other, I do so in order to validate its reality and penetrate it, or else to refute it as unreal. This explication is what puts the element of belief into play. By describing this process, Deleuze indicates the limit condition of the determination of the concept of the Other....

These relations of development, which form our commonalities as well as our disagreements with the other, also dissolve its structure and reduce it either to the status of an object or to the status of a subject. That is why, in order to grasp the other as such, we were right to insist upon special conditions of experience, however artificial—namely, the moment at which the expressed has (for us) no existence apart from that which expresses it: the Other as the expression of a possible world. (D. 1994: 260-61)

… and he concludes by recalling a fundamental maxim of his mode of reflection:

The rule invoked earlier—not to be explicated too much—meant, above all, not to explicate oneself too much with the other, not to explicate the other too much, but to maintain one's implicit values and multiply one's own world by populating it with all those expresseds that do not exist apart from their expressions. (D. 1994: 261)

Anthropology would profit from heeding this lesson. Keeping the values of the Other implicit does not mean celebrating whatever transcendent mystery it supposedly keeps enclosed in itself. It consists in refusing to actualize the possibles expressed by indigenous thought, making a decision to maintain them, infinitely, as possibles—neither derealizing them as fantasies of the other nor fantasizing that they are actual for us. The anthropological experiment, in that event, depends on the formal internalization of those specific and artificial conditions Deleuze spoke of: the moment the world of the other is no longer thought to exist outside its expression, it transforms into an eternal condition, which is to say one internal to the anthropological relation, which *realizes* this possible qua *virtual*. If there is something that *de jure* belongs to anthropology, it is not the task of explaining the world of the other but that of multiplying our world, "populating it with all these expresseds that do not exist outside their expressions." For we cannot think *like* Indians; at most, we can think *with* them. And on this point, (to attempt, but of course just for a moment, to think "like them"), it should be said that if there is a clear message in Amerindian perspectivism, it is that one should never try to actualize the world that is expressed in the gaze of the other.

196

Chapter Thirteen

Becomings of Structuralism

This book's question has often been the status of structuralism, and for good reason. Lévi-Strauss' structuralism ought to be understood as a structural transformation of Amerindian thought—the result of an inflection sustained by the latter inasmuch as it was amenable to being filtered through problems and concepts characteristic of Occidental *logopoiesis* (the same and the other, the continuous and the discrete, the sensible and the intelligible, nature and culture…), according to a movement of controlled equivocation and unstable equilibrium incessantly fertilized by corrupting translations. I will thus reprise my thesis from the first chapter concerning the intrinsically translational condition of anthropology, a discourse conceptually codetermined by the discourse about which it discourses. It would be inadvisable to consider Lévi-Strauss' anthropology without accounting for the conditions of its constitution, which is to say his contact with Saussurean linguistics or d'Arcy Thompson's morphology as well as the formative experience of living among Amerindian peoples, as much in the field as the library. "The Amerindian foundations of structuralism," to employ Anne-Christine Taylor's formula again, can be ignored only at the cost of losing a dimension vital for understanding Lévi-Strauss' work in its integrality. Which does not at all mean that the issue of the validity of its problems and concepts can be restricted to considerations of some "cultural atmosphere," however vast. No, Lévi-Strauss' work is on the contrary the moment when Amerindian thought casts its roll of the dice: through the good offices of its great conceptual mediator, it exceeds its own context and proves itself capable of inciting thought in the other, in everyone who, Persian or French, is prepared to think—nothing more, nothing less.

The big question opened up by the current reevaluation of the intellectual heritage of Lévi-Strauss is that of deciding if structuralism is one or multiple—or, to employ one of the great Lévi-Straussian dichotomies, continuous or discontinuous. Without ceasing to be in agreement with the interpreters who are in agreement with Lévi-Strauss about his work having a single inspiration and method, I see the theoretical personality of structuralism and its author as being divided into two, eternally unequal—but not opposed—twins: a cultural hero and a deceiver; a persona, on the one hand, of mediation (who just as much establishes order and the discrete) and, on the other, a counter-persona of separation (who is also at the same time the master of chromaticism and disorder). There really are two structuralisms. But as Lévi-Strauss himself showed, two is always more than two.

We are beginning to grasp that Lévi-Strauss' oeuvre is in active collaboration (and was so from its very beginning) with its future subversions. We can take as an example the idea that structural anthropology employs "a transformational rather than fluxional method." (See page 147) This became, throughout Lévi-Strauss' work, a true enough approximation, as this key concept of transformation was itself submitted to a progressive transformation … first, by gaining the upper hand over structure and, second, by gradually getting redressed in an outfit that is more and more analogical, and closer to dynamic fluxes than algebraic permutations. This conceptual transition is itself chromatic, being composed of small displacements and brief returns to the background, but its guiding thread is clear. The curve's point of inflection can be located, it seems to me, somewhere between the first and second volumes of the *Mythologiques*. A rather curious footnote in *From Honey to Ashes* is probably the first explicit indication of this change:

> Leach has accused me of [...] using exclusively binary patterns. As if the very notion of the transformation of which I make constant use and which I borrowed in the first instance from d'Arcy Wentworth Thompson were not entirely dependent on analogy... (1973: 90, n. 12)

An interview given over twenty years later sees Lévi-Strauss confirming that the notion derives not from logic or linguistics but from the great naturalist d'Arcy W. Thompson as well as, implicitly, Goethe and Dürer (Lévi-Strauss and Éribon 1991: 113-14). Transformation transforms into an aesthetic and dynamic—not logical and algebraic—operation. And with that, the opposition between the central conceptual paradigms of the classic phase of structuralism—{totemism, myth, discontinuity} vs. {sacrifice, ritual, continuity}—becomes far more fluid and unstable than what their author will nonetheless continue saying about it in certain passages from the later phase of his work, such as the celebrated discussion of the myth-ritual opposition found in the "Finale" of *The Naked Man.*

The parting of the waters is clearly located between, on one side, the finite algebra that was appropriate for the contents of kinship and, on the other, the intensive form of myth:

> The problem raised in *Elementary Structures of Kinship* was directly related to algebra and the theory of groups and substitutions. The problems raised by mythology seem impossible to dissociate from the aesthetic forms in which they are objectified. Now these forms are both continuous and discontinuous.... (Lévi-Strauss and Éribon 1991: 137-38)

We can draw the conclusion that the structuralist notion of transformation underwent a double, at once historical and structural, transformation—in truth, a single but complex transformation, a double twist that transformed it into a simultaneously "historical" and "structural" operation. This change owed much to the then-novel influence of mathematical innovations, like those of Thom and Petitot, exercised on Lévi-Strauss; but of far greater importance, I believe, was the fact that the kind of object his anthropology privileged changed. After getting an algebraic-combinatory figuration in the early work, transformation is progressively deformed and self-dephased, and ends up becoming a figure whose characteristics are more topological and dynamic than they were in that first draft. The borders between syntactical permutation and semantic innovation, logical displacement and morphogenetic condensation are rendered more torturous, contested, and complicated—in effect, more fractal. The opposition between form and force (between transformations and fluxions) loses its contours and in a certain way is weakened.

This does not mean that Lévi-Strauss emphasizes this change, or goes back on it, apart from his reflections on the subject of different problems treated by structural method. On the contrary, his tendency was always to emphasize "the continuity of the program I have been pursuing since I wrote *The Elementary Structures of Kinship*" (L.-S. 1969: 9). Continuity being, if there is one, an ambivalent notion in the vocabulary of structuralism.

Now it should be obvious that Lévi-Strauss was right; it would be a little ridiculous to correct him on what he had to say about himself. But the French master's insistence on the unity of inspiration underlying his work should not prevent us from proposing, as good structuralists would, that he be read in the key of continuity; less, though, in order to insist on unequivocal breaks or ruptures in his work than to suggest a complex coexistence or even intensive superposition of the "states" of structural discourse.

The discontinuities in the structuralist project could be distributed along two classic dimensions: on an axis of successions, following the idea that Lévi-Strauss' oeuvre is composed of successive phases; and on an axis of coexistences, following the idea that it enunciates a double discourse, and describes a double movement. The two discontinuities would then coexist to the extent that the oeuvre's *moments* can be distinguished on the basis of the importance each grants to two *movements* opposed in counterpoint throughout it.

We can start with diachrony, with the argument that structuralism is just like totemism: it never existed. Or to be more precise, like totemism, its mode of existence is not that of substances, but differences. In this case, the difference is, as the commentaries often remark, between the first of Lévi-Strauss' phases, that of the 1949 *Elementary Structures of Kinship*, which could be called prestructuralist, and a second, poststructuralist phase associated with the 1964-1971 *Mythologiques* and the three monographs that follow—1979's *The Way of The Masks*, 1985's *The Jealous Potter*, and the late, 1991 text *The Story of Lynx*.

This second phase can be considered poststructuralist because the brief, indisputably "structuralist" moment of the pair of studies on totemism precede it; books Lévi-Strauss himself described as constituting a pause—a discontinuity—between *The Elementary Structures* and the *Mythologiques*. These 1962 texts are where Lévi-Strauss identifies savage thought (in other words, the concrete conditions of human semiosis) with a gigantic, systematic enterprise of arranging the world, and also raises totemism, which had until then been the emblem of primitive irrationality, to the stature of the paragon of all rational activity. It is at this moment in the oeuvre that a certain malicious judgment of Deleuze and Guattari seems most applicable: "Structuralism represents a great revolution; the whole world becomes more rational" (1987: 237).

◊ In effect, it would be possible to raise an objection to *The Savage Mind* similar to the one Deleuze made against critical philosophy, which is that the Kantian transcendental field is traced from the empirical form of representation, on account of having been constructed through a sort of retrospective projection of the conditioned onto the condition. In Lévi-Strauss' case, the savage mind could be regarded as having been traced from the most rationalist form of domestic thought—science ("there are two distinct modes of scientific thought" [L.-S. 1966: 15])—even though it would have been necessary, on the contrary, to construct the concept of a properly savage thought *not at all resembling* its domesticated version (domesticated, it should be recalled, "for the purpose of yielding a return" (LS 1966: 219).[126] But one could also, in a more conciliatory spirit, entertain the idea that with structuralism, the world does not become more rational unless the rational at the same time becomes something else … something more worldly, perhaps, in the sense of in-the world and popular. But also more aesthetic, and less utilitarian and profitable.

The idea that *The Elementary Structures of Kinship* is a prestructuralist book should be understood, obviously, with reference to the late works of Lévi-Strauss, but will all the same have to be approached with surgical delicacy. In any case, I think that anthropologists of the caliber of David Schneider or Louis Dumont were right to categorize the 1949 text in this way, organized as

126. Deleuze (1974) reminds us that for Spinoza, the difference "between a racehorse and a draft horse [...] can perhaps be thought as greater than the difference between a draft horse and an ox."

it is around two of the founding dichotomies of the human sciences: the individual and society, on the one hand—the problem of social integration and totalization—and, on the other, Nature and Culture, the problem of instinct and institution. In other words, at the heart of *The Structures* lies the difference between the Enlightenment and Romanticism—between Hobbes and Herder, that is, or if more recent eponyms would be preferable, between Durkheim and Boas.[127] In his first great work, Lévi-Strauss' focus is the consummate anthropological problem of hominization: the emergence of the synthesis of culture as the transcendence of nature. And the "group," or Society, is maintained as the transcendental subject and final cause of every one of the phenomena under consideration. At least, of course, until the book's final chapter, when all of that, as Maniglier has emphasized, is suddenly dissolved into contingency:

> The multiple rules prohibiting or prescribing certain types of spouse, and the prohibition of incest, which embodies them all, become clear as soon as one grants that society must exist. But society might not have been. (L.-S. 1969: 490)

What follows is the great conclusive development in which it is at once established that society is coextensive with symbolic thought (and not its antecendent cause or *raison d'être*), that the sociology of kinship is a subdivision of semiology (every exchange is an exchange of signs; that is, of perspectives), and that all human order contains in itself a permanent impetus toward counter-order. These latter statements mark the appearance, still surreptitious, of what could be called Lévi-Strauss' other, second voice, the moment when the sociology of kinship begins to give way to an "anti-sociology,"[128] which is to say a cosmopolitical economy—to the regime, in other words, of the Amerindian plane of immanence that will be drawn in the *Mythologiques*.

---

127. Mediating between these polarities, naturally, is Rousseau, that philosophical *trickster*, whom Lévi-Strauss did not at all by chance choose for his patron saint.

128. "[We should] give up the idea that *The Elementary Structures* is a great work of sociology and instead acknowledge that it is the very dissolution of sociology" (Maniglier, 2005b: 768).

For it is with the *Mythologiques* that the inversion of the hierarchy between these voices is completed—or better, almost completed; it was probably not truly necessary to go any further: to take up Mauss' formula again, Lévi-Strauss was a Moses looking at the Promised Land…. The notion of society sees itself disinvested from in favor of a systematic focus on intersocietal narrative transformations; the Nature/Culture opposition ceases to be a universal (objective or subjective) anthropological condition and becomes a mythic theme internal to indigenous thought, a theme whose ambivalent status in said thought only deepens from volume to volume of the series; and those algebriform objects called "structures" assume more fluid contours, drifting, as we saw, toward an analogical notion of transformation.[129] And finally, instead of forming discretely distributed combinatory totalities having a concomitant variation and being in relational tension with socioethnographic *realia*, the relations constituting Amerindian myths evince, in exemplary fashion, the very principles of "connection and heterogeneity," "multiplicity," "asignifying rupture," and "cartography" that Deleuze and Guattari counterpose to structural models in the name of the rhizome—the concept supposed to have been anti-structure's proper name, and that became the battle-cry of poststructuralism.

The demonstrative itinerary of the *Mythologiques* is effectively that of a generalized heterogeneous transversality wherein the myth of one people transforms another's ritual and the technics of a third, the social organization of one is the body-painting of another (a.k.a., how to shuttle between cosmology and cosmetology without leaving politics), and the geometric curve of the Earth of mythology is constantly short-circuited by its geological porosity … on account of which the transformations appear to leap distant points on the Amerindian continent, spurting up here and there like isolated eruptions of a subterranean lava-sea.[130]

---

129. The word "structure" itself is put into a regime of continuous variation, cohabiting without big semantic distinctions with "schema," "system," "armature," and the like. See for example the inventive legends and diagrams that adorn the *Mythologiques*.

130. One of the most interesting paradoxes of the Panamerindian mythic system is the co-presence of the dense, connective metonymy of the transformational network and certain "effects of action at a distance," such as those made when the stories of Central Brazilian peoples reappear among Oregon and Washington tribes.

Pierre Clastres said that structuralism was "a sociology without society"; if this is accurate—and for Clastres, it was a reproach—then we encounter in the *Mythologiques* a structuralism without structure, which for me is a compliment. Anyone inclined to take the long trek that leads from *The Raw and The Cooked* to *The Story of Lynx* will notice that the Amerindian mythology charted in the series does not grow from a tree but a rhizome: it is a gigantic canvas with neither center nor origin, a collective and immemorial mega-assemblage of enunciation arranged in a "hyper-space" (L.-S. 1979: 105) endlessly traversed by "semiotic flows, material flows, and social flows" (D. G. 1987: 22-3); a rhizomatic network shot through with diverse lines of structuration but that is, in its interminable multiplicity and radical historical contingency, irreducible to a unifying law and impossible to represent via an arborescent structure. There exist innumerable structures *in* Amerindian myths, but there is not a (single) structure *of* Amerindian myth. No "elementary structures of mythology."

In the end, Amerindian mythology is an open multiplicity or multiplicity at n-1—or better still, we could say, at M-1, in homage to the reference myth M1, the Bororo myth that, as we discover very early on in *The Raw and The Cooked*, was only an *inverted, weakened* version of the Gé myths that follow it (M7-12). The reference myth is thus "any myth," a myth "without references," an M-1, like all myth. For every myth is a version of another, which in turn opens to a third and fourth myth, and the *n*-1 myths of indigenous America neither express an origin nor point to a destiny: they are without reference. A discourse on origins, myth is nonetheless precisely that which throws off the origin. The reference "myth" gives way to the sense of myth, to myth as sense machine: to myth as an instrument for converting one code to another, for projecting one problem onto an analogous problem, and for making "reference circulate" (as Latour would say), anagrammatically counter-effectuating sense.

Translation has been equally at issue in the present book. The first approach Lévi-Strauss outlines to the concept of myth emphasizes its full translatability: "Myth is the part of language where the formula *tradutore, tradittore* reaches its lowest truth value" (L.-S. 1963: 210). In *The Naked Man*, the definition is expanded, and transferred from the semantic to the pragmatic plane.

We learn at that point that far from being merely *translatable*, myth is primarily *translation*:

> Properly speaking, there is never any original: every myth is by its very nature a translation [...] it does not exist *in* a language and *in* a culture or subculture, but at their point of articulation with other languages or cultures. Therefore a myth never *belongs to its language*, but rather represents a perspective on *a different language* [...] (L.-S. 1981: 644-45).

Do we detect some Bakhtin in Lévi-Strauss...? One could say, to generalize in the characteristic manner of *A Thousand Plateaus'* authors, that "if there is language, it is fundamentally between those who do not speak the same tongue. Language is made for that, for translation, not for communication" (D. G. 1987: 430). The effectively perspectivist conception of myth in *The Naked Man* renders myth contiguous with anthropology itself, specifically with what constitutes it, as Lévi-Strauss had already remarked in 1954, as "the social science of the observed." We also know that the *Mythologiques* are "the myth of mythology." Now these two definitions in fact converge. *The discourse of structural mythology establishes the conditions for every possible anthropology.* Every anthropology is a transformation of the anthropologies that are its object, and both are always already situated at "the point of articulation of a culture with other cultures." What enables one to move from one myth to another and from one culture to another is of the same nature as what enables one to move from myth to the science of myths, and from culture to the science of culture. (I am generalizing one of Maniglier's core arguments [2000].) Transversality with symmetry ... an unanticipated link, that is, between the *Mythologiques* and Latour and Stenger's principle of generalized symmetry.

If myth is translation, this is because *it is above all not representation*; for a translation is not a representation but a *transformation*. "[A] mask is not primarily what it represents but what it transforms, that is to say, what it chooses not to represent" (L.-S. 1982: 144).[131] This is what gives to the metaobject of

---

131. The ultimate reason for the approximation between myth and music in the *Mythologiques* would thus be the fundamentally nonrepresentational character of both semiotic modes.

the *Mythologiques* its properly holographic character as the mythic rhizome with which it forms a rhizome, the network that contains in each of its myths a reduced image of the Panamerican mythic system (the "unique" myth). "It is because structure is more rigorously defined as a system of transformation that it cannot be represented without making the representation part of itself" (Maniglier 2000: 238). This leads us to a reconceptualization of structure as "transformalist" or, better, *"transformationalist"*— which is to say, neither formalist à la Propp nor transformational à la Chomsky:

> A structure is therefore always in between: between two variants, between two sequences of the same myth, and even between two levels internal to the same text. [...] The unity is thus not that of a form that would repeat itself identically in one variant or another, but that of a matrix enabling one to show what makes one precisely a real transformation of the other [...], and structure is rigorously coextensive with its actualizations. This is why Lévi-Strauss insists on the obstinately neglected difference between structuralism and formalism (Maniglier, op cit 234-235).[132]

A structuralism without structures? At least a structuralism animated by another notion of structure much closer to a rhizome than the kind of structure *A Thousand Plateaus* opposes to it—a notion, in truth, that had always been present in Lévi-Strauss' work. Or perhaps we should say that there are two different ways Lévi-Strauss employs the concept of structure: as a principle, on the one hand, of transcendental unification or formal law of invariance, and as an operator of divergence and modulator of continuous variation (of the variation of variation), on the other. In other words, structure both as a closed grammatical combinatory and as an open differential multiplicity.

---

132. This is why the quest for a "structure of myth" that would be a closed syntagmatic object is perfectly meaningless. As Maniglier's observation clearly shows (just as Almeida's [2008] does even more definitively), the consummate structural transformation, the canonical formula of myth, does not allow for a definition of the "internal structure" of a myth, since such a thing does not exist ("the principle remains the same"—see the decisive passage in Lévi-Strauss 1969: 307-10). A myth is not distinguishable from its versions, its "internal" composition has the same nature as its "external" transformations. The idea of a myth of myth is purely operational and provisional. What enables us to pass to the interior of a myth also enables us to pass from one myth to another. *Each and every myth* is a Klein bottle (L.-S. 1988: 157 et seq.).

It would be quite instructive to undertake a detailed study of what could be called the dialectic of analytic opening and closing in the *Mythologiques*, to borrow from the series one of its omnipresent motifs. If Lévi-Strauss believed he recognized a version of the anthropological problem of Nature and Culture in Amerindian mythology, it could be noted, conversely, that the dialectic of the open and closed he perceived to be at work in myth was also operant on the metamythological plane of anthropology. Because if the *Mythologiques* are indeed "the myth of mythology," then they should contain the themes developed in the myths of which they are a structural transformation; a transformation, in other words, allowing one to move from content to form and vice versa.

We saw that Lévi-Strauss often indicates that the myths he analyzes form "a closed group." The idea of *closure* sometimes appears to be consubstantial with structural analysis itself: it should, in his view, always be demonstrated that "the group closes itself," that there is always a return to the initial state of a chain of myths after a final transformation; that in truth, "the group" is closed on diverse axes. This insistence is bound up with the theme of the necessary redundancy of the language of mythical language, which is the condition for establishing mythology's grammar (as Lévi-Strauss sometimes enjoys casting his enterprise). And, finally, his avowed antipathy to the "open work" is well known.

It nonetheless happens that the proliferation of demonstrations of closure ends up giving the apparently paradoxical impression that there is a theoretically indefinite, or open, number of closed structures. The structures are closed, but both their number and the ways in which they are closed is open—there is neither a structure of structures, in the sense of a final level of structural totalization, nor an *a priori* determination of the semantic axes (the codes) mobilized in structure.[133] Every group of myths is in the end located at the intersection of an indeterminate number of other groups; in each group, each myth is equally an interconnection, and in each myth…. The groups should be able to *close*, but the analyst cannot allow them to become *locked*:

---

133. The nonexistence of any metastructure is declared as early as "Introduction to the Work of Marcel Mauss" and "The Notion of Structure in Ethnology." On the indetermination of the principles of the semantic axes of a mythic system, see the maxim in *The Savage Mind* that states that "the principle of a classification is never postulated."

[I]t is in the nature of any myth or group of myths to refuse to be treated as a closed entity: there inevitably comes a point during the analysis when a problem arises which cannot be solved except by breaking through the boundaries that the analysis has prescribed for itself. (L.-S. 1981: 602)[134]

Moreover and above all, the importance granted to the imperative of closure undergoes a strong relativization in diverse places in Lévi-Strauss' work that emphasizes the opposite: the interminable character of analysis, the spiral movement of transformations, dynamic disequilibrium, dissymmetry, structures laterally coopting each other, the plurality of levels the stories are spread over, their many supplementary dimensions, and the multiplicity and diversity of axes needed to arrange the myths…. The keyword in all of this is *disequilibrium*:

Disequilibrium is always present. (L.-S. 1973: 259)

Far from being isolated from the others, each structure conceals a disequilibrium, which can only be compensated for through recourse to some term borrowed from the adjacent structure. (L.-S. 1979: 358)

Even when the structure, in order to overcome some disequilibrium, changes or becomes more complex, it can never do so without creating some new disequilibrium on a different level. We observe once again that it is the unavoidable dissymmetry of the structure which gives it its power to create myth, which is nothing else but an attempt to correct or mask this inherent dissymmetry. (L.-S. 1979: 489)

As in South America, a condition of dynamic disequilibrium is visible at the center of a group of transformations. (L.-S. 1981: 103)

Such disequilibrium is not a simple formal property of mythology responding to the transformability or translatability of myth but, as we will soon see, a fundamental element of its content. In thinking among themselves, myths think *through* this disequilibrium itself, which is the very "disparity" of the "being of the

---

134. Note, in the same way indicated above in note 133, how Lévi-Strauss barely distinguishes between a "myth" and a "group of myths."

world" (L.-S. 1981: 603). Myths contain their own mythology or "immanent" theory, and it affirms

> an initial asymmetry, which shows itself in a variety of ways according to the perspective from which it is being apprehended: between the high and the low, the sky and the earth, land and water, the near and the far, left and right, male and female, etc. This inherent disparity of the world sets mythic speculation in motion, but it does so because, on the hither side of thought, it conditions the existence of every object of thought. (L.-S. 1981: 603)

Perpetual disequilibrium cuts through myth, then the myth of mythology, and finally reverberates through the whole of structuralism. We have already seen that the duality between the notions of structure as grammatical combinatory and as open differential multiplicity appears only in a very late phase of Lévi-Strauss. In truth, though, it traverses the entirety of his work; it is just the relative weight accorded to each of these conceptions that changes: the first of them predominates in *The Elementary Structures*, and the second attains preeminence in the *Mythologiques*.

Let's take a step back, or rather, connect this diachronic step to the synchronic discontinuity mentioned above. From very early on, Lévi-Strauss harbors an important poststructuralist subtext or counter-text. (If Lévi-Strauss is not the last prestructuralist—far from it, sorry—he should truly be taken as the first poststructuralist.) The supposed predilection of structuralism for symmetric, equipollent, discrete, dual, and reversible oppositions (such as those of the classic schema of totemism) is first refuted by the criticism, astonishing even today, of the concept of dualist organization made in the 1956 article of nearly the same name. Ternarism, asymmetry, and continuity are conceived there as being anterior to binarism, symmetry, and discontinuity. Then we have the canonical formula of myth, which comes as disconcertingly early, and that would seem to be everything desired—except something symmetric and reversible. Just as notable, finally, is the fact that Lévi-Strauss closes both of the two phases of the *Mythologiques* (the "Finale" of *The Naked Man* and *The Story of Lynx*) by expressing his reservations about the feasibility of accounting for mythic transformations with the vocabulary of extensional logic (L.-S. 1981: 635; 1995: 185).

Above all, it is surely not by chance that Lévi-Strauss' final two mythological books are developments of the two figures of unstable dualism: *The Jealous Potter* (1988) exhaustively illustrates the canonical formula, and *The Story of Lynx* is focused on dynamic instability—"perpetual disequilibrium," an expression that first appears in *The Elementary Structures* in order to describe the avuncular marriage of the Tupi—both of them being Amerindian cosmosociological dualities. Which leads me to presume that we are faced with the same initial intuition—the same virtual structure, if you will—of which the canonic formula (which predeconstructs totemic analogism of the A:B::C:D kind) and dynamic dualism (which destabilizes the static parity of binary oppositions) would only be two privileged expressions or actualizations. There are doubtlessly others; perhaps some "dead, pale, or obscure moons" in the firmament of structures, perhaps another firmament that would be less closed and more moving, more wavelike and vibratory—a hypostructural firmament demanding, so to speak, a subquantum structuralism. In any event, anthropologists have always practiced a kind of string theory—er, I mean, a theory of relations.

First of all, we have that twisted monument to mathematical perversity known as the canonical formula. Instead of confronting us with a simple opposition between totemic metaphor and sacrificial metonymy, it installs us from the outset in the equivalence between metaphoric and metonymic relations, via the twist that passes from metaphor to metonymy and back (L.-S. 1973: 248): a "double" or "supernumerary twist" which is in fact nothing other than structural transformation pure and simple (or rather, hybrid and complex): "the relation of disequilibrium [...] inherent in mythical transformations" (L.-S. 1987: 5) The asymmetric conversions between literal and figurative sense, term and function, container and contained, the continuous and the discontinuous, the system and its exterior are all themes present in both the entirety of Lévi-Strauss' analyses of mythology and what lies beyond them (2001). We dwelt in the last chapters on the Deleuzian concept of becoming, without truly knowing where it would lead us if it was forced, transversally of course, against the notions of classic structuralism. We now begin to see, however, that the canonical formula is an approximate translation, spoken with a cute, strangely inflected accent in a foreign language, an almost suprasegmentary dimension of Lévi-Strauss' theoretical discourse; or rather, a premonitory anticipation of the generality of that instantaneous movement-in-place that Deleuze will call becoming. *Becoming is a double twist.*

There is also, second, the dualism in dynamic or perpetual disequilibrium at the heart of *The Story of Lynx*. What it reveals is a conceptual movement whereby Amerindian myth accedes to what could be called its properly speculative moment. In effect, Lévi-Strauss shows how disequilibrium changes from myth's form to its content; or, in other words, how disequilibrium goes from being condition to theme, how an unconscious schema becomes a "profound inspiration":

> What, indeed, is the underlying inspiration for these myths? [...] These myths represent the progressive organization of the world and of society in the form of a series of bipartitions but without the resulting parts at each stage ever being truly equal. [...] The proper functioning of this system depends on this dynamic disequilibrium, for without it this system would at all times be in danger of falling into a state of inertia. What these myths implicitly proclaim is that the poles between which natural phenomena and social life are organized—such as sky and earth, fire and water, above and below, Indians and non-Indians, fellow citizens and strangers—could never be twins. The mind attempts to join them without succeeding at establishing parity between them. This is because it is these cascading differential gaps, such as mythical thought conceives them, that set in motion the machine of the universe. (L.-S. 1995: 63)

Myths, by thinking among themselves, think themselves as such, via a movement that, if it makes their "reflection" a good one—which is to say if it transforms itself—cannot escape the disequilibrium thus reflected. The imperfect duality around which Lévi-Strauss' last great analysis of myth turns—the twinhood that is "the key to the whole system"—is the realized expression of this self-propelling asymmetry. In the end, we learn from the dynamic disequilibrium of *The Story of Lynx* that the true duality of interest to structuralism is not the dialectical combat between nature and culture but the intensive, interminable difference between

211

unequal twins. The twins of *The Story of Lynx* are at once the key and the cipher [*la chiffre*], the password of Amerindian mythology and sociology. A (numerical) cipher, meaning: the fundamental disparity of the dyad, opposition as the inferior limit of difference, and the pair as a particular case of the multiple.

As Patrice Maniglier remarked about the difference between the two phases of the structuralist project:

> As much as the first moment of Lévi-Strauss' work appears to be characterized by an intense interrogation of both the problem of the passage from nature to culture and the discontinuity between the two orders—which alone would seem to Lévi-Strauss to guarantee social anthropology's specificity in the face of physical anthropology—the second moment is equally characterized by an obstinate denunciation of the constitution of humanity into a separate order.[135]

And in effect, we should consider the last paragraphs, already invoked above (page 130), of *The Elementary Structures of Kinship*, where the author observes that absolute joy, "eternally denied to social man," consists in "keeping to oneself." Let's compare this remark, which is after all still Freudian, to another that was also already cited—the one where Lévi-Strauss defines myth as the "story of the time before men and animals became distinct" (Lévi-Strauss and Éribon 1991: 139). The author adds there that humanity has never successfully resigned itself to not being in communication with the other species inhabiting the planet. Yet the nostalgia for an original communication between all species—for interspecific continuity—is not exactly the same thing as this nostalgia for a life of "keeping to oneself," itself behind the fantasy of posthumous incest—of intraspecific continuity. Very much to the contrary, I must say: the accent and meaning of what Lévi-Strauss understands to be human *counter-discourse* has changed. The second level of the anthropological discourse of structuralism surfaces.

The creative discord or tension between the two stucturalisms of Lévi-Strauss is internalized in a particularly complex way in the *Mythologiques*. We saw above that Lévi-Strauss opposed the algebra of kinship of *The Elementary Structures*, which would be completely on the side of the discrete, to the mythic dialectic

---

135. See, in the same sense, Schrempp's pioneering book (2002).

between the continuous and the discontinuous. This latter difference cannot be merely formal. For it is not only an aesthetic form of Amerindian mythology, a *mélange* of the continuous and the discontinuous, but also its philosophical content. And how, really, could a veritable structuralist separate form and content?

This is why we are forced to conclude that the *Mythologiques* are something more than an enterprise centered on the "the study of the mythic representations of the study of the passage from nature to culture," as the author modestly describes his project in *Anthropology & Myth* (L.-S. 1987b). Because as the *Mythologiques* are progressively drawn up, its author increasingly contests the relevance of a radical distinction between nature and culture, just as Maniglier observes. It would be a bit absurd to imagine that Lévi-Strauss transfers onto the Indians the same dementia he diagnoses as the fatal flaw of the West. Indeed, the *Mythologiques*, far from describing a clear, unequivocal passage between Nature and Culture, obliges their author to map a labyrinth of twisting, ambiguous pathways, transversal trails, tight alleys, obscure impasses, and even rivers that flow in both directions at once. The one way, nature-to-culture street stops where the first book of the tetralogy begins. Starting there, the seven books of the series are increasingly haunted by "mythologies of ambiguity" (*From Honey to Ashes*), "fluxional mythologies" (*The Origin of Table Manners*), by a reverse traffic going from culture to nature, zones where the two orders copenetrate, tiny intervals, brief periodicities, rhapsodic repetitions, analogic models, continuous deformations, perpetual disequilibriums, dualisms that split into semi-triadisms and shatter, without warning, into a multitude of transversal axes of transformation. Honey and sexual seduction, chromaticism and fish, the moon and androgyny, din and stench, eclipses and Klein bottles, culinary triangles that, when viewed up close, transform into Koch curves—into infinitely complex fractals, that is…. It could almost be said that the content of Amerindian mythology consists in a negation of the generative impulse of myth itself, insofar as this mythology thinks in an active fashion, and nostalgically contemplates, a continuum whose negation is in Lévi-Strauss' view the fundamental condition of thought. If Amerindian mythology possesses, as Lévi-Strauss more than once affirms, a right side and a reverse, a progressive and a regressive sense, this is also because these are the two senses or directions of structuralist discourse itself (and vice versa). The polemical distinction between myth and ritual made in the "Finale" of *The Naked Man* is in the end revealed to have been a recursive internalization of the message of myth itself: the grand Tupi myth of *The Story of Lynx* describes a trajectory identical to the one that defines the essence of every ritual (ritual and not myth, *nota bene*) as a cascading enchainment of oppositions of decreasing significance, a "desperate" attempt to make them do more than asymptotically converge and thereby capture the ultimate asymmetry of the real. As if the only myth that incontestably functions as a Lévi-Straussian myth is "the myth of mythology," by which I mean the *Mythologiques* themselves. Or not, since it must now be considered that they are not what they were long understood to be. A problem that will doubtlessly have to be returned to.

I offer as clarification a certain paragraph from the end of *The Naked Man*. On the subject of a North American myth concerning the conquest of the celestial fire, which sets in motion the utilization of an arrow-ladder that shatters the communication between sky and earth, Lévi-Strauss observes—the same author, recall, who begins *The Raw and the Cooked* with a eulogy to both the discrete and the logical enrichment achieved through the reduction of primordial contents—Lévi-Strauss observes and concludes:

> We must not forget, then, that these irreversible acts of mediation entail serious adverse consequences: first, a quantitative impoverishment of the natural order—in time, by the limit imposed on human life, and in space, by the reduction in the number of the animal species after their disastrous celestial escapade; and also a qualitative impoverishment, since by having conquered fire, the woodpecker loses most of his decorative red feathers (M729); and since the red breast acquired by the robin takes the form of an anatomical injury, resulting from his failure during the same mission. So, either through the destruction of an original harmony, or through the introduction of differential gaps which impair that harmony, humanity's accession to culture is accompanied, on the level of nature, by a form of deterioration entailing a transition from the continuous to the discrete. (L.-S. 1981: 498-99)

Here we have one of those crucial passages, almost completely lost in the jungle of the *Mythologiques*, where the ambiguity between the two discourses of structuralism—the triumphant hominization of *The Elementary Structures* and the denunciation of this self-separation of humanity—is analytically internalized and attributed to an immanent reflection of myth itself. These myths recount two stories, and the regressive movement is not as negative as might be expected, or at least not only negative. Would the genesis of culture then be degenerative, and the regression out of it regenerative? Or would the latter be impossible, or merely imaginary, or something worse? For there are moments where a nostalgia for the continuous appears to be for Lévi-Strauss the symptom of a real illness provoked by what could be called the uncontrolled proliferation of the discontinuous in the West, and not just a simple fantasy or imagined freedom. The global warming of history, the end of cold histories, would in that case be the end of Nature.

Whatever the case may be, if Amerindian mythology has, as Lévi-Strauss affirms several times over, a right side and its reverse, a progressive, totemic sense and a regressive, sacrificial one (those again, being the two orientations of structuralism itself), then shamanism and Amerindian perspectivism unequivocally belong to the reverse, to a world whose direction is regressive. It will be recalled that the civilizing complex of the origin of fire and cooking presupposes the following schemas: the sky/earth disjuncture, the establishing of seasonal periods, and the differentiation of natural species. But shamanic perspectivism operates in the reverse, regressive element of the twilight chromaticism of the sky and the earth (i.e., the shamanic voyage), the universal background humanity of all beings, and a pharmaceutical technique (tobacco) that radically scrambles the nature/culture distinction by defining a province of "supernature," of nature thought qua culture. (Supernature—a rather crucial rare concept in the *Mythologiques*.) We are reminded of the ironic, anti-Sartrean definition (L.-S. 1966, ch. 9) of stucturalist method as "progressive-regressive not once but twice-over." A method, moreover, enthusiastically practiced by myths themselves.[136] Against the myth of method, then, the method of myth.

136. See *From Honey to Ashes*: "In connection with the Ofaié myth about the origin of honey (M192), I pointed out a progressive-regressive movement which I now see is characteristic of all the myths we have studied up till now" (L.-S. 1973: 153).

The body, finally, has often been at issue in this book. In truth, the final phase of Lévi-Strauss' work is the theater of a closely fought match between the unity of the human mind and the multiplicity of the Amerindian body. When things get underway in the Overture to *The Raw and The Cooked*, the mind starts with an advantage, but the body progressively gets the upper hand and then carries the long match, although only by points—by means of a little *clinamen* that intensifies in the final rounds, which are played out in *The Story of Lynx*. The psychology of the human mind cedes its place to an anti-sociology of the indigenous body.

Which is how, at the very end of the long voyage of Lévi-Strauss' structural mythology and at the moment where it gives the impression of having at last cut its ambitions down to modest size,[137] what could be regarded as its theoretical enterprise's greatest destiny is realized: to restore the thinking of the others in its own terms, to practice this "opening to the Other" that (in another "remarkable reversal") anthropology discovers to be the attitude characteristic of the others it studies—the others that for so long it complacently imagined to lie dormant in atemporal ethnocentric cocoons. The disturbing final message of *The Story of Lynx* is that the other of the others is *also* Other: that there is space for a "we" only if it is already determined by alterity. And if there is a more general conclusion to be drawn, it is that anthropology has access to no other possible position except a "coplaneness" of principles with savage thought, a plane of immanence that it would hold in common with its object. In defining the *Mythologiques* as the myth of mythology and anthropological knowledge as a transformation of indigenous praxis, Lévi-Strauss' anthropology projects a philosophy to come: *Anti-Narcissus*.

The final quarter of the last century saw the structuralist theory of marriage alliance, which dominated the scene in the 1960s, fall

---

137. *The Story of Lynx* ends, in its very last chapter, with "the bipartite ideology of Amerindians" rather than any "elementary structures of mythology," which it explicitly rejects as empty and unhelpful.

into growing critical disrepute. *Anti-Oedipus* contributed much to this decline, again (Chapter 8), inasmuch as it vigorously expressed an intransigent refusal of every exchangeist conception of the socius. Yet even if it is indisputable that this attitude persisted in *A Thousand Plateaus*, the terms of the problem had by then radically changed. In *Anti-Oedipus*, exchange was discarded as a general model of action in favor of production, and circulation (to which Deleuze and Guattari unilaterally assimilated exchange in Mauss' sense) was subordinated to inscription.[138] In *A Thousand Plateaus*, as we have seen, production ceded its place to another nonrepresentational relationship, that of becoming. Where production had been filiative, becoming would evince an affinity with alliance. But then what happened to the anti-exchange position?

Even if some find it convenient to forget this, *Anti-Oedipus'* notion of production is not *exactly* identical with its Marxist homonym. "Desiring production" should not be confused with Hegelian-Marxist "necessitarian production" and its notion of need (D. G. 1983: 25 et seq.), and the difference between them is emphasized multiple times. "Our problem was never a return to Marx; it is much more a forgetting, a forgetting of Marx included. But, in the forgetting, small fragments floated...." We can add that the flux/break system of desiring production in *Anti-Oedipus* is poorly distinguished from a process of generalized circulation; as Jean-François Lyotard suggested in a certain teasing spirit, "This configuration of *Kapital*, the circulation of flows, is imposed by the predominance of the point of view of circulation over that of production" (1977: 15).

The finitist (or "finitive" rather than infinitive) and necessitarian conception of production is still valid currency in anthropological circles, as it is generally in its name and that of its accessories that "exchangeist" positions are critiqued in anthropology. Yet if it proved both desirable and even necessary to distinguish between the need-based production of political economy and the desiring production of machinic economy, between labor-production and function-production, it could be proposed, by analogy, that it might be just as interesting to distinguish between

138. *Anti-Oedipus* takes back up the Marxist cliché via a pretend "reduction of social reproduction to the sphere of circulation" (1983: 188) that condemned ethnology of the Maussian and structuralist kind.

alliance-structure and alliance-becoming, contract-exchange and "change-exchange." Such distinctions would allow us to isolate and displace the contractualist conception of alliance by deliberately playing on the equivocal homonymy between the intensive alliance of Amazonian sociocosmologies, for example, and the extensive alliance of classical theories of kinship, structuralism's included. There is, naturally, something more than a homonymy in each case, given that there is a filiation (even if monstrous rather than reproductive) between the pairs of concepts respectively implicated. *Anti-Oedipus'* notion of production owes a great deal to political economic production, even if it subverts it. In the same way, Amazonian potential alliance exists in filigree (virtually, so to speak) in Lévi-Strauss, and the latter's anti-oedipal and (self-) subversive potential should be fully brought out.

The problem, in the last analysis, is that of constructing a non-contractualist, nondialectic concept of exchange that would make it neither a rational interest nor an *a priori* synthesis of the gift—not an unconscious teleology, work of meaning, inclusive *fitness*, desire of the desire of the other, conflict, or contract, but rather a becoming-other.[139] Alliance is the becoming-other proper to kinship.

The machinic, rhizomatic laterality of alliance is, at the end of the day, much closer to Deleuze's philosophy than the organic and arborescent verticality of filiation. The challenge, then, is to liberate alliance both from the task of organizing filiation and, reciprocally, from being dominated by filiation, and to do so by releasing its "monstrous"—which is to say, creative—powers. Where alliance's twin, exchange, is concerned, I think something has recently become clear: it never really was postulated as the contrary of production, whatever current dogma says. On the contrary, the anthropology of exchange has always treated it as production's most eminent form: the production of Society. So the question is not to unveil the naked truth about production supposedly concealed under the hypocritical cover of exchange and reciprocity but, rather, to free these concepts from their equivocal functions in the machine of filiative, subjectivating production by presenting them with their (counter-) natural element, which is becoming. Exchange, then, as the infinite circulation of

139. If "the expression 'difference of intensity' is a tautology" (D. 1994: 222), then "becoming-other" is yet another, or maybe the same, tautology.

perspectives—exchange of exchange, metamorphosis of meta-morphosis, perspective on perspective: again, becoming.

A double movement, therefore, for a double heritage that rests above all else on a monstrous alliance or counter-natural nuptials: Lévi-Strauss *with* Deleuze. Those two names are in fact intensities, and it is from the virtual reserve of their liaison that came (the book we at once let happen and elaborated) *Anti-Narcissus*.

BIBLIOGRAPHY

Adler, Alfred, and Michel Cartry (1971), "La Transgression et sa dérision." *L'Homme* 11(3):5-63.

Albert, Bruce (1985), *Temps du sang, temps des cendres: représentation de la maladie, système rituel et espace politique chez les Yanomani du Sud-Est (Amazonie brésilienne)*, Ph.D. dissertation, Ethnologie et sociologie comparative, Université de Paris X.

Almeida, Mauro (2008), "La formule canonique du mythe." *Lévi-Strauss: leituras brasileiras*. R.C. de Queiroz and R.F. Nobre, eds. pp. 147-82. Belo Horizonte: Editora de UGMG.

Andrello, Geraldo (2006), *Cidade do índio : transformações e cotidiano em Iauaretê*. São Paulo: Editora Unesp/NUTI.

Århem, Kajn (1993), "Ecosofia Makuna." *La Selva Humanizada: ecología alternativa en el trópico húmedo colombiano*. F. Correa, ed. pp. 105-22. Bogotà: Instituto Colombiano de Antropología.

Asad, Talal (1986), "The Concept of Cultural Translation in British Social Anthropology." *Writing Culture: The Poetics and Politics of Ethnography*. J. Clifford and G. Marcus, eds. pp. 141-64. Berkeley: University of California Press.

Baer, Gerhard (1994), *Cosmologia y shamanismo de los Matsiguenga*. Quito: Abya-Yala.

Bateson, Gregory (1958/1936), *Naven: A Survey of the Problems suggested by a Composite Picture of the Culture of a New Guinea Tribe Drawn from Three Points of View*. Stanford: Stanford University Press.

Carneiro da Cunha, Manuela (1978), *Os Mortos e os outros: uma análise do sistema funerario e da noção de pessoa entre os índios Krahó*. São Paulo: Hucitec.

— (1998), "Pontos de vista sobre a floresta amazônica: xamanismo e tradução." *Mana* 4(1):7-22.

Chaumeil, Jean-Pierre (1985), "Échange d'énergie: guerre, identité et reproduction sociale chez les Yagua de l'Amazonie péruvienne." *Journal de la Société des Américanistes* 71:143-57.

Clastres, Hélène (1968), "Rites funéraires Guayaki". *Journal de la Société des Américanistes* 57:63-72.

— (1972), "Les beaux-frères ennemis: à propos du cannibalisme Tupinambá." *Nouvelle Revue de Psychanalyse* 6:71-82.

Clastres, Pierre (1987/1962), "Exchange and Power: Philosophy of the Indian Chieftainship." *Society Against the State: Essays in Political Anthropology*. New York: Zone Books.

— (2010), "Archeology of Violence: War in Primitive Societies." *Archeology of Violence*. Los Angeles: Semiotext(e).

Clastres, Pierre, and Lucien Sebag (1963), "Cannibalisme et mort chez les Guayakis." *Revista do Museu Paulista* 14:174-81.

Conklin, Beth A. (2001), *Consuming Grief: Compassionate Canibalism in an Amazonian Society*. Austin: University of Texas Press.

de Almeida Mauro, William Barbosa (2008), "A fórmula canônica do mito." *Levi-Strauss: leituras brasileiras*. R.C. de Queiroz and R.F. Nobre, eds. pp. 147-82. Belo Horizonte: Editora UFMG.

de Andrade, Oswald (1997/1928), "Anthropophagite Manifesto." *The Oxford Book of Latin American Essays*. I. Stavans, ed. pp. 96-99. New York: Oxford University Press.

DeLanda, Manuel (2002), *Intensive Science and Virtual Philosophy*. London: Continuum.

— (2003), "1000 Years of War: CTHEORY Interview with Manuel De Landa." www.ctheory.net/articles.aspx?id=383.

— (2006), *A New Philosophy of Society*. London: Continuum.

Deleuze, Gilles (1973), Deleuze: Anti Oedipe et Mille Plateaux. Cours Vincennes, 28 May. http://www.webdeleuze.com/php/texte.php?cle=171&groupe=Anti%20Oedipe%20et%20Mille%20Plateaux&langue=1.

— (1974), "Deleuze: Anti Oedipe et Mille Plateaux." Cours Vincennes, 14 January. http://www.webdeleuze.com/php/texte.php?cle=176&groupe=Anti%20Oedipe%20et%20Mille%20Plateaux&langue=2.

— (1983), "Deleuze: Image mouvement image temps." Cours Vincennes - St Denis, 12 April. http://www.webdeleuze.com/php/texte.php?-cle=72&groupe=Image%20Mouvement%20Image%20Temps&langue=1.

— (1983), *Nietzsche and Philosophy*. New York: Columbia University Press.

— (1988), *Bergsonism*. New York: Zone Books.

— (1990 a), "Michel Tournier and World Without Others." *The Logic of Sense*. pp. 301-20. New York: Columbia University Press.

— (1990 b), "Plato and the Simulacrum." *The Logic of Sense*. pp. 253-65. New York: Columbia University Press.

— (1990 c), "Klossowski or Bodies-Language." *The Logic of Sense*. pp. 280-300. New York: Columbia University Press.

— (1990 d), *The Logic of Sense*. New York: Columbia University Press.

— (1993), *The Fold: Leibniz and the Baroque*. Minneapolis: University of Minnesota Press.

— (1994), *Difference and Repetition*. New York: Columbia University Press.

— (1997), "Bartleby; or, The Formula." *Essays Critical and Clinical*. pp. 68-90. Minneapolis: University of Minnesota Press.

— (2004/1972), "How Do We Recognize Structuralism?" *Desert Islands and Other Texts*. D. Lapoujade, ed. pp. 170-92. Los Angeles: Semiotext(e).

— (2006), "May '68 Did Not Take Place." *Two Regimes of Madness: Texts and Interviews 1975-1995*. D. Lapoujade, ed. pp. 233-36. Los Angeles: Semiotext(e).

— (2006), "Preface for the Italian Edition of A Thousand Plateaus." *Two Regimes of Madness: Texts and Interviews 1975-1995*. D. Lapoujade, ed. pp. 313-16. Los Angeles: Semiotext(e).

Deleuze, Gilles, and Félix Guattari (1983), *Anti-Oedipus: Capitalism and Schizophrenia*. Minneapolis: University of Minnesota Press.

— (1986), *Kafka: Toward a Minor Literature*. Minneapolis: University of Minnesota Press.

— (1987), *A Thousand Plateaus: Capitalism and Schizophrenia*. Minneapolis: University of Minnesota Press.

— (1994) *What Is Philosophy?* New York: Columbia University Press.

Deleuze, Gilles, and Claire Parnet (1987), *Dialogues*. New York: Columbia University Press.

Dennett, Daniel C. (1978), *Brainstorms: Philosophical Essays on Mind and Psychology*. Harmondsworth, UK: Penguin.

Derrida, Jacques (2008), *The Animal That Therefore I Am*. New York: Fordham University Press.

Descola, Philippe (1992), "Societies of Nature and the Nature of Society." *Conceptualizing Society*. A. Kuper, ed. pp. 107-26. London: Routledge.

— (1996), "Constructing Natures: Symbolic Ecology and Social Practice." *Nature and Society: Anthropological Perspectives*. P. Descola and G. Palsson, eds. pp. 82-102. London: Routledge.

— (2013), *Beyond Nature and Culture*. Chicago: University of Chicago Press.

Detienne, Marcel (1996/1967), *The Masters of Truth in Archaic Greece*. New York: Zone Books.

Donzelot, Jacques (1977), "An Anti-Sociology." Sémiotext(e) 2(3):27-44.

Duffy, Simon, ed. (2006), *Virtual Mathematics: The Logic of Difference*. Bolton, UK: Clinamen Press.

Dumont, Louis (2006), *An Introduction to Two Theories of Social Anthropology: Descent Groups and Marriage Alliance*. New York: Berghahn Books.

Englund, Harri, and James Leach (2000), "Ethnography and the Meta-Narratives of Modernity." *Current Anthropology* 41(2):225-48.

Erikson, Philippe (1986), "Altérité, tatouage et anthropophagie chez les Pano : la belliqueuse quête du soi." *Journal de la Société des Américanistes* 1986:185-210.

Fabian, Johannes (1983), *Time and the Other: How Anthropology makes its Object*. New York: Columbia University Press.

Favret-Saada, Jeanne (2000), "La-pensée-Lévi-Strauss." *Journal des anthropologues* (82-83):53-70.

Fernandes, Florestan (1970/1952), *A Função Social da Guerra na Sociedade Tupinambá*. São Paulo: Livraria Pioneira Editora/EDUSP.

Fortes, Meyer (1969), *Kinship and the Social Order: The Legacy of Lewis Henry Morgan*. London: Routledge & Kegan Paul.

— (1983), *Rules and the Emergence of Society*. London: Royal Anthropological Institute of Great Britain and Ireland.

Gell, Alfred (1998), *Art and Agency: An Anthropological Theory*. Oxford: Clarendon.

— (1999), "Strathernograms, or the Semiotics of Mixed Metaphors." *The Art of Anthropology: Essays and Diagrams*. pp. 29-75. London: Athlone.

Goldman, Marcio (2005) "Formas do saber e modos do ser: observações sobre multiplicidade e ontologia no candomblé." *Religião e Sociedade* 25(2):102-20.

Gregory, Chriss (1982) *Gifts and Commodities*. London: Academic Press.

Griaule, Marcel, and Germaine Dieterlen (1986) *The Pale Fox*. Chino Valley, AZ: Continuum Foundation.

Hallowell, A. Irving (1960), "Ojibwa Ontology, Behavior, and World View." *Culture in History: Essays in Honor of Paul Radin*. S. Diamond, ed. pp. 49-82. New York: Columbia University Press.

Hamberger, Klaus (2004), "La pensée objectivée." *Lévi-Strauss*. M. Izard, ed. pp. 339-46. Paris: Éditions de l'Herne.

Héritier, Françoise (1981), *L'exercice de la parenté*. Paris: Gallimard/Le Seuil.

Herzfeld, Michael (2001), "Orientations: Anthropology as a Practice of Theory." *Anthropology: Theoretical Practice in Culture and Society*. M. Herzfeld, ed. London: Blackwell.

— (2003), "The Unspeakable in Pursuit of the Ineffable: Representations of Untranslability in Ethnographic Discourse." *Translating Cultures: Perspectives on Translation and Anthropology*. P.G. Rubel and A. Rosman, eds. pp. 109-34. Oxford: Berg.

Holbraad, Martin (2003), "Estimando a necessidade: os oráculos de ifá e a verdade em Havana." *Mana* 9(2):39-77.

Holbraad, Martin, and Rane Willerslev (2007), "(Afterword) Transcendental Perspectivism: Anonymous Viewpoints from Inner Asia." *Inner Asia* 9(2):311-28.

Hubert, Henri, and Marcel Mauss (1964), *Sacrifice: Its Nature and Function*. Chicago: University of Chicago Press.

Hugh-Jones, Stephen (1979), *The Palm and the Pleiades: Initiation and Cosmology in North-West Amazonia*. Cambridge, UK: Cambridge University Press.

— (1996), "Shamans, Prophets, Priests and Pastors." *Shaminsm, History, and the State*. N. Thomas and C. Humphrey, eds. pp. 32-75. Ann Arbor: University of Michigan Press.

Ingold, Tim (1991), "Becoming Persons: Consciousness and Sociality in Human Evolution." *Cultural Dynamics* 4(3):355-78.

— (1992), *Editorial. Mana* 27(4):693-96.

— (2000), *The Perception of the Environment: Essays on Livelihood, Dwelling and Skill*. London: Routledge.

Irving, Hallowell A. (1960), *Ojibwa Ontology, Behavior, and Worldview. In Culture in History: Essays in Honor of Paul Rand*. S. Diamon, ed. pp. 49-82. New York: Columbia University Press.

Jameson, Frederic (1997), "Marxism and Dualism in Deleuze." *The South Atlantic Quarterly* 96(3):393-416.

Jensen, Casper B. (2003), "Latour and Pickering: Post-Human Perspectives on Science, Becoming, and Normativity." *Chasing Technoscience: Matrix for Materiality*. D. Ihde and E. Selinger, eds. pp. 225-40. Bloomington, IN: Indiana University Press.

— (2004), "A Nonhumanist Disposition: On Performativity, Practical Ontology, and Intervention." *Configurations* 12:229-61.

Jullien, François (2008), *De l'universel, de l'uniforme, du commun et du dialogue entre les cultures*. Paris: Fayard.

Jullien, François, and Thierry Marchaisse (2000), *Penser d'un dehors, la Chine: entretiens d'Extrême-Occident*. Paris: Éditions du Seuil.

Kohn, Eduardo (2002), *Natural Engagements and Ecological Aesthetics Among the Ávila Runa of Amazonian Ecuador*. Ph.D. dissertation, Department of Anthropology, University of Wisconsin–Madison.

— (2005), "Runa Realsim: Upper Amazonian Attitudes to Nature Knowing." *Ethnos* 70(2):171-96.

Kuper, Adam (2003), "The Return of the Native." *Current Anthropology* 44(3):389-402.

Kwa, Chunglin (2002), "Romantic and Baroque Conceptions of Complex Wholes in the Sciences." *Complexities: Social Studies of Knowledge Practices*. J. Law and A. Mol, eds. pp. 23-52. Durham, NC: Duke University Press.

Lambek, Michael (1998), "Body and Mind in Mind, Body and Mind in Body: Some Anthropological Interventions in a Long Conversation." *Bodies and Persons: Comparative Perspectives from Africa and Melanesia*. M. Lambek and A. Strathern, eds. pp. 103-22. Cambridge, UK: Cambridge University Press.

Lapoujade, David (2006), "Le structuralisme dissident de Deleuze." *Gilles Deleuze içi / Pour Gilles Deleuze*. A. Akay, ed. pp. 27-36. Istanbul: Akbank Sanat.

Latour, Bruno (1993), "An Interview with Bruno Latour (with T.H. Crawford)." *Configurations* 1(2):247-68.
— (1993), *We Have Never Been Modern*. Cambridge, Mass.: Harvard University Press.
— (1996), "Not the Question." *Anthropology Newsletter* 37(3):1, 5.
— (2002), *War of the Worlds: What about Peace?* Chicago: Prickly Paradigm Press.
— (2004), *Politics of Nature: How to Bring the Sciences into Democracy*. Cambridge, MA: Harvard University Press.
— (2005), *Reassembling the Social: An Introduction to Actor-Network Theory*. Oxford: Oxford University Press.
— (2010), *On the Modern Cult of the Factish Gods. Durham*. NC: Duke University Press.
Lawlor, Leonard (2003), "The Beginnings of Thought: The Fundamental Experience in Derrida and Deleuze." *Between Deleuze and Derrida*. P. Patton and J. Protevi, eds. pp. 67-83. London: Continuum.
Leach, Edmund (1961/1951), "Rethinking Anthropology." *Rethinking Anthropology*. pp. 1-27. London: Athlone.
Lévi-Strauss, Claude (1943), "The Social Use of Kinship Terms among Brazilian Indians." *American Anthropologist* 45(3):398-409.
— (1944), "Reciprocity and Hierarchy." *American Anthropologist* 46(2):266-8.
— (1963a), *Totemism*. Boston: Beacon Press.
— (1963b), *Structural Anthropology*. New York: Basic Books.
— (1963c/1952), "Social Structure." *Structural Anthropology*. pp. 277-323. New York: Basic Books.
— (1963d/1954), "The Place of Anthropology in the Social Sciences and Problems Raised in Teaching It." *Structural Anthropology*. pp. 346-81. New York: Basic Books.
— (1963e/1955), "The Structural Study of Myth." *Structural Anthropology*. pp. 206-231. New York: Basic Books.
— (1966), *The Savage Mind*. Chicago: University of Chicago Press.
— (1969) *The Elementary Structures of Kinship*. Boston: Beacon Press.
— (1969), *The Raw and the Cooked*. New York: Harper & Row.
— (1973), *From Honey to Ashes*. New York: Harper & Row.
— (1978), *Structural Anthropology, Volume 2*. Harmondsworth, UK: Penguin.
— (1978/1952), "Race and History." *Structural Anthropology, Volume 2*. Harmondsworth, UK: Penguin.
— (1978/1960), "The Scope of Anthropology." *Structural Anthropology, Volume 2*. Harmondsworth, UK: Penguin.
— (1978/1964), "Scientific Criteria in the Social and Human Disciplines." *Structural Anthropology, Volume 2*. Harmondsworth, UK: Penguin.
— (1979), *The Origin of Table Manners*. New York: Harper & Row.
— (1981), *The Naked Man*. New York: Harper & Row.
— (1982), *The Way of the Masks*. Seattle: University of Washington Press.
— (1987a), *Introduction to the Work of Marcel Mauss*. London: Routledge & Kegan Paul.
— (1987b), *Anthropology and Myth: Lectures, 1951-1982*. Oxford: Blackwell.
— (1988), *The Jealous Potter*. Chicago: University of Chicago Press.
— (1992), *Tristes Tropiques*. New York: Penguin.
— (1995), *The Story of Lynx*. Chicago: University of Chicago Press.
— (2000), "Postface." *L'Homme* 154-155:713-20.
— (2001), "Hourglass Configurations." *The Double Twist: From Ethnography to Morphodynamics*. P. Maranda, ed. pp. 15-32. Toronto: University of Toronto Press.

— (2004), "Pensée mythique et pensée scientifique." Lévi-Strauss. M. Izard, ed. pp. 40-2. Paris: Éditions de l'Herne.

— (2008), *Œuvres*. Paris: Gallimard.

Lévi-Strauss, Claude, and Georges Charbonnier (1969), *Conversations with Claude Lévi-Strauss*. London: Cape.

Lévi-Strauss, Claude, and Didier Éribon (1991), *Conversations with Claude Lévi-Strauss*. Chicago: University of Chicago Press.

Lienhardt, Godfrey (1961), *Divinity and Experience: The Religion of the Dinka*. Oxford: Oxford University Press.

Lima, Tânia Stolze (1999/1996), "The Two and Its Many: Reflections on Perspectivism in a Tupi Cosmology." *Ethnos* 64(1):107-31.

— (2005), *Um peixe olhou para mim : o povo Yudjá e a perspectiva*. São Paulo: Edunesp/NuTI/ISA.

Lyotard, Jean-François (1977), "Energumen Capitalism." Semiotext(e) 2(3):11-26.

Maniglier, Patrice (2000), "L'humanisme interminable de Lévi-Strauss." *Les Temps modernes* 609:216-41.

— (2005a), "Des us et des signes. Lévi-Strauss : philosophie pratique." *Revue de Métaphysique et de Morale* 1/2005:89-108.

— (2005b), "La parenté des autres. (À propos de Maurice Godelier, *Metamorphoses de la parenté*)." *Critique* 701, octobre 2005:758-74.

— (2006), *La vie énigmatique des signes. Saussure et la naissance du structuralisme*. Paris: Léo Scheer.

— (2010), "The Structuralist Legacy." *The History of Continental Philosophy*, vol. 7. R. Braidotti, ed. Chicago: University of Chicago Press.

Mauss, Marcel (2001), *A General Theory of Magic*. London: Routledge.

Menget, Patrick (1985a), "Guerres, sociétés et vision du monde dans les basses terres de l'Amérique du Sud." *Journal de la Société des Américanistes* 71:129-208.

— (1985b), "Jalons pour une étude comparative (dossier 'Guerre, société et vision du monde dans les basses terres de l'Amérique du Sud')." *Journal de la Société des Américanistes* 71(131-41).

— (1988), "Note sur l'adoption chez les Txicão du Brésil central." *Anthropologie et Sociétés* 12(2):63-72.

Merleau-Ponty (2003), *Nature: Course Notes from the Collège de France*. Evanston, IL: Northwestern University Press.

Munn, Nancy (1992/1986), *The Fame of Gawa: A Symbolic Study of Value Transformation in a Massim (Papua New Guinea) Society*. Durham, NC: Duke University Press.

Nadaud, Stéphane (2004), "Love Story between an Orchid and a Wasp." *The Anti-Œdipus papers*. F. Guattari, ed. New York: Semiotext(e).

Overing, Joanna (1983), "Elementary Structures of Reciprocity: A Comparative Note on Guianese, Central Brazilian, and North-West Amazon Sociopolitical Thought." *Antropologica* 59-62:331-48.

— (1984), "Dualism as an Expression of Differences and Danger. Marriage Exchange and Reciprocity among the Piaroa of Venezuela." *Marriage Practices in Lowland South America*. K. Kensinger, ed. pp. 127-55. Urbana, IL: University of Illinois Press.

— (1986), "Images of Cannibalism, Death and Domination in a "Non Violent" Society." *Journal de la Société des Américanistes* 72(1): 133-56.

Pagden, Anthony (1982), *The Fall of Natural Man: The American Indian and the Origins of Comparative Ethnology*. Cambridge, UK: Cambridge University Press.

Pedersen, Morten A. (2001), "Totemism, Animism and North Asian Indigenous Ontologies." *Journal of the Royal Anthropological Institute* 7(3):411-27.

Petitot, Jean (1999), "La généalogie morphologique du structuralisme." *Critique* 55(620-621):97-122.

Pignarre, Philippe , and Isabelle Stengers (2011), *Capitalist Sorcery: Breaking the Spell*. New York: Palgrave Macmillan: Palgrave Macmillan.

Richir, Marc (1994), "Qu'est-ce qu'un dieu? Mythologie et question de la pensée." *Philosophie de la mythologie*. F.-W. Schelling, ed. pp. 7-85. Paris: Jérôme Millon.

Rivière, Peter (1984), *Individual and Society in Guiana: A Comparative Study of Amerindian Social Organization*. Cambridge, UK: Cambridge University Press.

Rodgers, David (2002), "A soma anômala : a questão do suplemento no xamanismo e menstruação ikpeng." *Mana* 8(2):91-125.

— (2004), *Foil*. Unpublished MS.

Sahlins, Marshall (1985), *Islands of History*. Chicago: University of Chicago Press.

— (1995), *How "Natives" Think: About Captain Cook, for Example*. Chicago: University of Chicago Press.

— (2000), "What Is Anthropological Enlightenment? Some Lessons from the Twentieth Centry." *Culture in Practice: Selected Essays*. pp. 501-26. New York: Zone Books.

Salmon, Gildas (2013), *Les structures de l'esprit: Lévi-Strauss et les mythes*. Paris: Presses universitaires de France.

Schrempp, Gregory (2002), *Magical Arrows: The Māori, the Greeks, and the Folklore of the Universe*. Madison: University of Wisconsin Press.

Seeger, Anthony, Roberto DaMatta, and Eduardo Viveiros de Castro (1979), "A construção da pessoa nas sociedades indígenas brasileiras." *Boletim do Museu Nacional* 32:2-19.

Sloterdijk, Peter (2000), *La domestication de l'Être*. Paris: Mille et Une Nuits.

Smith, David W. (2006), "Axiomatics and Problematics as Two Modes of Formalisation: Deleuze's Epistemology of Mathematics." *Virtual Mathematics: The Logic of Difference*. S. Duffy, ed. pp. 145-68. Bolton: Clinamen Press.

Soares de Souza, Gabriel (1972/1587), *Tratado descritivo do Brasil em 1587*. São Paulo: Cia Editora Nacional/Edusp.

Stasch, Rupert (2009), *Society of Others: Kinship and Mourning in a West Papuan Place*. Berkeley: University of California Press.

Stengers, Isabelle (2010/1996), *Cosmopolitics I*. Minneapolis: University of Minnesota Press.

— (2011), *Thinking with Whitehead: A Free and Wild Creation of Concepts*. Cambridge, MA: Harvard University Press.

Strathern, Marilyn (1987), "The Limits of Auto-Anthropology." *Anthropology at Home*. A. Jackson, ed. pp. 59-67. London: Tavistock.

— (1988), *The Gender of the Gift*. Berkeley: University of California Press.

— (1991), *Partial Connections*. Savage, MD: Rowman & Littlefield.

— (1992a), *After Nature: English Kinship in the Late Twentieth Centruy*. Cambridge, UK: Cambridge University Press.

— (1992b), "Parts and Wholes: Refiguring Relationships in a Post-Plural World." *Reproducing the Future: Anthropology, Kinship, and the New Reproductive Technologies*. pp. 90-116. New York: Routledge.

— (1992c), "Future Kinship and the Study of Culture." *Reproducing the Future: Anthropology, Kinship, and the New Reproductive Technology*. pp. 46-63. New York: Routledge.

— (1995), "The Nice Thing About Culture Is That Everyone Has It." *Shifting Contexts: Transformations in Anthropological Knowledge*. M. Strathern, ed. pp. 153-76. London: Routledge.

— (1996), "Cutting the Network." *Journal of the Royal Anthropological Institute* 2(4):517-35.

— (1999), *Property, Substance and Effect: Anthropological Essays on Persons and Things*. London: Athlone.

— (2001), "Same-Sex and Cross-Sex Relations: Some Internal Comparisons." *Gender in Amazonia and Melanesia: An Exploration of the Comparative Method*. T. Gregor and D. Tuzin, eds. pp. 221-44. Berkeley: University of California Press.

— (2005), *Kinship, Law, and the Unexpected: Relatives Are Always a Surprise*. Cambridge, UK: Cambridge University Press.

Strathern, Marilyn, et al. (1996/1989), "The Concept of Society is Theoretically Obsolete." *Key Debates in Anthropology*. T. Ingold, ed. pp. 55-98. London: Routledge.

Tarde, Gabriel (1999/1895), *Œuvres de Gabriel Tarde, Volume I: Monadologie et sociologie*. Le Plessis-Robinson: Institut Synthélabo.

Taylor, Anne-Christine (1985), "L'art de la réduction." *Journal de la Société des Américanistes* 71:159-73.

— (1993), "Les bons ennemis et les mauvais parents: le traitement symbolique de l'alliance dans les rituels de chasse aux têtes des Jivaros de l'Equateur." *Les complexités de l'alliance, IV: Économie, politique et fondements symboliques de l'alliance*. E. Copet and F. H.ritier-Augé, eds. pp. 73-105. Paris: Archives contemporaines.

— (2000), "Le sexe de la proie : représentations jivaro du lien de parenté." *L'Homme* 154-155:309-34.

— (2004), "Don Quichotte en Amerique." *Lévi-Strauss*. M. Izard, ed. pp. 92-8. Paris: Éd. de L'Herne.

— (2009), *Corps, sexe et parente : une perspective amazonienne*. Unpublished MS.

— (n.d.), *Perspectives de recherche: l'anthropologie du sujet*. Unpublished MS.

Taylor, Anne-Christine, and Eduardo Viveiros de Castro (2006), "Un corps fait de regards." *Qu'est-ce qu'un corps ? (Afrique de l'Ouest/Europe occidentale/Nouvelle-Guinée/Amazonie)*. S. Breton, J.-M. Schaeffer, M. Houseman, A.-C. Taylor, and E. Viveiros de Castro, eds. pp. 148-99. Paris: Musée du Quai-Branly/Flammarion.

Thevet, André (1953/1575), "Cosmographie universelle." *Les Français en Amérique pendant la deuxième moitié du XVIeme siècle: le Brésil et les brésiliens*. S. Lussagnet, ed. pp. 1-236. Paris: PUF.

Vernant, Jean-Pierre (1996/1966), "Raisons d'hier et d'aujourd'hui." *Entre mythe et politique*. pp. 229-36. Paris: Le Seuil.

Viveiros de Castro, Eduardo (1990), "Princípios e parâmetros: um comentário a *L'Exercice de la parenté*." *Comunicações do PPGAS* 17:1-106.

— (1992/1986), *From the Enemy's Point of View: Humanity and Divinity in an Amazonian Society*. Chicago: University of Chicago Press.

— (1998), "Cosmological Perspectivism in Amazonia and Elsewhere." Conférences inédites. Cambridge, UK.

— (1998/1996), "Cosmological Deixis and Ameridian Perspectivism." *Journal of the Royal Anthropological Institute* 4(3):469-88.

— (2001a), "A propriedade do conceito: sobre o plano de imanência amerindio." XXV Encontro Annual da ANPOCS, Caxambu.

— (2001b), "GUT Feelings about Amazonia: Potential Affinity and the Construction of Sociality." *Beyond the Visible and the Material: The Amerindianization of Society in the Work of Peter Rivière*. L. Rival and N. Whitehead, eds. pp. 19-43. Oxford: Oxford University Press.

— (2002a), "Perspectivismo e multinaturalismo na América indígena." *A inconstância da alma selvagem*. pp. 345-99. São Paulo: Cosac & Naify.

— (2002b), "O problema afinidade na Amazônia." *A inconstância da alma selvagem*. pp. 87-180. São Paulo: Cosac & Naify.

— (2002c), "O nativo relativo." *Mana* 8(1):113-48.

— (2003), "And." *Manchester Papers in Social Anthropology* 7:1-20.

— (2004a), "Perspectival Anthropology and the Method of Controlled Equivocation." *Tipití* 2(1):3-22.

— (2004b), "Exchanging Perspectives: The Transformation of Objects into Subjects in Amerindian Cosmologies." *Common Knowledge* 10(3):463-84.

— (2006), "Une figure humaine peut cacher une affection-jaguar. Réponse à une question de Didier Muguet." *Multitudes* 24:41-52.

— (2008a), "The Gift and the Given: Three Nano-Essays on Kinship and Magic." *Kinship and Beyond: The Genealogical Model Reconsidered*. S. Bamford and J. Leach, eds. pp. 237-68. Oxford: Berghahn Books.

— (2008b), "Immanence and Fear, or, The Enemy First." "Indigeneities and Cosmopolitanisms." *Keynote address* Canadian Anthropological Society and American Ethnological Society, Toronto.

— (2008c), "Xamanismo transversal: Lévi-Strauss e a cosmopolítica amazônica." *Lévi-Strauss: leituras brasileiras*. R.C. de Queiroz and R.F. Nobre, eds. pp. 79-124. Belo Horizonte: Editora de UGMG.

Wagner, Roy (1972), "Incest and Identity: A Critique and Theory on the Subject of Exogamy and Incest Prohibition." *Man* 7(4):601-13.

— (1977), "Analogic Kinship: A Daribi Example." *American Ethnologist* 4(4):623-42.

— (1978), *Lethal Speech: Daribi Myth as Symbolic Obviation*. Ithaca: Cornell University Press.

— (1981/1975), *The Invention of Culture*. Chicago: University of Chicago Press.

— (1986), *Symbols that Stand for Themselves*. Chicago: Chicago University Press.

— (1991), "The Fractal Person." *Big Men and Great Men: Personification of Power in Melanesia*. M. Godelier and M. Strathern, eds. pp. 159-73. Cambridge, UK: Cambridge University Press.

Weiss, Gerald (1972), "Campa Cosmology." *Ethnology* 11(2):157-172.

Willerslev, Rane (2004), "Not Animal, Not Not-Human: Hunting and Empathetic Knowledge among the Siberian Yukaghirs." *Journal of the Royal Anthropological Institute* 10(3):629-52.

Wolff, Francis (2000), *L'être, l'homme, le disciple*. Paris: PUF – "Quadrige."

Zourabichvili, François (2003), *Le vocabulaire de Deleuze*. Paris: Ellipses.

— (2004/1994), "Deleuze. Une philosophic de l'événement." *La philosophie de Deleuze*. F. Zourabichvili, A. Sauvargnargues, and P. Marrati, eds. pp. 1-116. Paris: PUF.

Eduardo Viveiros de Castro is a Brazilian anthropologist and professor at the National Museum of the Federal University of Rio de Janeiro.

Peter Skafish is Andrew W. Mellon postdoctoral fellow in the anthropology department at McGill University.